Bonds and Bond Derivatives

For Fiona Featherston

Bonds and Bond Derivatives

Miles Livingston

First published 1999
Reprinted 1999, 2001, 2002

Blackwell Publishers Inc.
350 Main Street
Malden, Massachusetts 02148
USA

Blackwell Publishers Ltd
108 Cowley Road
Oxford OX4 1JF
UK

Library of Congress Cataloging-in-Publication Data

Livingston, Miles
        Bonds and bond derivatives / Miles Livingston.
            p.   cm.
        Includes bibliographical references and index.
        ISBN 0–631–20755–4 (hardcover : alk. paper). — ISBN 0–631–20756–2
(pbk. : alk. paper)
        1. Bonds.   2. Bond market.   3. Financial futures.   4. Government
securities.   5. Portfolio management.   I. Title.
        HG4651.L58   1998
        332.63'23—dc21   98–22988
                                                                                                        CIP

British Library Cataloguing in Publication Data

A CIP catalogue record for this book is available from the British Library.

Typeset in 10 on 12 pt Sabon
By Newgen Imaging Systems (P) Ltd, Chennai, India
Printed in Great Britain by T. J. International Ltd, Padstow, Cornwall
This book is printed on acid-free paper.

Contents

Preface

In the last 30 years, the size and the complexity of the bond markets have increased significantly. The two major causes are the enormous growth of the level of debt and the high variability of interest rates. Because of interest rate variability, the potential losses to borrowers and lenders from poor debt choices have greatly increased.

This book is an introduction to bond markets and bond derivatives for college and university students and executives in commercial businesses and financial institutions. While many topics about debt instruments involve considerable mathematics, the purpose of this text is to present the essential elements in an intuitive and relatively non-mathematical way. The book is designed to be the main text for a course in debt markets. In recent years, more and more universities and colleges have been offering such courses. In addition, the text can be used as a supplementary book in courses on investments, money and banking, and financial institutions. It can be used as a training manual and reference source for firms involved in the debt markets.

Bonds and Bond Derivatives describes bond markets, bond derivatives, and institutions involved in these markets. The book begins with a discussion of the major macroeconomic determinants of interest rates. Next, the role of financial institutions in the debt markets is presented, including the Federal Reserve, the US Treasury, brokers, dealers, investment bankers, mutual funds, banks, pension funds, and insurance companies. Present value calculations for flat and nonflat term structures are carefully described. Several chapters cover specialized instruments such as money market debt, mortgages, international debt, options, futures, and swaps. The important concept of arbitrage is shown to link many different types of markets.

This book presents difficult material about debt instruments in an intuitive way. The individual chapters contain practice problems that have been extensively tested in student classes at the University of Florida. The material is a mixture of theory and practical information, and the style of writing is concise and to the point.

Compared with my previous book, *Money and Capital Markets*, this present book excludes nonessential institutional information. Also, present value and bond yield calculations are initially presented for flat term structures. Once students have a grasp of this material, the more difficult cases of nonflat term structures and term structure theories are presented.

M.L.

───── Acknowledgments

I should like to thank the staff at Blackwell Publishers for all their help in the production of this book. I should particularly like to thank Al Bruckner and Katie Byrne, and reviewer George W. Trivoli, Jacksonville State University.

The author and publishers would like to thank the editor of the *Journal of Financial Research*, and the editor of the *Wall Street Journal* for permission to reproduce copyright material. Every effort has been made to trace all copyright holders, but the publishers would be grateful to be notified of any additional copyright information that should be incorporated in the next edition or reprint of this book.

Introduction

This book focuses on bond markets and bond derivatives. The importance of these topics has grown considerably over the last 25 years because of increases in the levels of debt, considerable variability of interest rates, and development of many new varieties of debt instruments. Consequently, involvement of individuals and firms in the debt markets has expanded and there is a high risk of incorrect decisions being made.

The Growth of Debt

The debt obligations of households, businesses, and government are individually large and have been growing at rapid rates in recent years. Because of this increase in the size of the debt market, events in the debt market can have wide-ranging impacts upon the entire economic system.

To provide some indication of the size of the debt markets, figure I.1 shows debt as a percentage of Gross National Product (GNP). The categories of debt are federal government debt, tax-exempt debt issued by state and local governments, corporate bonds, mortgage debt, and consumer credit.

Several important things are revealed by this figure. First, the absolute size of these debts is huge, especially US government debt and mortgage debt. Second, federal government debt and mortgage debt since 1980 have not only been increasing in absolute size, but also as a percentage of GNP.

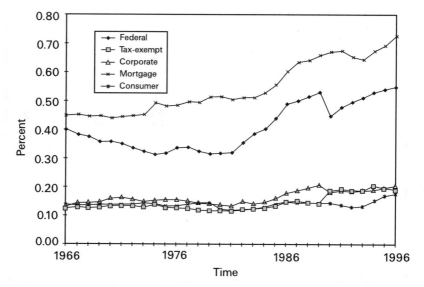

Figure I.1   Debt as a percent of GDP (1966–96)

The Variability of Interest Rates

Figure I.2 shows the behavior of short-term and long-term interest rates since 1946. It can be seen that interest rates have changed considerably over time.

The considerable variability of interest rates significantly increases the importance of debt financing decisions to both borrowers and lenders. For all the participants in the financial markets (i.e. households, businesses, government, and financial institutions), the stakes in the interest-rate game are large. In an environment of variable interest rates, two interrelated decisions are important to borrowers and lenders: (1) When is the best time to issue debt? (2) Should short-term or long-term debt be used? The risk of making errors in these decisions has been called **interest-rate risk**, a topic playing a central role in this book.

The best strategies for borrowers are shown in table I.1. The cost of errors can be considerable. For example, suppose a borrower believes current interest rates are high and are likely to drop in the future. The best strategy is to borrow short-term and roll-over the loan in the future at a lower interest rate. However, if interest rates rise considerably, the loan must be refinanced at much higher rates and the potential consequences for the borrower may be catastrophic.

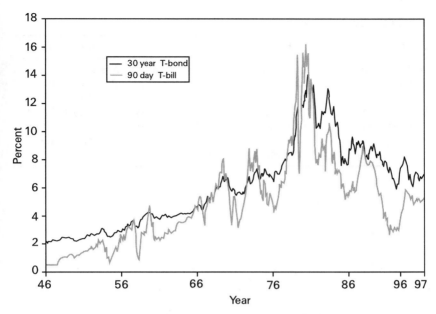

Figure I.2 Interest rates since 1946

Table I.1 Strategies of borrowers

Borrower's forecast	Best strategy	What can go wrong
High current interest rates	Borrow short-term, and roll-over loan	Interest rates may rise and new loan is at higher interest rates
Low current interest rates	Borrow long-term, locking-in the interest rate	Interest rates may fall and the opportunity to borrow at lower rates is lost

The best strategies for lenders are shown in Table I.2. Suppose the lender thinks current interest rates are low and will rise in the future. The best strategy is to lend short-term and roll-over the loan at future higher interest rates. If the forecast is wrong and interest rates fall, the loan must be rolled-over at lower interest rates.

When the economy is expanding, interest rates tend to rise. When the economy is contracting or in recesssion, interest rates tend to decline. This pattern is shown in figure I.3.

Table I.2   Strategies of lenders

Lender's forecast	Best strategy	What can go wrong
High current interest rates	Lend long-term and lock-in high interest rate	Interest rates may rise and opportunity to lend at higher interest rate is lost
Low current interest rates	Lend short-term, expecting to roll-over at higher future interest rates	Interest rates may fall and the loan must be rolled-over at a lower interest rate

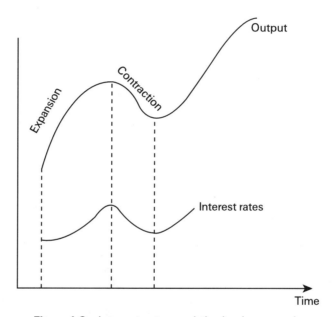

Figure I.3   Interest rates and the business cycle

In an informationally efficient market, all current information is reflected in current interest rates, suggesting that changes in interest rates in the future are essentially random. In an efficient market, there is no way of consistently knowing whether today's rates are high or low relative to future interest rates. Since considerable evidence shows interest rates to be essentially random and unpredictable, there is no easy way to consistently implement the timing strategies described above. The best predictor of tomorrow's interest rate is today's interest rate.

Just simply extrapolating the current interest rate has smaller errors than following the advice of the typical expert forecaster.

New Varieties of Debt

Since consistently accurate prediction of the future course of interest rates is unlikely, market participants have developed other ways of reducing their exposure to changes in rates. The result is the development of many types of financial instruments that allow the transfer of risks. These instruments include options, futures, swaps, and mortgage derivatives. These risk transfer tools allow borrowers and lenders to deal with changing interest rates. The use of these tools for risk transfer is a major focus of this book.

Call options are securities that provide insurance against price increases. A call option is the right to purchase an asset at a specific exercise price during an agreed time interval. This allows the buyer of the call option to lock-in an upper bound on the purchase price. If the price goes above the specific exercise price, the call buyer can exercise the call option and pay only the specified exercise price. If the price is below the exercise price, the option lapses. Thus, purchase of a call option provides a type of insurance against price increases.

Put options are securities that provide insurance against price declines. A put is an option to sell an asset at a specified exercise price. If the market price declines below the exercise price, the put can be exercised and the asset sold at the exercise price. This puts a lower bound on the selling price.

Futures contracts are agreements to buy or sell an asset at a future date at a price set today. This type of contract allows buyers and sellers to lock-in a price today. This type of insurance against price changes dramatically reduces the riskiness of businesses for which price changes can be catastrophic. Many businesses find it better to give up the potential of gains from favorable price changes in exchange for avoiding catastrophic loss from unfavorable price changes.

Swaps allow borrowers to exchange debt obligations. A borrower with a fixed-rate loan may find it advantageous to exchange debt obligations with another borrower with a variable-rate loan. An intermediary, called a swaps dealer, expedites the transaction.

In recent years, many nonmarketable debt instruments have become marketable. The gain of marketability is a reduction in the effective interest rate. The most dramatic example has occurred in the mortgage market. Mortgages that used to be held by the original lender are now packaged into portfolios with default guarantees and sold to investors.

Plan of the Book

The goal of this book is to provide readers with a working knowledge of bond markets, interest rates, present and future value calculations, and interest rate derivatives. Chapter 1 discusses the macroeconomic determinants of interest rates and the effect of the Federal Reserve upon interest rates. Chapter 2 describes the major issuers of debt instruments. Financial intermediaries are covered in chapter 3. Present value calculations and the term structure of interest rates are presented in chapters 4–9. Chapter 10 covers default risk. Options, futures, and other derivatives are described in chapters 11 through 15. Chapter 16 analyzes the impact of international exchange rates on bond investments.

1

Determinants of the Level of Interest Rates

While many varieties of debt instruments exist, all debt instruments are affected by macroeconomic factors determining the underlying interest rate. This chapter discusses macroeconomic factors affecting interest rates. The first part discusses the Federal Reserve and its impact upon rates. Next, the loanable funds approach shows the impact of the supply of, and demand for, funds upon interest rates. The impact of inflation is the focus of the last part of the chapter.

Federal Reserve

The Federal Reserve is the central bank of the United States. The major function of the Federal Reserve in the bond market is to set and administer monetary policy. This involves controlling the money supply and/or interest rates.

The Federal Reserve system consists of two major parts: the Board of Governors in Washington, DC and the 12 Federal Reserve district banks and branches. The Federal Reserve Board is composed of seven members appointed by the President for 14-year terms. The terms are staggered so that a new governor must be appointed every two years. One of the governors is appointed by the President as Chairman of the Board of Governors for a four-year term. In practice, the Chairman has considerable power in setting the course of monetary policy.

The Federal Reserve system is composed of 12 districts, each of which has a Federal Reserve district bank and branches. These Federal Reserve banks are privately owned by the commercial banks that are Federal Reserve members in that district. Each district bank has a president who participates in the Federal Open Market Committee.

The Federal Open Market Committee (FOMC) sets monetary policy. The voting members of the FOMC are the seven governors, the president of the Federal Reserve district bank of New York, and, on a rotating basis, four presidents of the other Federal Reserve district banks. The FOMC has eight regular meetings a year. The primary task of these FOMC meetings is to draft a monetary policy directive, which sets guidelines for the growth rate of the money supply and the level of interest rates.

The goals of monetary policy are to promote economic growth, full employment, and low inflation. Economic growth is desirable because it means an increase in the wealth of the nation. Full employment is desirable for two reasons: (1) more people working means more output; (2) able-bodied people are entitled to have the opportunity to work for equity reasons. Low inflation is good because low inflation promotes incentives to work and increase output.

These policy goals can be competing, forcing the Federal Reserve to make difficult policy choices. For example, it may be hard to achieve both full employment and low inflation. In order to keep the inflation rate relatively low, the Federal Reserve may have to follow a tight monetary policy, keeping the money supply growing at a slow rate and pushing up interest rates. A small money supply (and high interest rates) reduces investment, income, and employment. The Federal Reserve typically adopts a compromise policy.

Technically, there are three possible tools of monetary policy available: (1) changing reserve requirements; (2) changing the interest rates on loans to banks through the Federal Reserve's discount window; and (3) open market operations. In practice, the Federal Reserve concentrates on open market operations. These can be used effectively to make small adjustments in policy. In contrast, changing reserve requirements or changing the discount rate tends to result in large and inflexible changes in policy.

Open market operations involve the purchase and sale by the Federal Reserve of US Treasury securities in the open market. If the Federal Reserve buys bonds in the open market from an individual, the seller's commercial bank account is increased by the sale price. Since the money in this account can be spent, the money supply increases, and, other things being equal, interest rates are reduced. If the Federal Reserve sells bonds to an individual, the buyer's bank account is reduced; the money supply goes down, and interest rates tend to go up.

When the Federal Reserve buys securities from a commercial bank, it pays for them by increasing the bank's balance at the Federal Reserve.

Balances at the Federal Reserve in excess of required reserves can be withdrawn and used to make loans to bank customers, causing an increase in the money supply.

In practice, the Federal Reserve has unlimited buying power, because it can create balances in any amount with the stroke of a pen. In carrying out monetary policy, the Federal Reserve tends to accumulate a large portfolio of US Treasury securities, upon which it earns interest. Part of this interest is used by the Federal Reserve to pay its operating expenses, and the rest is returned to the Treasury.

Foreign Central Banks

Foreign central banks operate in much the same way as the Federal Reserve. A 1990 study by the International Monetary Fund found similar operating procedures for the central banks of France, Germany, Japan, the United Kingdom, and the United States.

Central banks differ in their degree of independence from the rest of the government. The central banks of Germany and Japan are more independent than the US Federal Reserve. The central banks of the United Kingdom and France are more subject to politics than the US Federal Reserve. The evidence shows countries with more independent central banks have lower inflation rates.

Loanable Funds Approach

According to the loanable funds approach, the interest rate is determined by the supply of and the demand for loanable funds. This approach is shown schematically in figure 1.1. The demand curve shows the relationship between the demand for funds and the interest rate. This curve is drawn with a downward slope, indicating a greater demand for funds at lower interest rates. The supply curve shows the relationship between the supply of funds and the interest rate. The supply curve has an upward slope; at higher interest rates more funds are supplied to the market. The interest rate and the amount of funds changing hands are determined by the point where the two curves cross.

The demand for funds

The total demand for funds has several components: business investment in plant and equipment, consumer borrowing for consumption, and

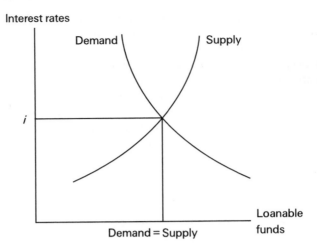

Figure 1.1 Loanable funds approach

governmental budget deficits. We have drawn the total demand curve as downward-sloping, but considerable controversy exists about the demand curves for the components.

Business investment in plant and equipment is affected by the level of the interest rate. Businesses estimate the rates of return on their investments and then list the investments from the highest to the lowest rate of return. The return on investments is then compared to the cost of financing these investments. In the loanable funds framework, the cost of financing is assumed to be the interest rate. Investments with returns higher than the interest rate are profitable and are undertaken. Investments with returns less than the interest rate are rejected. As the interest rate falls (rises), some investments become profitable (unprofitable). Thus, with low interest rates, there is greater business investment in plant and equipment. With high interest rates, business investment is curtailed. This pattern translates into a downward-sloping demand curve.

Consumer borrowing for "big ticket" items is interest-rate sensitive. High interest rates cause reductions in consumer purchases of homes and automobiles, but purchases of relatively low-priced items may not be substantially affected by interest rates. Thus, the demand curve for expensive consumer goods is downward-sloping. For other consumer goods, the slope is unclear. For the aggregate of all consumer goods, the demand curve is probably downward-sloping.

Government borrowing is also included in the demand for funds. Federal government borrowing is probably not substantially affected by interest rates. Expenditure and tax decisions are only indirectly affected by the interest rate. Thus, federal government borrowing can be added as a constant to business and consumer borrowing. State and local governments borrow substantial amounts for capital expenditures. These expenditures are somewhat affected by the interest rate. When interest rates are quite low, state and local governments are more willing to borrow. Thus, the demand for state and local government borrowing is interest sensitive.

The supply of funds

The total amount of funds supplied to the market includes savings from individual consumers, business savings, and increases in the money supply. The supply curve has been drawn with an upward slope; higher interest rates lead to a larger supply of funds, but economists debate the slopes of the components of the supply curve.

Consumers save out of current income for future consumption. The amount of individual saving depends upon preferences, current income, wealth, and interest rates. The major determinants of savings are thought to be preferences, income, and wealth. As described in the next paragraph, interest rates may have only a secondary impact upon savings by consumers.

The direction of the effect of interest rates on savings is debatable. On the one hand, higher interest rates may attract funds from people who are willing to give up current consumption for a more attractive rate of return and resulting higher consumption in the future; this is called the **substitution effect** and implies an upward-sloping supply curve. On the other hand, some savers have a target goal for total future income derived from savings. These individuals are able to reduce the amount saved and maintain the same future income level as interest rates rise. This is called the **income effect** and implies a downward-sloping supply curve. The net impact of these two effects upon total savings is not clear on purely deductive grounds.

In addition, the market value of existing wealth is a function of interest rates. For example, as interest rates decline, the market value of debt instruments (and probably equity as well) increases. Thus, wealth and interest rates interact.

The impact of the interest rate on business savings is not entirely clear either. Business savings represent retained earnings and depreciation. Depreciation is a function of physical wear and tear on equipment and is probably not substantially affected by interest rates. The impact of the interest rate on retained earnings is ambiguous. Retained earnings equal

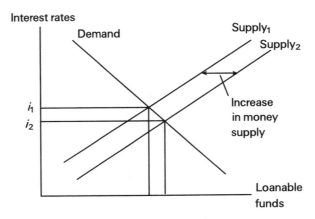

Figure 1.2   An increase in the money supply

earnings minus dividends. Thus, the impact of the interest rate on retained earnings can be decomposed into the impact of the interest rate on earnings and on dividends. Each of these impacts has an unclear direction. For example, the earnings of some firms, such as banks, may be very sensitive to interest rates, whereas other firms' earnings may be totally unaffected by interest rates. Most likely, interest rates are a minor determinant of retained earnings.

Government policies and interest rates

The actions of the government can significantly affect the level of interest rates. The following discussion focuses upon two government policies – increases in the money supply and increases in government borrowing.

Increases in the money supply   The money supply in the economy is largely determined by the central bank (Federal Reserve) as it carries out monetary policy. Increases in the supply of money shift the supply curve of funds to the right, resulting in a lower interest rate (see figure 1.2).

The initial decline in interest rates tends to stimulate business investment, shifting the demand for funds to the right and offsetting part of the initial decline in interest rates. In addition, large increases in the money supply may generate expectations of inflation. These inflationary expectations may raise interest rates as described later in the chapter. Thus, the net impact of increases in the money supply upon interest rates is somewhat ambiguous.

Increases in government borrowing   In the loanable funds framework, an increase in the government deficit (financed by additional

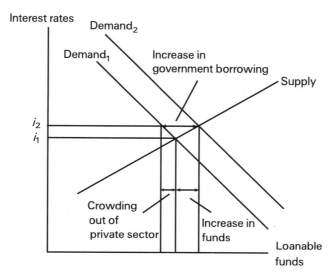

Figure 1.3   Increased government borrowing

borrowing) raises the total demand for funds, resulting in a shift to the right of the demand curve for funds. As shown in figure 1.3, the shift in the demand curve causes a rise in the interest rate. Unless the supply curve is perfectly flat, the total amount of funds supplied to the market does not increase as much as government borrowing. Some nongovernment borrowers are crowded out by the government borrowing. Consequently, increased government borrowing tends to make consumer and business borrowing more expensive, thus reducing consumer expenditures and business capital expenditures in the private economy. The added government borrowing shifts resources from the private sector to the government.

In the crowding-out view, large government deficits reduce business investment in plant and equipment below the level otherwise attainable. Since business investment is a primary ingredient for increasing productivity (output per man hour) and economic growth, large deficits and resulting higher interest rates slow the growth rate of the economy. Thus by borrowing more money, the government may reduce the growth rate of the incomes of the people.

Inflation and Interest Rates

The term **inflation** means a process with a continual increase in the general price level. As prices go up, individuals try to protect their purchasing power and take actions which may inadvertently perpetuate the inflation. For example, employees may try to protect themselves from inflation by having their wages tied to the cost of living. As prices rise, wages are forced up, which raises production costs, which raises selling prices, and so on, in a never-ending cycle. Throughout history, inflation has been a frequent occurrence. Generally, inflation has a significant impact upon economic activity, including interest rates.

Inflation is undesirable for two reasons. First, during inflationary periods, people try to stay ahead of inflation or even benefit in real terms. Strategies include trying to increase wages and prices and purchasing real assets. If some people are smarter or luckier than others, inflation may result in a redistribution of wealth, meaning that some people may be poorer and some people wealthier in real terms as a result of inflation. Second, people's efforts may be directed at keeping ahead of inflation and deflected from productive economic activity. The real wealth and the growth in that wealth may suffer. In effect, inflation may reduce real economic growth, curtailing the total wealth. Thus, inflation can reduce the total economic pie and alter its distribution.

Precisely measuring the rate of inflation is a difficult task. The consumer inflation rate depends upon the price changes of individual consumer goods and the amounts consumed by actual consumers. Since consumer choices change as relative prices change, the basket of goods purchased by the average consumer changes over time. Finding the correct basket of goods is a major problem in measuring the inflation rate. Thus, considerable disagreement exists about the true inflation rate. Government statistics provide several price indexes – a consumer price index, a producer price index, and a GNP deflator. The rate of change in these indexes should each measure the inflation rate. But these rates of change can differ considerably. This discussion overlooks these pragmatic problems in measuring the inflation rate and assumes a hypothetical inflation rate.

Complete certainty

Intelligent investors try to forecast important factors affecting their investment returns. Because inflation affects returns, investors form expectations of the future inflation rate, based upon all available current information. These anticipations of the future inflation rate are reflected immediately in security prices and interest rates.

The most clear-cut relationship between inflation and interest rates occurs when the future inflation rate is completely certain. As will be explained shortly, lenders add an inflation premium to the interest rate to compensate for declining purchasing power in this case.

The inflation-free (real) rate of interest is defined as the rate that would prevail in an inflation-free world. Denote the inflation-free interest rate by r. Let the completely certain inflation rate be denoted by p. Let the observed, nominal (that is, money terms) interest rate be i.

In order to compensate lenders exactly for the declining purchasing power of money, the following condition must hold:

$$i = r + p + rp \tag{1}$$

The following example illustrates this expression. The inflation-free interest rate is 5 percent and the inflation rate is 10 percent. Then the nominal rate, i, must equal the inflation-free rate, r (0.05), plus the inflation rate, p (0.10), plus the product of the two, rp (0.05)(0.10).

$$i = 0.05 + 0.10 + (0.05)(0.10) = 0.155 \tag{2}$$

Adding the inflation rate, p, compensates the lender for the declining value of the principal (10 percent). Adding the term rp compensates the lender for the declining value of the inflation-free interest (0.5 percent). This last term is frequently omitted, since the product of two rates has small absolute value. Thus, in the example, the nominal rate is frequently approximated by the first two terms as 15 percent.

Uncertainty

If the inflation rate is uncertain, the impact of inflation upon interest rates is not as clear-cut. In a widely held view, the anticipated inflation rate is added to the real interest rate. In addition, a risk premium should be added, so that:

$$i = r + E(p) + h \tag{3}$$

where $E(p)$ is the expected inflation rate and h is a risk premium. This premium compensates the lender for the possibility of a higher actual inflation rate than expected rate. To illustrate, if the real interest rate is 5 percent, the expected inflation rate is 10 percent, and the risk premium is 4 percent, the nominal interest rate is

$$i = 0.05 + 0.10 + 0.04 = 0.19 = 19\% \tag{4}$$

Empirical tests

Empirically testing the relationship between inflation and interest rates is difficult because the anticipated inflation rate is not directly observable. Several ways of estimating anticipations have been suggested, but none is completely suitable. Some researchers have tried to see whether the nominal interest rate changes in unison with the observed inflation rate. The evidence indicates a positive, but imprecise relationship between current and recent inflation rates. Thus, if the recent inflation rate is 10 percent, current interest rates increase by some proportion of this 10 percent, but not by exactly 10 percent.

Summary

The Federal Reserve is the central bank of the United States. Its primary role is to set and administer monetary policy in order to keep inflation low, and to encourage economic growth and full employment. The Federal Reserve controls interest rates and the growth rate of the money supply. Its main tool is open market operations.

The interest rate is determined by the demand for investment funds by businesses, by consumers, and by government, and by the supply of savings from individuals and businesses and the supply of money.

Because investors include anticipations of the future in current security prices, anticipated inflation rates have an impact upon the current interest rate. In the case of complete certainty about future inflation, the inflation rate is added to the real interest rate to arrive at the observed nominal interest rate. If the future is uncertain, the nominal interest rate equals the real interest rate plus the anticipated inflation rate plus some risk premium.

Questions and Problems

1   Explain the conflicting policy goals of the Federal Reserve.
2   Describe the determinants of the demand for funds and the supply of funds in the loanable funds framework.
3   Assume that the inflation-free rate of interest is 3 percent and that the inflation rate is 10 percent with complete certainty and no taxes. Determine the nominal interest rate.
4   In a world of certainty with no taxes, the nominal interest rate is 10 percent and the inflation-free interest rate is 5 percent. What is the inflation rate?
5   Assume no taxes. Suppose the inflation-free interest rate is 5 percent. The market forecasts a deflation rate of 15 percent. What is the nominal interest rate?

2

Issuers

This chapter discusses the issuers of securities. In the United States, this list includes the US Treasury, municipalities, corporations, US government and government-sponsored agencies, and mortgage issuers. The security issuers in foreign countries are quite similar, although the existence of particular types of issuers depends upon the size and sophistication of financial markets. Countries such as Japan, Germany, the United Kingdom, and Canada are quite similar to the US. Other countries have fewer similarities.

The US Treasury

The US Treasury has the responsibility of paying US federal government expenditures, collecting taxes, and borrowing to meet the deficit between expenditures and taxes. This borrowing is accomplished by selling debt securities of various types. The large federal deficits of recent years have greatly increased the total amount outstanding of US Treasury debt. Since 1980, annual deficits of over $100 billion have been the norm. The total debt has ballooned to over $5 trillion.

Because of the enormous growth in the federal debt, the Treasury plays an increasingly important role in the debt markets. Treasury debt obligations are the dominant force in the bond market for two reasons. First, the total Treasury debt is enormous. Second, each Treasury issue is large compared to corporate and municipal debt. Treasury issues of $10 billion dollars or more are common. The average corporate bond issue is approximately $130 million. Thus, the typical Treasury bond issue is about 75 times larger than the typical corporate bond issue. Large size for each Treasury debt issue implies a large volume of trading and a liquid market, that is, a market in which dealers make active markets and in which buyers and sellers can trade rapidly without affecting prices.

Treasury securities are held by the Federal Reserve, by foreigners, by commercial banks, by nonbank financial institutions, and by individuals. The Federal Reserve buys and sells Treasury securities in the course of open market operations. In order to effectively control monetary conditions, the Federal Reserve must have sizable holdings of Treasury securities. Foreigners hold Treasury securities because they are default-free and denominated in dollars, a relatively safe currency. Commercial banks hold Treasury securities as secondary reserves, that is, assets that can readily be turned into cash as the need arises. Nonbank financial institutions include pension funds, insurance companies, and finance companies. These institutions are large holders of debt obligations. These obligations allow nonbank financial institutions to control their risk by matching the institutions' fixed obligations to pensioners or policyholders with fixed income investments in bonds. Individual investors hold Treasury securities because they are default-free, free of state income tax, and highly marketable. However, individuals hold a relatively small proportion of Treasury debt directly in their portfolios.

Types of Treasury securities

The Treasury issues nonmarketable and marketable debt.

Nonmarketable debt   About one quarter of the Treasury debt is nonmarketable. The original buyer cannot resell it. Nonmarketable is primarily of two types – savings bonds and bonds sold to government agencies. The US Treasury sells some nonmarketable bonds in the form of savings bonds. Savings bonds have a fixed interest rate, cannot be resold (although they can be redeemed early with penalty), and generally are held until maturity. Only a small part of Treasury borrowing is in the form of savings bonds. A large part of the nonmarketable debt is securities sold to government retirement funds for civil service employees and the military.

Marketable debt   The Treasury sells three major types of marketable debt: (1) bills, (2) notes, and (3) bonds. Treasury bills have maturities up to one year. They are issued on a discount basis, meaning no coupon payments. The buyer pays the purchase price and receives the par value at maturity. The difference is interest.

Treasury notes and bonds are originally issued with maturities exceeding one year. Notes and bonds pay semiannual coupon interest to the owners. The distinction between notes and bonds is largely semantic.

Notes have original maturities of up to 10 years. Bonds have original maturities of between 10 and 30 years.

There are some legal restrictions on the Treasury's ability to issue debt. Congress has put a ceiling on the national debt. As the total debt has grown, Congress has been forced to raise the debt ceiling.

Treasury debt management issues

Issue pattern Every year the Treasury needs to sell over $1.5 trillion of debt. Part of the sales results from the current deficit (recently about $0.25 trillion). The rest is from refinancing of maturing issues.

Because of the enormous sums to be raised, the Treasury spreads its issues out over the course of the year. In addition, the Treasury regularizes its pattern for issuing securities so that the market is not surprised by a particular issue. The Treasury feels that a regular pattern results in lower yields on average. To illustrate, the Treasury might announce the following issue pattern: 13-week and 26-week bills every week, 52-week bills every fourth week, two-year notes every month, etc.

Debt maturity The maturity of its debt is an important issue for the Treasury for two reasons. First, since short-term interest rates usually are lower than long-term interest rates, issuing short-term debt results in lower interest costs on average. Figure 2.1 shows an upward sloping yield curve that has been typical in recent years. Since the long-term interest rate has recently been 1 to 4 percent higher than the short-term interest rate, the short-term securities have an immediate cost saving with a rising yield curve.

Second, short-term debt has to be refinanced more frequently than long-term debt. Since short-term interest rates fluctuate considerably, the rollover of short maturity debt may take place at very high interest rates. A policy of issuing exclusively short maturities has lower total interest cost on average – but greater variability of total interest cost – than issuing long maturities.

Since a considerable part of the current deficit is interest on outstanding debt, the question of debt maturity affects the level and variability of deficits themselves. If the Treasury followed a policy of issuing only short-term debt, the average interest cost of the debt would be relatively low compared to issuing exclusively long-term debt. However, the interest cost of the debt would be closely tied to the level of interest rates. When rates were high, the interest cost of the debt would be very high. The political consequences might be considerable, if the interest on the debt increased at the same time that the other components of the federal deficit were high. A policy of issuing long-term debt exclusively

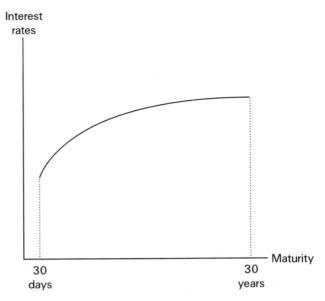

Figure 2.1   Upward sloping yield curve

would stabilize interest costs but make them relatively high on the average. In practice, the Treasury issues debt with many different maturities. The maturity composition is about 25 percent bills, 50 percent notes, and 25 percent bonds.

Procedures for issuing Treasury securities

Because of the enormous amounts of money involved, the procedures for issuing Treasury securities are quite important. The Treasury sells bills, notes, and bonds at weekly auctions. Prospective buyers must submit sealed bids by a specified time. Bids may be competitive or noncompetitive.

Noncompetitive bids   Noncompetitive bids must not exceed $5 million par value. The noncompetitive bidder does not specify a price, but merely specifies the par value of the securities desired. Noncompetitive bidders agree to accept the average price of the accepted competitive bids. All noncompetitive bids are accepted by the Treasury.

Competitive bids   All bids for $5 million or more of par value are competitive. The bidder specifies the price. The Treasury accepts the competitive bids with highest prices (and lowest interest rates) and rejects the others (see figure 2.2). To illustrate the acceptance procedure,

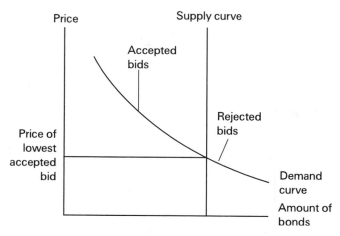

Figure 2.2

suppose the Treasury announces a sale of $5 billion par value of 52-week Treasury bills. One billion dollars of noncompetitive bids and $8 billion of competitive bids are received. The $1 billion of noncompetitive bids are accepted and the $4 billion of competitive bids with the highest prices (lowest yields) are accepted.

Discriminatory auctions   In determining the prices paid by competitive bidders the Treasury has used two procedures. Historically, all accepted competitive bidders have paid the price bid. This type of auction has been called a discriminatory auction because each bidder can pay a different price. The noncompetitive bidders pay the average of these accepted competitive bid prices.

In practical terms, the difference between the highest and lowest accepted competitive bids tends to be small. In technical terms, the demand curve tends to be relatively flat, since new issues must be competitively priced relative to traded old issues. For example, every week the Treasury issues a new 13-week Treasury bill. The bidders for a new 13-week bill can observe yields on the 12-week bill, issued the previous week. These 12-week bill yields provide a good estimate of the fair prices for 13-week bills.

Single-price or Dutch auctions   Recently, the Treasury has used a single-price or Dutch auction in some offers. With a single-price auction, each accepted bid pays the price of the lowest accepted bid.

A single-price auction may increase the total revenue received. On the one hand, the Treasury receives lower revenue with a single-price auction for a given set of bids, since everyone pays the lowest accepted price. On the other hand, in a single-price auction the average bidder

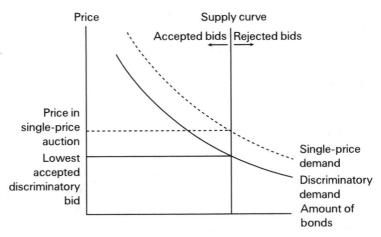

Figure 2.3 Impact of single-price auction upon demand curve

may bid a higher price, shifting the demand curve to the right, off-setting and perhaps overwhelming the first effect (see figure 2.3). The reason for the demand curve shift is the problem of the **winner's curse** in a discriminatory auction. Imagine yourself as a bidder in a discriminatory auction. If you bid a high price, your bid wins but you are cursed with a high price. If you bid a low price, the probability of rejection is higher, but an accepted bid receives a low price. Risk-averse bidders may elect to place low bids to avoid the winner's curse. The average bid is lower. A discriminatory auction shifts the demand curve to the left.

When-issued trading Between the time a Treasury auction is announced and the time the securities are actually sold, trading in unissued, or when-issued, securities occurs. In the when-issued market, the buyers and sellers agree on a price to be paid in the future after the securities are sold at the auction. Since when-issued trading occurs before auction bids are submitted to the Treasury, auction bidders, who can observe prices in the when-issued market, have a good idea of market prices for the new securities. Figure 2.4 shows the timing of the announcement of an issue, auction date, and issue date.

Issuing notes and bonds Issuing coupon-bearing Treasury notes and bonds presents a special problem. Notes and bonds repay a stated par value to the owner at maturity. If these securities were originally issued at nonpar prices, the tax law provides that they would have special tax liabilities that many investors would like to avoid. To ensure issue prices of par, a special bidding procedure is necessary. Bids are solicited in terms of yields. The Treasury selects the winning bids, that is, the ones

Figure 2.4   The announcement date, auction date, and issue date

with the lowest yields. The coupon on the bond issue is set equal to the yield on the average winning bid. If the coupon rate equals the yield, the bonds and notes must sell at par.

Limits on bidders   The competitive bidders in Treasury auctions are typically dealers who intend to resell the securities in the secondary market. If one dealer were able to purchase an entire new issue, that dealer might be able to charge unfairly high prices in the secondary market. To prevent dealer monopolies, the Treasury limits the percentage of a particular issue purchased by a single bidder. Recently, Salomon Brothers, a large dealer, violated Treasury restrictions and purchased a large proportion of an issue. Salomon Brothers was penalized severely for this transgression.

Index-Linked Bonds

Index-linked bonds are inflation-protected bonds. The coupons and par value are adjusted to reflect actual inflation experience. Recently, the US Treasury has issued several inflation-indexed bonds.

To illustrate inflation protection, suppose the US government issues a one-year bond with an annual coupon and par value increased by the realized inflation rate. If the inflation-free interest rate at the time of issue is 5 percent, the index-linked bond has a coupon rate of 5 percent. Suppose par and the issue price are $100, implying a coupon of $5: if the actual inflation rate is 10 percent over the bond's one-year life, the inflation-adjusted coupon is $5.50, that is, $100(0.05)(1.10). The inflation-adjusted par value is $110, that is, $100(1.10). In real terms, the bond buyer receives a return of 5 percent.

In the case of a multi-period bond, the coupons and the par value are adjusted by the cumulative amount of inflation between the issue date of the bond and the payment date. If the actual inflation rates are i_1 for period 1, i_2 for period 2, and so on, then the nominal payment for period n is the stated payment times $(1 + i_1)(1 + i_2) \cdots (1 + i_n)$. Suppose a 20-year bond with a 5 percent stated interest rate is issued; for a par value of $100, the coupon is $5. The actual inflation rates during the next three years are 10 percent, 8 percent, and 7 percent. Then, the coupon payment in year three is $5(1.10)(1.08)(1.07) = 6.3558.

Attractions of index-linked bonds

Index-linked bonds have several attractions. First, for retired persons on a fixed income, index-linked bonds provide a low-risk investment with inflation protection. Standard bonds do not provide the same type of inflation protection. Suppose that the interest rate on a standard bond is set by the market to be the inflation-free interest rate plus the expected inflation rate plus a risk premium for the uncertainty surrounding inflation. If inflation expectations are realized on average, fixed-income investors earn the inflation-free interest rate plus a fair risk premium on average.

Unfortunately, in individual periods, the returns to fixed-income investors can be markedly affected by changes in inflationary expectations. Suppose we have an initial inflation-free interest rate of 5 percent, an expected inflation rate of 5 percent, and an inflation risk premium of 2 percent. The nominal interest rate on nonindexed bonds is 12.25 percent (i.e. the real rate of 5 percent plus the inflation rate of 5 percent plus the product of the two rates plus the 2 percent inflation risk premium). If inflationary expectations change because of new information, the prices of nonindexed bonds adjust and the realized return is affected. As an example, suppose inflation expectations increase from 5 percent to 10 percent, interest rates increase from 12.25 percent to 17.50 percent, and the realized returns for bond investors are reduced for the period in which inflation expectations rose. In general, realized returns on long-term nonindexed bonds are significantly affected by changes in interest rates; long-term bonds can have negative returns when interest rates rise.

Index-linked bonds protect investors from the risks of changing inflationary expectations. Although the holder of an index-linked bond is compensated for realized inflation, indexation of bonds does not protect investors from changes in inflation-free interest rates.

In addition, the issuer of index-linked bonds is protected from inflation risk. An issuer of nonindexed bonds loses if inflationary expectations drop after the bond is issued. In our previous example, the initial interest rate for standard bonds was 12.25 percent because the inflation-free interest rate was 5 percent, expected inflation was 5 percent, and the inflation premium was 2 percent. Suppose the expected inflation rate drops to zero. The nominal interest rate on newly issued bonds drops to 7 percent, but the bond issuer is forced to pay the contractually binding 12.25 percent coupon on the nonindexed debt. The real burden of the debt for the issuer has risen.

Nonindexed bonds contain a premium for inflation risk. Inflation risk premiums are unnecessary with index-linked bonds. By issuing index-linked bonds, the issuer reduces interest costs.

The problems with index-linked debt

Currently, index-linked bonds are not widely issued. Issuance of such bonds is largely confined to British and Israeli government bonds and a few issues of US Treasury bonds. The lack of indexed-linked bonds results from the following problems.

Taxation of the indexed part of the return presents one problem. In the United States, coupon interest is fully taxable; bond principal repayment is tax-free. If the coupon is indexed, the investor earns the inflation rate times one minus the tax rate, which is necessarily less than the inflation rate. If consumption costs rise by the inflation rate, the investor has a shortfall because of taxes. A similar problem occurs with indexation of the principal. If the indexed amount is a capital gain, the investor loses in real terms. A remedy is to make the indexation tax-free.

Tax exemption for the indexation of coupons presents a further problem. Coupons on standard bonds are taxed. If inflationary expectations are included in the coupon of standard bonds and are grossed-up, there is an inconsistency between standard and index-linked bonds. A possible solution is to make indexation of principal tax-free, but make indexation of coupon taxable.

Individual firms are reluctant to issue inflation-linked debt because the firm's inflation rate can differ from the inflation rate for the overall economy. For example, consider a firm issuing a bond linked to the overall price index. If the overall inflation rate is 10 percent but the firm's inflation rate is only 5 percent, the firm loses; it is required to pay 10 percent more interest, but its assets increase by only 5 percent in value. Issuing bonds tied to a broad inflation index increases the firm's risk unless the firm's inflation rate is highly correlated with the overall inflation rate.

Corporations are able to issue floating-rate bonds tied to a short-term interest rate. If the short-term interest rate is highly correlated with realized inflation rates, the firm is able to inflation-index the coupon, although not the principal. Thus, floating-rate bonds provide partial indexation protection.

Municipalities

Municipalities are state and local governments. These governmental units are sizable issuers of debt instruments. There are many varieties of municipal debt. Some municipal bonds are general obligation (GO) bonds, which are backed by the full taxing power of the municipality.

Other municipal bonds are revenue bonds, which are sold to finance a specific project. Only the revenues from that project are used to repay the revenue bonds. An example would be a toll highway; the revenues from the tolls are used to repay the bondholders. Revenue bonds are higher-risk and carry higher yields than general obligation bonds.

The interest paid on most municipal bonds is exempt from federal income taxes. Consequently, the (before-tax) yields on municipal bonds are relatively low. In effect, the federal government provides a tax subsidy to state and local governments. In recent years, the federal government has restricted the federal tax exemption to bonds that are intended to finance truly governmental activities.

Because most municipal bonds are small issues, they are relatively illiquid. There is a "thin" market in them, meaning that trading is relatively infrequent. Many municipal bonds are serial issues. That is, a particular issue has staggered maturities. The amount of each maturity outstanding is often quite small, reducing liquidity further.

Municipal bonds are typically issued through an auction. The entire issue is sold to an investment banker, a firm which resells the bonds to the public. Investment banking is discussed in more detail in a later chapter.

Corporations

Corporations are large issuers of debt and equity. Since 1980, issues of corporate debt have skyrocketed. Part of this increase in debt is explained by merger activity in which many corporate mergers were heavily financed by debt. The use of very small amounts of equity and large amounts of debt makes the debt very risky. Bonds with high default risk are called junk bonds. Junk bond financing has increased markedly.

Corporate debt obligates the issuing firm to make fixed payments to debtholders. A fixed payment obligation may be advantageous or disadvantageous to stockholders depending upon the fortunes of the firm. If a corporation does extremely well, all incremental returns above the payments to the bondholders go to the stockholders, who earn high returns. If the corporation does poorly, there may be little or nothing left for stockholders after paying the fixed obligations to bondholders. The stockholders may lose everything invested. Consequently, use of debt financing tends to magnify the returns to stockholders. If the firm does well, stockholders do *very* well; if the firm does poorly, stockholders do *very* poorly.

Textbooks on corporate finance devote considerable attention to the question of the optimal, or best, amount of debt financing for a firm. These texts do not provide any simple solution to the problem. Besides the question of the increased risk from magnification of stockholders' returns, a major controversy concerns the so-called tax advantage of debt. Because interest payments on corporation debt are deductible in computing corporate income taxes, there are possible tax advantages of debt. But expert opinions vary on measuring this possible benefit.

For some firms, the managers of the firms may have better information about the firm's prospects than the market. The decision to issue bonds or stock is affected by this difference in information, so-called **asymmetric information**. For example, if *only* the management knows of extremely attractive investment opportunities, the stock price of the firm does not reflect the profits from these opportunities and is relatively low. Sale of stock at this depressed price is a mistake; issuing debt is a better idea.

In large corporations, the stockholders typically hire managers to act as agents on behalf of the stockholders. The gain to the agent from a particular corporate strategy may differ from the gain to the stockholders. Rational agents can be expected to act in their own personal interest, not in the stockholders' interest, creating an **agency problem**. This conflict of interest may affect the decision to issue stock or bonds.

Government Agencies

Several agencies of the federal government issue debt obligations. These include the Government National Mortgage Association (GNMA), the Export–Import Bank, and the Tennessee Valley Authority.

There are several agencies which are privately owned but sponsored and backed by the federal government. Several of these are large borrowers in the debt markets, including the Federal Home Loan Banks, the Federal National Mortgage Association (FNMA), the Federal Home Loan Mortgage Corporation (FHLMC), and the Farm Credit Bank. The first three were set up to promote the inflow of credit to the housing market and the last one to promote the flow of funds into the farming industry.

The securities of government agencies are the direct obligations of private agencies. They are not the direct obligations of the federal government and, therefore, are not default-free in the same sense as Treasury securities. But in practical terms, the chance for default is very tiny. The federal government would not allow any of these agencies to fail. Consequently, agency securities are almost interchangeable with Treasury securities. Agency securities are usually smaller-sized issues than Treasury securities and are somewhat less marketable. The securities of the government-sponsored agencies have a slightly higher default risk than the government agencies (e.g. GNMA). In practical terms, default risk on the government-sponsored agencies is minimal because of the high probability of a government bailout.

Mortgages

Mortgages are loans backed by real estate as collateral. The total amount of real estate loans outstanding is enormous.

Historically, thrift institutions were the major financial institution in the mortgage market. Traditionally, thrifts made real estate loans and then held these loans as assets until the mortgage matured. In recent years, thrifts have begun to sell mortgages in the secondary market. The usual procedure is for a sizable number of mortgages to be guaranteed against default, put together into a pool, and then sold to investors. Claims on this mortgage pool are typically marketable and can be exchanged between investors. The thrift institution which originates the securities in the pool no longer holds the mortgage but often continues to process the collection of mortgage payments for the pool.

This process of selling mortgages is called securitization because the mortgages are effectively changed into securities that can be bought and sold in the resale market. Sometimes this type of security is called asset-backed. Securitization has several important consequences. First, the originating thrift no longer bears the risk of default on the mortgage or the risk that interest rates might change adversely in the future. The default risk is covered by insurance. The interest rate risk is borne by the buyers of the mortgages. Second, securitization opens up the market for mortgages to many more lenders, increasing the availability of funds to the mortgage market and reducing interest costs to borrowers. In effect, the efficiency of the borrowing and lending process has been improved.

Government agencies have played a major role in the development of a national mortgage market. Government guarantees have eliminated the default risk of mortgages and greatly increased their marketability.

In recent years, so-called derivative mortgage products have expanded dramatically. Derivatives are securities based upon mortgages. However, the cash flows from the underlying mortgages are broken into separate packages. Some derivatives are low-risk. Some derivatives are extremely high-risk; their prices can change dramatically as interest rates change. Some buyers of mortgage derivatives have incurred huge losses after interest rates changed.

Summary

The US Treasury issues debt to finance federal budget deficits. Given the large cumulative total of the deficits over time, the total amount of debt is large. The Treasury has a serious task to issue debt to cover new deficits and roll-over the maturing debt from previous deficits. Given the magnitude of Treasury operations, the impacts upon interest rates can be considerable.

Other large issuers of securities include government agencies, government-sponsored agencies, municipalities, corporations, and mortgage issuers.

Questions and Problems

1 Since 1980, the market for Treasury debt has become increasingly important. Why?
2 What types of entities are the major holders of Treasury securities and why?
3 Explain the procedure by which the Treasury auctions securities. What are the pros and cons for a discriminatory auction versus a one-price auction?
4 The Treasury announces an auction of $10 billion par value of 52-week Treasury bills. $2 billion of noncompetitive bids are received. The competitive bids are as follows:

Price per $1 of par	Par value
0.9200	$3 billion
0.9194	$3 billion
0.9188	$4 billion
0.9180	$2 billion
0.9180	$2 billion
0.9178	$6 billion

Compute the price per dollar of par paid by noncompetitive bidders with a discriminatory auction.

5 The Treasury auctions $12 billion of 52-week Treasury bills. Three billion dollars of noncompetitive bids are received. The competitive bids are:

Price per $1 of par	Par value
0.9200	$5 billion
0.9180	$4 billion
0.9170	$3 billion
0.9160	$2 billion

What is the price paid per dollar of par (to 4 decimals) by noncompetitive bidders with a discriminatory auction? If a single-price (Dutch) auction were used, the bid prices would increase proportionally by 1 percent. Would the Treasury receive higher revenue with a discriminatory auction or a one-price auction? Suppose that a single-price auction increased the bids proportionally compared to a discriminatory auction. By what percent would the bids have to increase for the total revenue to be the same with a discriminatory and single-price auction?

3

Financial Intermediaries

Many financial intermediaries play an important role in the debt markets. Investment banking firms market debt securities on behalf of issuers. Dealers make markets in the resale (secondary) market. Brokers act as agents for buyers and sellers in the resale markets. Mutual funds, insurance companies, pension funds, commercial banks, and thrifts are large lenders in the debt markets. The purpose of this chapter is to describe the major functions of these intermediaries in the debt markets.

A long literature discusses the reasons for the existence of these financial intermediaries. Financial intermediaries exist because they expedite the flow of funds from economic sectors with surpluses to sectors with deficits. Financial intermediaries provide a number of advantages including the following: (1) pooling of small savings, (2) diversification of risks, (3) economies of scale in monitoring information and evaluating investment risks, (4) lower transactions costs.

Initial Sale of Securities (Primary Market)

When securities are issued, they may be sold directly to buyers, as in the case of the US Treasury, which sells securities directly to the public and to bond dealers. Alternatively, security issues are sold to investment banking firms, which market the securities.

Original issues of securities are classified as public or private offerings. The exact meaning of the term public is a technical legal question. In practical terms, a public offering has a sufficiently large size and has a sufficiently large number of buyers. Issues failing to meet the conditions for public offerings are considered private offerings. Public offerings of securities have to be registered with the Securities and Exchange

Commission (SEC) before the securities can be sold, whereas private offerings are not registered. The purpose of SEC registration is to have the SEC verify the factual accuracy of the information about the securities to reduce the chance of fraud by issuers of securities. SEC endorsement does not indicate desirable investments but rather represents a confirmation of informational accuracy. Several types of public offerings of securities do not have to be registered with the SEC. These include US Treasury securities, municipal bonds, and debt with maturities of less than 270 days.

Investment bankers typically use syndicates to sell securities. A syndicate is a group of investment bankers who combine their efforts to market an issue. A particular investment banker organizes the syndicate and is called the lead underwriter. A larger syndicate gives access to a larger group of potential buyers. Syndicates are usually employed for issues of common stock since the stock is sold to many small buyers, who are more easily reached with more syndicate members. Syndicates are smaller, or nonexistent, for debt issues since bonds have relatively low resale risk for the investment banker. The marketing of bonds tends to be easier since bonds are often purchased by a small number of large financial institutions.

Firm commitments

Firm commitments involve the outright purchase of an entire security issue by an investment banker (or syndicate), which takes on the risks of reselling the issue to the public. The underwriter purchases the issue and tries to resell it publicly at a higher price, earning the difference as an underwriting fee or spread. Since the resale price is not guaranteed, the underwriter runs the risk of being forced to sell the issue below the purchase price. Part of the underwriting fee is compensation for this risk.

The underwriter pays SEC registration expenses. A public registration may take several weeks or more. During this period, market conditions may change, and the underwriter may be exposed to considerable risks from a declining market.

In order to speed up the issuing process, a procedure called a shelf registration is now permitted. With a shelf registration, securities are effectively preregistered with the SEC for the following two years. Once the registration is approved, the issue can be brought to market on very short notice. This allows an issuer to try to time an issue as market conditions change. For example, a firm issuing bonds would like to reduce its financing costs by selling the bonds when interest rates are low. With a shelf-registered issue, the firm can rapidly bring the bonds to market if conditions become very favorable. Investment banking fees are lower for shelf registration because the resale risk is lower. That is, the risk of price decline is small because the investment banker holds the debt for only one or two days.

Best efforts

Public offerings may involve best-efforts selling. In this case, an investment banking firm tries to sell as much of an issue as possible. Any unsold amount reverts back to the issuer. The investment banking firm does not bear much risk with best-efforts selling. Best-efforts selling appears to be concentrated among the low-risk and the high-risk offerings. For low-risk offerings, the issuer does not need an underwriter to absorb the risk, since the risk is small. For high-risk offerings, underwriters are unwilling to absorb the risk. Moderate-risk offerings tend to be firm commitments.

Private placements

Some corporate securities are sold directly to buyers in what is called a private offering. An example would be the direct sale of a corporate bond issue to an insurance company. Insurance companies are large buyers of private offerings of bonds.

Private offerings may have advantages. First, the issuer does not have to bear the cost of registration of a public offering. Second, the issue can be tailor-made to the needs of the issuer and buyer. An insurance company may find a particular privately-offered bond attractive because of its specific maturity, e.g. 13 years, not easily found in the market.

Private offerings have disadvantages as well. First, private offerings cannot be widely traded; the resale market is limited. Private offerings are relatively illiquid. Second, the interest rate on a private placement is higher than an otherwise identical public issue. The higher interest rate is a disadvantage to the issuer, although an advantage to the buyer.

Rule 144a offerings

A rule 144a offering is a sale of securities to qualified institutional buyers, typically insurance companies, mutual funds, or pension funds. Because these institutional buyers are assumed to be informed investors, these securities do not have to undergo a public registration with the SEC. Rule 144a securities can be resold to other institutional buyers. Thus,

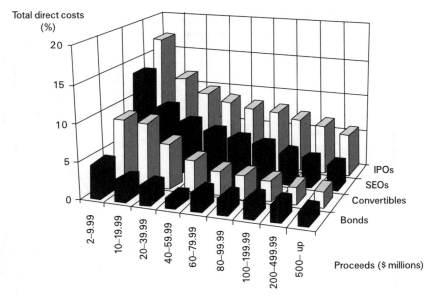

Note: Total direct costs as a proceeds. The total direct costs for initial public offerings (IPOs), seasoned equity offerings (SEOs), convertible bonds, and straight bonds are composed of underwriter spreads and other direct expenses.

Source: Inmoo Lee, Scott Lochhead, Jay Ritter and Quanshui Zhao, "The Cost of Raising Capital," *Journal of Financial Research*, XIX (Spring 1996), pp. 59–74.

Figure 3.1 Underwriter costs versus issue size

they have somewhat more liquidity and somewhat lower yields than private placements. Rule 144a offerings are largely debt obligations.

Cost of public offerings

Figure 3.1 shows the underwriter costs in percent versus the size of the offering. For larger offerings, the percent cost is lower. The cost also depends upon the type of security issued; it is greatest for IPOs (initial public offerings of stock). SEOs (seasoned equity offerings) have lower costs; these are additional sales of stock by companies with existing publicly traded stock. The next highest cost is for convertible bonds. Finally, straight bonds have the lowest costs.

Figure 3.2 shows the costs of issuing debt as a function of bond rating. The rating is an indicator of the probability of default. The highest

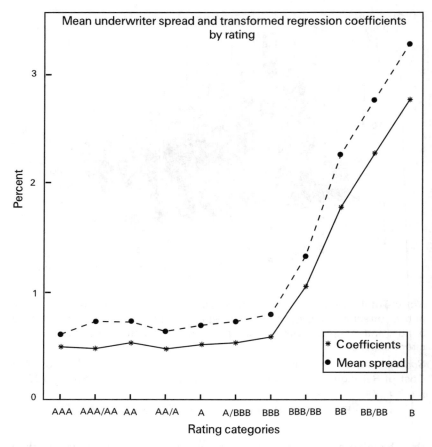

Source: S. Jewell and M. Livingston, "Split Ratings, Bond Yields, and Underwriter Spreads," *Journal of Financial Research*, XXI (Summer 1998).
Figure 3.2   Underwriter fees versus bond rating

rating is AAA and the lowest is B. The underwriter costs are virtually the same for all ratings of BBB and above; these are sometimes called investment-grade. Ratings of BB and B have considerably higher underwriter fees because the default risk of these bonds is much higher. BB and B rated bonds are sometimes called junk bonds.

The figure also shows the underwriter fees for cases where the two largest rating agencies (Moody's and Standard & Poors) disagree on the rating. Thus, a rating of BBB/BB means that one agency rates the bond BBB and the other agency rates the agency BB. The underwriter fees for these "split-rated" bonds lie between the fees for the higher and lower rating.

Dealers and Brokers (Secondary Market)

Resale markets for securities have an important function. The opportunity for investors to buy or sell securities rapidly without affecting the price makes securities more liquid and the ownership of securities more desirable. Increased liquidity reduces the returns required by investors, making the cost of funds lower for business and governmental borrowers.

Security dealers are market makers. They have an inventory of securities and buy and sell. Dealers quote bid prices, at which they are willing to buy, and asked prices, at which they are willing to sell. On average, the dealer hopes to make the difference between the bid and the asked prices. Brokers act as agents for buyers and sellers.

Brokers carry out transactions for a fee or commission. There are three basic types of brokers. Full-service brokers both give advice to clients and carry out transactions. Discount brokers merely execute transactions; their fees might be one-third those of a full-service broker. Deep discount brokers handle large transactions. Because the transaction size is large, the commission as a percentage of the transaction size is quite low for deep discount brokers. Thus, large traders using deep discount brokers receive relatively low commissions.

Organized exchanges

For common stocks, a large proportion of security trading takes place on organized exchanges. Access to trading on organized exchanges is restricted to exchange members. Nonmembers pay members a commission to brokers to execute orders on the floor of the exchange.

The New York Stock Exchange (NYSE) is the largest organized stock exchange in the United States by volume of trading, and it dominates common stock trading. The American Stock Exchange (AMEX) is the second-largest organized stock exchange in the United States. Members of an exchange are described as having a seat. This is not a place to sit, but represents the right to trade on the floor of the exchange. Exchange seats are traded and their market value fluctuates as market conditions change. To trade on the floor of the exchange, one must purchase a seat and pass other standards set by the exchange. Members of the exchange may have more than one seat, if they have a great deal of business on the floor of the exchange.

There are several types of stock exchange members. The largest group is commission brokers who execute buy and sell orders for the public for a fee. Some members are odd-lot brokers. An odd-lot is defined as a transaction of less than 100 shares. A round lot is 100 shares or a multiple of 100 shares. Transactions for less than 100 shares have to go through odd-lot brokers who charge a fee. Odd-lot brokers break round lots into odd-lots and vice versa. Another type of member is a registered trader, who trades for his own account. Because the cost of a seat is quite high, registered traders must be individuals who do enough trading to cover the large investment required to own a seat. Registered traders probably feel that proximity to the action on the exchange floor gives them the advantage of speedy execution.

Specialist firms are the final type of exchange members. Specialists are designated market makers for individual securities listed on the NYSE. Every listed security has one, and only one, specialist who has a monopoly position as market maker. Specialist firms are typically market makers for several different securities. To be a specialist, a firm has to have enough capital to maintain an inventory of the traded securities. The stated purpose of the specialist system is to reduce the variability of security prices. When too many sellers exist, the specialist is supposed to be a buyer to keep prices from falling temporarily. When too many buyers exist, the specialist is supposed to be a seller to prevent prices from rising temporarily. Proponents of the specialist system claim that a monopoly position for a market maker is desirable. However, the Chicago Board Options Exchange operates very effectively with several market makers. In addition, over-the-counter markets typically have several market makers for any one security.

There are several ways of placing orders. A market order allows the commission broker to execute the order at the most favorable price at the time that the order hits the exchange floor. The advantage of a market order is that the order will definitely be carried out. The disadvantage is that the price might change adversely. For example, an investor may place a market order to buy at 2:00 p.m. when the price is $40. By the time that the order is executed at 2:02, prices may have changed. The best purchase price available at the time may be $41. The order will be executed by the broker at this price.

Another type of order is a limit order. This represents an order with some constraints. The order will be executed only if the constraints are met. For example, at 2:00 p.m. a limit buy order may be placed to purchase at $40 or less. If the best purchase price exceeds $40 when the order reaches the exchange floor, the order will not be executed. The limit order can specify if it is to be canceled if not executed immediately (called fill-or-kill). A limit order can also be left outstanding indefinitely. The order would then be executed if the price reaches $40.

In some situations, investors may want to place a stop order, which is an order to close out an existing position. For example, an investor may purchase a stock at $40 but with great fear that the price might decline sharply. To provide downside protection, the investor might place a stop order at $37 to sell this stock. If the price declines to $37, the stop order will be executed.

If an investor feels that the price of a security is going to decline, the investor can try to benefit through a shortsale. In a shortsale, a security is borrowed and sold in expectation of buying this security back later at a lower price. In effect, the investor tries to sell high and buy low, making the difference. For example, if an investor feels that IBM stock is overpriced at $135, the investor can shortsell, hoping to purchase IBM at $120 for a $15 profit.

In general, the proceeds from a shortsale cannot be used by the shortseller but must be left on deposit with the broker. The shortseller must pay any cash dividends to the lender of the securities. This rule results from the fact that a stock usually goes down by approximately the after-tax amount of a cash dividend on the ex-dividend (dividend payment) date.

In addition, the NYSE has a rule that shortsales cannot take place following a downtick in prices. The NYSE keeps a record of every transaction price for every security, and every shortsale must be designated as such. The downtick rule says that if prices have dropped, the next transaction cannot be a shortsale. In technical terms, the downtick rule says that a shortsale is prohibited if the last, previous, different price was higher. For example, if the price sequence is 40, 41, 41 or 40, 41, the next sale can be a shortsale. If the past price sequence was 41, 40, a downtick has occurred and the next transaction cannot be a shortsale.

The motivation for the downtick restriction on shortsales is to preclude a deluge of shortsales from driving prices sharply lower. In the past, unscrupulous traders have been able to create panic selling in a particular security by shortselling large quantities of the stock. After the panic has driven prices to extremely low levels, the shortsellers can then buy back the stock for huge gains. The downtick rule has been instituted to prevent this type of price manipulation.

The organized exchanges have a set of requirements for a security to be traded, or, as it is usually called, listed. These requirements deal with a minimum size, a minimum number of shareholders, and a minimum period of existence. In the past, being listed on an exchange was considered an advantage. Some investigators believed that listing by itself raised the stock price. Currently, listing is regarded as less desirable. Many large and well-known firms are not traded on the NYSE or AMEX but over-the-counter (discussed below).

Over time, transactions on the NYSE are becoming increasingly automated. Thus, small buy and sell orders are matched by computer. In addition, the stock exchange and the futures exchanges are linked by computer so that transactions on both exchanges can be executed simultaneously.

For many years, the NYSE had a fixed set of commission rates charged by all member firms. Because these commissions were quite high for large transactions, a market developed for over-the-counter trading of stocks listed on the NYSE. This market has been called the Third Market. The competition from the Third Market forced the NYSE and AMEX to move to a negotiated commission schedule, with lower fees for large transactions.

Trading of options and futures takes place on organized exchanges. Since participants in the options and futures markets may have possible financial liabilities exceeding their original cash commitments, a special organization called a clearinghouse is required to guarantee performance. Clearinghouses are discussed more fully in the chapters on options (chapter 11) and futures contracts (chapter 13).

Trading of securities on organized exchanges in the United States is conducted by continuous auction. For a number of hours during the day, the exchange remains open and trading can occur continuously, as often as buyers and sellers enter the market. On some other exchanges, trading occurs for only a short period during the day. All the buyers and sellers get together at the designated time and agree to one price at which all purchases and sales are executed. Examples of this type of trading include the London Gold Market and the Israeli Stock Exchange.

While most trading on the New York Stock Exchange is stocks, a number of corporate bonds are also traded. In general, the trading of bonds on the New York Stock Exchange involves small-volume transactions and may not be representative of larger-volume prices.

Over-the-counter

Over-the-counter (OTC) trading involves a network of dealers who make markets in individual securities. OTC dealers stand ready to buy at the bid price and sell at the (higher) asked price, hoping to profit on average by the difference. A sizable amount of trading of stocks is done over-the-counter. Virtually all bond trading is carried out over-the-counter.

Apart from New York Stock Exchange corporate bond trading, the resale market for debt instruments is essentially an OTC market composed of dealers and brokers. Dealers make markets in securities. That is, dealers maintain inventories and risk their own funds. Dealers stand ready to buy at the bid price and sell at the asked price, hoping on the average to make this difference or spread.

In contrast to dealers who risk their own funds, brokers do not own securities; instead they try to match buyers and sellers for a fee. Frequently, brokers will serve as a middleman expediting trades between dealers.

A dealer hopes to make the bid–asked spread on average. However, on an individual transaction, a dealer may buy at the current bid price of $100 and a few hours later sell at the then-current asked price of $99. This inventory loss is the primary risk of being a dealer. Hopefully, gains on profitable trades at least offset losses on unprofitable trades, but there is no guarantee of profit.

Dealers can try to make money by gambling on the direction of price movements – so-called positioning. For example, if a bond dealer feels that interest rates are going to fall, the dealer can buy bonds in expectation of selling the bonds back at future higher prices. If the dealer's forecast is wrong, the dealer must close the position at unfavorable prices and absorb a loss.

Security dealers are heavily levered. That is, the dealer's equity is a small percentage of the market value of his inventory. Most dealer financing is in the form of debt. For US Treasury bond dealers, a small proportion of debt financing is in the form of bank loans. The majority of dealer (debt) financing is in the form of repurchase agreements (repos).

A repurchase agreement involves the sale of a US Treasury security with an agreement to repurchase the same security the next day at the sale price plus overnight interest. Some repurchase agreements may be for longer than overnight; these are called term repos. Repurchase agreements are discussed in more detail in chapter 5.

Because dealers are so highly levered, the risk of dealer bankruptcy cannot be neglected. Several dealers have gone bankrupt in recent years. Some dealer losses have exceeded dealer equity, meaning that someone besides the dealer has had to absorb part of the dealer losses.

Until recently, regulation of government bond dealers has been minimal. Entry into the dealer market has been free, with minimal official restrictions on dealer behavior. Because of recent bankruptcies, new legislation requires the US Treasury to regulate dealers.

A considerable amount of stock trading occurs over-the-counter. The NASDAQ (National Association of Security Dealers Automated Quotation) system serves two functions. First, information about bid–asked prices is exchanged over NASDAQ. An investor wishing to transact in a particular OTC stock can see the prices quotes of market-making dealers. The most favorable price can be found. Second, small trades are matched and consummated by computer.

Several computerized trading systems have been developed for large blocks of stock. The buyers and sellers place their orders anonymously. Other investors are able to search the posted quotes for desirable prices and consummate transactions. The transactions costs for these large-block computerized systems are extremely low.

Bid–asked spreads

Dealers quote a bid price (at which they are willing to buy) and an asked price (at which they are willing to sell). The bid–asked spread represents the price of dealer services. Since spreads differ for particular securities, an interesting and important question is the determination of these spreads.

Spreads have been found to be related to the risks borne by dealers. First, spreads are inversely related to the volume of trading. For example, spreads tend to be large if trading is infrequent (a so-called thin market). An inactive resale market implies a longer holding period for dealer inventory. The longer the holding period, the greater the chance of price change. The likelihood of an unfavorable event increases for longer holding periods and the bid–asked spread increases.

In the bond market, US Treasury securities have active markets. In contrast, the majority of corporate and municipal bonds are infrequently traded and have large bid–asked spreads. To a considerable extent, this difference between Treasury securities and corporate and municipal bonds results from the size of each issue. Individual Treasury issues have total par values in the billions of dollars, whereas corporate and municipal bond issues have total par values in the millions of dollars.

Second, spreads are positively related to the inherent price risk of individual securities. Some securities can be expected to have a bigger percentage price change over a particular time interval compared to other securities. For example, short-term (30-day) US Treasury bills tend to have smaller percentage price changes than long-term (30-year) US Treasury bonds. As a consequence, the bid–asked spreads on bills will be much smaller than the bid–asked spreads on bonds.

Third, the bid–asked spread should be a function of dealer financing costs. When rates of interest are high, bid–asked spreads would, other things being equal, be relatively high to compensate the dealer for the high cost of financing inventory. Since most of a bond dealer's inventory is financed with bank loans and repurchase agreements, changes in these interest rates would tend to be reflected in bid–asked spreads.

Fourth, the bid–asked spread may depend upon the possibility that the dealer is trading against an informed investor who knows more than the dealer. In such circumstances, the dealer has an incentive to increase the size of the bid–asked spread. For example, if a dealer believes that a sell order is from an informed trader, the dealer has an incentive to drop the bid price and widen the spread.

The flow of information

In an over-the-counter market, transactions typically occur over the telephone. Maintaining up-to-date information on prices is critical in this type of market. As a consequence, electronic quotation systems have developed. These systems allow dealers to feed the latest bid–asked quotations into the system. They also allow dealers, brokers, buyers, and sellers to see the price quotes of competing dealers.

In OTC stock trading, the NASDAQ system was developed. This is an automated system for quoting the bid and asked prices of dealers in the OTC market. In the bond market, competing services provide quotations. Inactively traded securities do not have prices quoted electronically. Price information for inactive securities is disseminated in the old fashioned way – by paper quote sheets.

Every transaction on the New York Stock Exchange is recorded and a highly accurate record of prices is available. In contrast, the bond market is an OTC market with no centralized record of actual transaction prices. The available price quotations on bonds observed in business newspapers are really bid–asked quotes rather than actual transactions prices. For example, the *Wall Street Journal* provides price quotes for US Treasury bills, notes, and bonds. These are average bid–asked quotes based upon a survey of several bond dealers at midafternoon. Actual transaction prices might be significantly different. Active bond market participants subscribe to a quotation service providing up-to-the-minute bid–asked quotes on debt instruments.

Mutual Funds

Mutual funds provide a clear example of the diversification role played by financial intermediaries. A mutual fund is a pooling of the funds of many small savers. Each investor has a proportional claim on the assets of the fund. These funds are then invested by the managers of the mutual fund in stocks, bonds, and other financial claims, as allowed by the fund's prospectus. The management charges a fee which varies with the investment objective of the fund. Funds requiring a great deal of managerial effort charge higher fees.

Closed-end mutual funds have an initial offering of shares, and no additional shares are sold. Existing shares cannot be redeemed. Thus, a closed-end fund has no new cash inflows or redemptions. Shares of closed-end funds trade on the open market at prices that may differ from their net asset value. The net asset value (NAV) of a mutual fund is the liquidating value, or the amount available to distribute if all the fund's assets were sold off. Typically, closed-end fund shares trade at a discount from their net asset value, although sometimes they may trade at premiums. Closed-end fund discounts from net asset value cannot get too large, since very large discounts would provide a profit opportunity to a large investor, who would buy all the shares of the fund at a discount and then liquidate the fund for a profit.

Korea Fund is an interesting example of a closed-end fund. An offering of Korea Fund shares was made in the United States. The proceeds were invested in Korean stocks with the special permission of the Korean government. Since ownership of Korean stocks is generally restricted to Korean residents, Korea Fund was given special access to the Korean markets. Consequently, the shares of Korea Fund typically trade at a premium above the net asset value. The net asset value is determined by the prices of the stocks as traded in Korea, that is, the value of Korean stocks to Koreans. The shares of the Korea fund sell in the United States at their value to US residents; this value is higher than the value to Koreans.

Most mutual funds are open-end funds; the fund continuously stands ready to sell new shares and redeem old shares. For open-end funds, additional shares can be sold, or existing shares can be redeemed by investors.

Many open-end mutual funds have front-end loads. Front-end loads are sales commissions that are deducted from the money invested. For example, a $10,000 investment with an 8.5 percent commission would result in a net investment of $9,150. A sizable number of mutual funds are no-load funds. These funds charge no sales commissions. Other things being equal, a investor should clearly prefer a no-load fund to one with a load. Someone investing in a no-load fund has to investigate the fund himself, since a security salesperson has a strong incentive to suggest a load fund. No-load mutual funds are typically purchased through the mail. Three especially informative sources about mutual funds are: *Mutual Fund Sourcebook* by Morningstar, *Investment Companies* by Arthur Weisenberger, and *The Handbook for No-Load Investors*.

The investment objectives of mutual funds vary. Some funds invest exclusively in stocks; some exclusively in bonds; some in a combination of stocks and bonds. Within these broader categories of funds, there are many specialized objectives. In the area of bond funds, specialties include US Treasury securities, corporate bonds, high-risk corporate bonds, municipal (tax-free) bonds, foreign bonds, and money market funds. For many people, money market mutual funds have provided an attractive alternative to bank savings and time deposit accounts. Money market mutual fund accounts typically provide a number of attractive services, including limited check-writing privileges and the ability to transfer funds by telephone between mutual funds or between the mutual fund and a bank. For stock mutual funds, specialized objectives include small company funds, growth funds, value funds, foreign funds, and global funds. Index funds try to duplicate the returns on a broad stock index.

Mutual funds provide several advantages over direct investment by savers. First, the mutual fund is large enough to be able to invest in a number of different securities and thus diversify away some of the risk. Using direct purchase of securities, individual investors might be too small to buy enough securities to diversify, since probably ten or more different securities are required to achieve most of the benefits of diversification. Second, mutual funds provide economies of scale, including efficient record keeping and, more importantly, economies in information search. For small portfolios, the amount of time required to monitor an efficient portfolio can be large relative to the absolute benefits of monitoring, implying significant advantages of having a mutual fund manager carry out the task. For example, an investor with $10,000 to invest might have to spend 10 hours per week, or over 500 hours per year, to monitor a portfolio of direct investments. Even if the rate of return were 20 percent, the total return of $2,000 may be too small to justify spending 500 hours per year monitoring the investments. A mutual fund can spend the same 500 hours and pro-rate the cost.

Because mutual funds can trade securities in large quantities, brokerage commissions are significantly lower than for individual small investors. On the other hand, mutual funds trade in larger-size transactions. Larger transactions may result in price concessions. Large sellers may have to sell at lower prices and larger buyers purchase at higher prices than small individual investors. These price concessions for large transactions are sometimes called market impact fees.

Insurance Companies

Insurance companies are another type of financial intermediary providing the important function of risk diversification. An insurance company agrees to make a financial payment to insured individuals if a particular event occurs.

Life and casualty are the major types of insurance. Life insurance is of two varieties. Permanent life insurance (whole life or universal life) has a constant premium; term insurance has a premium that varies as the risks change. A 25-year-old person pays a lower initial premium for term insurance than for permanent life insurance. As time elapses and the risk of death increases, the premium on the term insurance rises and eventually surpasses the level premium on permanent life insurance. For permanent life insurance, the insurance company invests the extra premium in the early years to earn enough to cover the added risks in later years. Permanent life incorporates an element of saving, whereas term insurance is pure insurance.

Property and casualty insurance companies insure against losses from fire, theft, flood, automobile accidents, and many others. Because property and casualty insurance risks are harder to predict than life insurance risks, these companies make lower risk investments than life insurance companies.

Regulation of insurance companies is left to the states. Regulators curtail unfair sales practices, require liquid assets to meet loss payments, and limit investment in risky assets.

The insurance company charges a fee, called a premium. An insurance company insures a large number of individuals. On the basis of statistical evidence, the insurance company can predict with a high degree of accuracy the likelihood of a particular event occurring to the entire group of insured individuals. The insurance premium is set at a level high enough to cover the expected payments to the insured individuals, plus a profit margin. By spreading the risk over a large number of insured individuals, insurance companies can protect people against the financial consequences of disastrous events. The insurance premium is the cost of this protection for the individual.

For example, consider an insurance company selling flood insurance exclusively. The insurance company sells insurance policies in widely diverse geographical areas. On the basis of historical evidence, the company can predict with great accuracy the number of areas likely to flood in any one year. The insurance company can also forecast the probability of flooding in a particular area and can estimate the likely losses. The historical evidence can be used to set insurance premiums at a high enough level to cover the predicted losses. The insured entities then pay a premium reflecting the average expected losses.

The advantage of insurance to the insured is the payment of a relatively small, periodic, and stable amount. The insured prefers this small loss from paying an insurance premium to a possibly large, and potentially catastrophic, loss if there is no insurance. An uninsured entity can expect to occasionally suffer severe and catastrophic losses. For risk averters, protection against a devastating loss makes insurance very attractive. The insured accepts a regular small loss (the insurance premium) in order to avoid a major loss.

Insurance companies invest insurance premiums, using the proceeds from investments to pay off claims. Because insurance companies are large investors, insurance companies in the aggregate channel a large flow of savings into investment.

Life insurance companies provide a large inflow of funds into the security markets. Life insurance typically involves a long-term contract. The insured individual pays a premium for an agreed time period. If the individual dies, the insurance company pays the principal. For permanent life insurance, the premium in the initial years exceeds the expected payouts by the insurance company. The excess is invested to provide sufficient funds in the later years of the contract to pay the expected claims. This investment of premiums provides a large flow of funds. Insurance companies are large buyers of debt instruments, including public and private bonds and mortgages.

Insurance companies face the problem of adverse selection. That is, individuals with the greatest risk to the insurance company are most likely to seek insurance. For example, someone with a known medical condition is most likely to buy life insurance. In addition, insurance may induce riskier behavior for the insured (the moral hazard problem). A car driver with insurance may be less careful than the uninsured (self-insured) driver.

Insurance companies do several things to reduce the company's risk. The extremely-high-risk insurance applicants may be denied insurance. The premium may be adjusted for the individual's risk. Restrictive covenants may be included in the insurance contract. Thus, life insurance may not apply when the insured operates an airplane. Coinsurance can be used to require the insured to bear some percentage of the losses. Coinsurance may be in the form of a deductible, meaning that part of a loss is not covered by insurance. In addition, the insurance policy may have a maximum total payment.

Pension Funds

Pension funds represent savings for payment of employee retirement benefits. Pension funds differ in the vesting period. An employee who leaves employment before the required vesting period loses all retirement benefits. Some plans are immediately vested. Some require a period of 5 or 10 years before vesting occurs.

For defined contribution plans, the employer contribution is specified. The actual payment received by the employee at retirement depends upon the actual investment performance of the funds. If the investment returns are high, the employee retirement benefit is high; if the returns are low, the payment is low.

Defined benefit plans specify the amount to be paid to employees at retirement. For example, a pension fund for state employees might specify the benefit to be 1.8 percent times the number of years employed times the average salary for the last five years employed. Someone employed for 20 years, earning $40,000 average salary for the last five years, would receive $14,400 (0.018 × 20 × 40,000).

Determining the appropriate amount of pension fund contributions is difficult with defined benefit plans. The employer must estimate the probable payments to employees at retirement. The current contributions necessary to achieve this goal depend upon the rate of return until the retirement date. Consequently, employers have some discretion to determine the current contributions to the pension fund. For example, if interest rates are assumed to be high, lower current contributions are necessary.

Many employers fully fund their defined benefit plans. That is, current pension fund contributions are sufficient to meet all contingencies. Other employers have underfunded their plans by contributing insufficient funds. Since pension fund contributions are a business expense reducing reported income, some firms with low earnings have reduced pension fund contributions to boost reported earnings. In some cases, firms with underfunded pension funds have gone bankrupt, leaving insufficient funds to make payments to retirees. Many states have underfunded their defined benefit plans. Underfunding reduces taxes in the short run but creates a tax liability for future tax-payers.

The Employee Retirement Income Security Act (ERISA) of 1974 sets minimum standards for corporate disclosure of pension fund information, contains rules for vesting and restrictions on underfunding, and controls pension fund investments. The Act established the Pension Benefit Guarantee Corporation to insure pension funds against underfunding. In the view of some experts, the Pension Benefit Guarantee Corporation has insufficient funds to cover expected underfunding from future corporate bankruptcies. Inadequate auditing of covered pension funds has contributed to the problem. Careful auditing by the Guarantee Corporation should allow underfunded pension funds to be detected early and funding adjustments made before the insurance company incurs losses.

Commercial Banks and Thrifts

Commercial banks and thrift institutions are the largest variety of financial intermediary. A commercial bank is an institution that has checking deposits and makes commercial loans. A thrift institution offers savings deposits.

The thrift industry is composed of three types of savings institutions: savings and loan associations, mutual savings banks, and credit unions. Savings and loan associations (S&Ls) and mutual savings banks take deposits and make primarily real estate loans. Mutual savings banks are owned by the depositors. S&Ls and mutual savings banks were created to funnel more funds into home mortgages. During the era of deregulation in the 1980s, riskier types of loans were allowed for things other than home mortgages. Losses on these risky loans contributed significantly to the many failures after 1980. Since 1970, more than two-thirds of the S&Ls have disappeared.

Credit unions are depository institutions for some group with a common bond. They take deposits from these individuals and make consumer loans to them. As an example, educators in a particular town might establish a credit union. All educators would be allowed to make deposits and borrow from this credit union. Noneducators would not have access.

By taking deposits and making loans, commercial banks and thrift institutions expedite the flow of funds from savers (depositors) to investors (borrowers). Banks offer several advantages compared to direct transfers of funds between savers and final investors. First, banks allow the pooling of small amounts of funds. Second, because of the large size of a bank relative to an individual saver, banks provide the advantage of loan diversification. Diversification is a process by which risks are spread among many investments. The bank is able to make a large number of loans. Although the bank loses money on some of these loans because of default by the borrower, on the entire portfolio of bank loans, the bank can realize a nice profit. In contrast, a small saver making a single loan might suffer devastating losses if there is a default. The bank is able to spread this risk of default over many loans. The small lender cannot spread the risk.

Third, banks have the advantage of low costs resulting from economies of scale. Because of large size, a bank is able to spread fixed costs over many units. Besides operating economies, banks have the advantage of economies of information production about prospective loan applicants. On a per unit basis, investigating many loan applicants is cheaper than investigating one or two applicants. By dealing in large volumes of funds, banks can achieve lower transactions costs.

A major reason for the existence of commercial banks is their ability to offer a special service – namely, checking deposits. For depositors, the ability to write checks against checking deposits is extremely desirable for mail payments and for large transactions since payment with currency is ponderous and poses a risk of theft. From the viewpoint of the overall economy, checking deposits perform a valuable function. They allow otherwise idle transactions balances to be pooled together by the banks and then used to finance loans.

Since commercial banks are one of the major means by which the Federal Reserve controls the money supply and interest rates, commercial banks perform a valuable function for the entire economy. Partly because of this role in monetary policy, commercial banks are very heavily regulated. Regulation restricts the activities of banks, but regulation also protects banks from market forces.

Besides pure banking activities, commercial banks engage in some of the activities of other nonbank financial intermediaries. For example, a number of banks engage in investment banking for municipal bonds. Some banks engage in discount brokerage. Over time, banks have tried to enter more and more nonbanking activities. The allowable activities of banks are regulated by the Federal Reserve.

Commercial banks and thrifts are heavily regulated for several reasons. First, the safety of deposits is considered important. Banks are viewed as trustees for deposited funds and thus should be regulated. Second, bank failures may have widespread and adverse effects upon the entire economy.

Banks are regulated by four types of regulators. Each state has bank regulatory agencies. Federally, the Federal Reserve examines banks and regulates nonbanking activities, the Federal Deposit Insurance Corporation (FDIC) provides deposit insurance and closes failing banks, and the Comptroller of the Currency gives some banks their charter, or right to operate. The United States has a very high rate of bank failure for an industrialized country. A major reason is that there have been many small, inefficient banks – over 10,000 of them. Recent legislation has put pressure on the banking system to consolidate high-cost banks into larger, more cost-effective banks.

Comparing Types of Debt Financing

Business debt includes the following four types:

1 Public offerings of debt are made by large, established firms that are relatively easy to monitor. Public offerings have long maturities, have

relatively few restrictive covenants, and are callable. The size of the issue is large, typically over $100 million. Large size is necessary to spread the sizable cost of a public offering and registration with the SEC over many bonds. Of the four types of debt, public offerings have the lowest interest rates.

2   Bank loans are the major source of debt financing for small firms and firms with relatively poor credit quality. They have short maturities. The interest rate is adjustable. The bank places many restrictive covenants on the actions of the borrower and closely monitors the firm.

3   Private placements of debt are often made by medium-size firms with a credit history that is too weak to justify public offerings of debt, but strong enough to justify private placement. The maturities are intermediate. The debt has many restrictive covenants and typically cannot be refinanced. The typical purchaser of the bonds is a life insurance company, which monitors the firm closely and holds the bonds until final maturity. Private placements are typically less than $50 million in size. The interest rate on private placements is between the rates on public offerings and the rates on bank loans.

4   Rule 144a offerings fall somewhere between public offerings and private offerings. The debt is purchased by qualified financial institutions and can be resold to other qualified financial institutions. Thus, it is partially marketable. It is typically sold by more established firms that do not want to go through the expense of a public offering.

Summary

Financial intermediaries expedite the flow of savings from savers to ultimate investors in physical assets. They offer some advantages, including pooling of savings, diversification of investment risks, economies of scale in monitoring information and evaluating investment risks, and lower transactions costs. In addition, individual types of intermediaries provide specialized services.

Investment bankers are engaged in the original sale of securities to the public. Dealers make markets in individual securities, trying on average to make a profit by buying at the bid price and selling at the asked price. Brokers match buyers and sellers of securities for a fee.

Mutual funds, insurance companies, and pension funds invest heavily in the debt markets. Mutual funds pool the funds of many investors and invest in stocks, bonds, or some combination, depending upon the stated investment objectives of the fund. Insurance companies charge premiums to cover financial losses. Pension funds invest retirement money.

Banks and thrifts make loans. Thrifts specialize in real estate loans. Commercial banks make all varieties of business loans.

Questions and Problems

1 Describe the reasons why financial intermediaries exist.
2 Explain the meaning of the term diversification. Under what circumstances is there a benefit from diversifying?
3 What role do investment bankers play in the financial system? What are the economic benefits of investment bankers? Why are the underwriter fees for high-yield bonds higher than the fees for investment-grade bonds?
4 Describe the various types of orders for securities, including market order, limit order, stop order, and a shortsale.
5 Differentiate between a full service broker, a discount broker, and a deep discount broker.
6 Explain the economic reasons for the existence of bid-asked spreads. What are the major determinants of bid–asked spreads charged by security dealers? Compare the bid–asked on corporate bonds with US Treasury bonds and the spreads on short-term Treasuries with long-term Treasuries.
7 What are the differences between a commercial bank and a thrift?
8 Describe the differences between a defined benefit and defined contribution pension plan. Which plan would likely be better in a period of unanticipated inflation?
9 Explain how insurance companies try to deal with the problems of adverse selection and moral hazard.

4

Time Values

Most securities involve cash flows at different points in time. To compare different securities, the cash flows on each security can be transformed into an equivalent value at the present time (i.e. present value) or at some future point in time (i.e. future value). Then, these present (or future) values can be compared and the best security chosen.

This chapter presents future value and present value computations assuming the same interest rate or discount rate for all periods. This assumption is usually called a flat term (or maturity) structure of interest rates. Later chapters extend the analysis to the case where the interest rates differ by maturity.

A Time Line

Since cash flows for securities occur at different points in time, it is important for the reader to have a clear understanding of the time line in figure 4.1. Points in time are shown above the line, and periods in time are shown below the line. Point in time 0 is the present (or now). Point in time 1 is one period from now. Period 1 begins at time 0 and

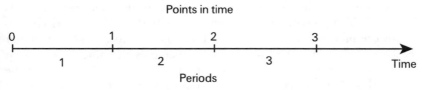

Figure 4.1 Example of a time line

extends until time 1. The length of a period is arbitrary and depends upon the particular situation under consideration. The length of a period may be a day, a month, a half year, or a year.

We will always assume that cash flows occur at the end of a period. Cash flows occurring at time zero are denoted with a subscript of 0, cash flows at time 1 have a subscript of 1, etc.

Future Value

Suppose we have a dollar at time zero. That dollar can be invested and earn interest. If the interest rate is R, the dollar invested at interest has a total value of $1 + R$ dollars after one period. If R is 10 percent, a dollar invested for one period is worth \$1.10.

If the dollar is invested for two periods, the future value is $(1 + R)^2$ if the first period's interest is reinvested. If the interest rate is 10 percent, the total value is $(1.10)^2$ or \$1.21. Formally,

$$\text{Future value at time } 2 = (1 + R)^2 = 1 + 2R + R^2 \tag{1}$$

$$(1.10)^2 = 1 + 2(0.10) + (0.10)^2 = 1 + 0.20 + 0.01 = 1.21 \tag{2}$$

On the right, the 1 represents the original dollar. $2R$ ($2(0.10)$) is the interest on the original principal for each of the two periods. R^2 ($(0.10)^2$) is the interest-on-interest, i.e. the interest earned in the second period on the first period's interest.

If a dollar is invested for n periods, the total value at the end of n periods equals $(1 + R)^n$. The total value equals \$1 principal plus the interest on original principal (n times R) plus many other terms for the interest on interest.

Present Value

Present value is the opposite (or reciprocal) of future value. Suppose an investor will receive a dollar at time 1. The present value at time 0 is $1/(1 + R)$. For a 10 percent interest rate, the present value of a dollar is $1/(1.10) = 0.9091$. Notice that \$0.9091 at time 0 and \$1 at time 1 represent equivalent values for investors with a 10 percent interest rate.

The present value of a dollar received n periods from now is $1/(1 + R)^n$. The present value gets smaller as the number of periods into the future increases because n is in the denominator. That is, a dollar received farther into the future has a lower present value. The present value also decreases as the interest rate increases. The Appendix at the end of this chapter (see pp. 66–9) contains a present value table for a variety of interest rates. Notice that present value decreases as maturity increases and as the interest rate increases.

Adding present values

Present values of cash flows at different points in time are additive. Thus, the present value of a dollar at time 1 and another dollar at time 2 is the sum of the present values.

$$Present\ Value = \frac{1}{1+R} + \frac{1}{(1+R)^2} \tag{3}$$

$$Present\ Value = \frac{1}{1.10} + \frac{1}{(1.10)^2} = \$1.74 \tag{4}$$

If the future cash flows are something other than one dollar, the present values are simply the cash flows times the present value of one dollar. Suppose we want to know the present value of $30 received one period from now and $40 received two periods from now. Then, the present values are

$$Present\ Value = \frac{30}{1+R} + \frac{40}{(1+R)^2} \tag{5}$$

$$Present\ Value = \frac{30}{1.10} + \frac{40}{(1.10)^2} = \$60.33 \tag{6}$$

Present value of an annuity

An annuity is a stream of constant cash flows over a period of time. Suppose the cash flows are one dollar per period beginning at time 1 and continuing until time n (i.e. a total of n payments of one dollar). The present value of this annuity can be found by adding the present value of the individual dollars. We will abbreviate the present value of an annuity as PVA.

$$Present\ value\ of\ annuity = PVA = \frac{1}{1+R} + \frac{1}{(1+R)^2} + \cdots + \frac{1}{(1+R)^n}$$

$$= \begin{bmatrix} PV \\ \$1 \\ at \\ time\ 1 \end{bmatrix} + \begin{bmatrix} PV \\ \$1 \\ at \\ time\ 2 \end{bmatrix} + \cdots + \begin{bmatrix} PV \\ \$1 \\ at \\ time\ n \end{bmatrix} \tag{7}$$

By the rules of algebra, this simplifies to

$$PVA = \left[\frac{1}{R} \right] \left[1 - \frac{1}{(1+R)^n} \right] \tag{8}$$

Suppose we have a two-period annuity of $1 per period and the interest rate is 10 percent. Then

$$PVA = \frac{1}{1.10} + \frac{1}{(1.10)^2} = \left[\frac{1}{0.10} \right] \left[1 - \frac{1}{(1.10)^2} \right] = \$1.7355 \tag{9}$$

If the annuity is $10 per period, the present value is simply $10 times the present value of a $1 annuity, or $17.36.

Because annuities occur so often, the Appendix contains a table of the present value of an n-period annuity. Notice that the present value of the annuity increases as the number of periods increases and as the interest rate gets smaller. The present value of an annuity can also be found using a financial calculator. The reader is encouraged to verify numbers in the Appendix using a financial calculator.

Price of a Bond

A bond is a loan for n periods. The cash flows from the lender's viewpoint are shown in table 4.1. The lender pays the borrower the price (P) at time 0. From time 1 through time n, the borrower repays in the form of a coupon (c). (This is an annuity.) At maturity (time n), the borrower pays the par (face) value to the lender. The price of bond is the present value of the cash flows. Namely,

$$Price = P = \frac{c}{1+R} + \frac{c}{(1+R)^2} + \cdots + \frac{c+par}{(1+R)^n}$$

$$= \begin{bmatrix} PV \\ c \\ time\ 1 \end{bmatrix} + \begin{bmatrix} PV \\ c \\ time\ 2 \end{bmatrix} + \cdots + \begin{bmatrix} PV \\ c + par \\ time\ n \end{bmatrix} \tag{10}$$

$$Price = P = c \begin{bmatrix} present\ value \\ of\ annuity \end{bmatrix} + \frac{par}{(1+R)^n} \tag{11}$$

$$P = c \left[\frac{1}{R} \right] \left[1 - \frac{1}{(1+R)^n} \right] + \frac{par}{(1+R)^n} \tag{12}$$

Table 4.1 Bond cash flows received by lender

	Points in time			
0	1	2	...	n
$-P$	$+c$	$+c$	...	$+c+par$

Suppose we have a two-period bond with an annual coupon of $8 per period, a par value of $100, and interest rate of 10 percent. Then,

$$P = \frac{8}{1.10} + \frac{8+100}{(1.10)^2} = \$96.53 \tag{13}$$

$$P = 8\left[\frac{1}{0.10}\right]\left[1 - \frac{1}{(1.10)^2}\right] + \frac{100}{(1.10)^2} \tag{14}$$

Treasury strips have no coupons, but simply pay par value at maturity. They are often called zero coupon bonds. The price of a strip is simply the present value of par.

$$Price_{strip} = \frac{par}{(1+R)^n} \tag{15}$$

Bond Yield to Maturity

If the price of a bond, its coupon, par value, and maturity are known, the yield to maturity (y) can be computed by solving the following equation.[1]

$$Price = P = \frac{c}{1+y} + \frac{c}{(1+y)^2} + \cdots + \frac{c+par}{(1+y)^n}$$

$$= \left[\begin{array}{c} PV \\ c \\ time\ 1 \end{array}\right] + \left[\begin{array}{c} PV \\ c \\ time\ 2 \end{array}\right] + \cdots + \left[\begin{array}{c} PV \\ c+par \\ time\ n \end{array}\right] \tag{16}$$

Financial calculators are able to solve this equation rapidly. The procedure used by the calculator is trial and error. To illustrate how this works, suppose we have a two-period bond with price of $98.26, coupon of $9, and par value of $100. We need to solve the following equation for the yield to maturity, y:

$$\$98.26 = \frac{\$9}{1+y} + \frac{\$109}{(1+y)^2} \tag{17}$$

Suppose we select a trial rate of 9 percent and compute the present value (PV).

$$PV = \frac{9}{1.09} + \frac{109}{(1.09)^2} = 100 \qquad (18)$$

This present value exceeds the price of the bond. Therefore, we need to try a higher rate to get the present value closer to the bond price. Try 10 percent.

$$PV = \frac{9}{1.10} + \frac{109}{(1.10)^2} = 98.26 \qquad (19)$$

Since the present value of the future cash flows from the bonds equals its price, we have found the yield to maturity. Finding the yield to maturity is not so easy in general. The typical calculator follows a trial and error rule that stops searching when the error is tiny.

The yield to maturity on a Treasury strip can be found directly. For a strip,

$$Price_{strip} = \frac{par}{(1+y)^n} \qquad (20)$$

Solving this for yield to maturity,

$$1+y = \left[\frac{par}{Price_{strip}} \right]^{1/n} \qquad (21)$$

To illustrate, suppose we have a two-period strip with $100 par value and price of $85.73. We need to solve the following equation.

$$1+y = \left[\frac{\$100}{\$85.73} \right]^{1/2} = 1.08$$
$$y = 0.08 = 8\% \qquad (22)$$

Other Yield Measures

Bond investors typically compute two other yields. The current yield is the ratio of the coupon divided by the price, c/P. The current yield represents the return on the bond from coupon and overlooks any return from price change. The stated yield (or coupon rate) is the coupon divided by par, c/par. The yield to maturity, current yield, and stated yield are linked as we shall see shortly.

A bond selling at par is typically called a par bond. A bond selling below par is called a discount bond. A bond selling above par is called

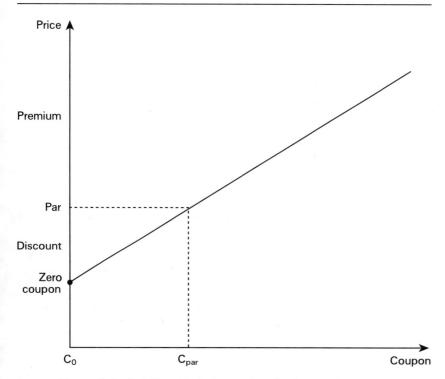

Figure 4.2 Relationship between bond prices and coupons

a premium bond. Figure 4.2 shows the relationship between bond price and coupon. Higher coupon bonds have higher prices. Thus, discount bonds have low coupons and premium bonds have high coupons.

In figure 4.2, the relationship between bond price and coupon is linear.[2] That is, each dollar of coupon adds a constant amount to price. When the coupon is zero, the bond is often called a zero coupon bond. Treasury strips and bills are examples of zero coupon bonds.

Bonds selling at par have the important characteristic that their yield to maturity, current yield, and stated yield are the same, i.e. $y = c/P = c/par$. This follows from the mathematics of yield to maturity. The link between yield to maturity, current yield, and stated yield for nonpar bonds is shown in table 4.2.

Finding the yield to maturity for a par bond is easy. Simply divide the coupon by par. Table 4.2 provides bounds on the yields to maturity for nonpar bonds. To find the yield to maturity for a discount bond, the lowest possible trial rate is c/P. Similarly for premium bonds, the highest possible trial rate is c/P.

Table 4.2 Yield to maturity (y), current yield (c/P) and stated yield (c/par)

Discount bond $P < par$	$y > c/P > c/par$
Par bond $P = par$	$y = c/P = c/par$
Premium bond $P > par$	$y < c/P < c/par$

Table 4.3 Comparison of yield to maturity, current yield, and stated yield for 2-period bonds

Coupon ($)	Maturity	Par ($)	Price ($)	Yield to maturity (y) (%)	Current yield (c/P) (%)	Stated yield (c/par) (%)
8	2	100	96.5289	10	8.29	8
10	2	100	100.00	10	10	10
12	2	100	103.4711	10	11.60	12

Most bonds are issued at par largely for tax reasons. They subsequently trade at a discount from par if interest rates rise after issue. If interest rates fall after issue, the bond sells at a premium.

To illustrate the relationship between the yield to maturity, current yield, and stated yield, consider the example in table 4.3 of three 2-period bonds with different coupons. The reader should verify the calculations. For the discount bond with $8 coupon, $y > c/P > c/par$. For the par bond with $10 coupon, all three yields are equal. For the premium bond with $12 coupon, $y < c/P < c/par$.

Perpetual Bonds

A perpetual bond never matures. It pays a periodic coupon indefinitely. The price of a perpetual bond in terms of its yield to maturity can be expressed as follows:

$$Price = P = \frac{c}{1+y} + \frac{c}{(1+y)^2} + \cdots \tag{23}$$

By the rules of algebra, this simplifies to

$$Price = P = \frac{c}{y} = \frac{coupon}{yield} \qquad (24)$$

Thus, if a perpetual bond has an annual coupon of $8 and a yield to maturity of 10 percent, its price is

$$Price = P = \frac{c}{y} = \frac{\$8}{0.10} = \$80 \qquad (25)$$

Only a small number of perpetual bonds exist. However, perpetual bonds are interesting because they serve as a limiting case. Long-term bonds approach perpetual bonds as the maturity gets longer. As in the case of par bonds, the yield to maturity for a perpetual bond equals the coupon divided by the price ($y = c/P$). Since a long-term bond is similar to a perpetual bond, the yield to maturity for a long-term bond is close to the yield to maturity for a perpetual bond. As an illustration, look up the listings of Treasury bonds in the newspaper and compare the current yield (i.e. c/P) for the longest-maturity Treasury bond (often called the "long bond") to the yield to maturity.

Holding Period Returns

The yield to maturity is a measure of return if a bond is held until maturity. The holding period return measures return for a shorter period of time. We consider holding period returns for a single period.

$$Holding\ Period\ Return = \frac{Ending\ Price - Beginning\ Price + Coupon}{Beginning\ Price}$$

$$HPR = \frac{P_1 - P_0 + c}{P_0} \qquad (26)$$

where P_0 is the price at time 0 and P_1 is the price at time 1. Notice that the holding period return can be decomposed into two parts.

$$Holding\ Period\ Return = \frac{Ending\ Price - Beginning\ Price}{Beginning\ Price}$$

$$+ \frac{Coupon}{Beginning\ Price}$$

$$HPR = \frac{P_1 - P_0}{P_0} + \frac{c}{P_0} \qquad (27)$$

$$HPR = [Percent\ Capital\ Gain\ (Loss)] + [Current\ Yield]$$

The holding period return is the percentage capital gain or loss plus the current yield. Let's consider two cases: (1) constant interest rates over the holding period; (2) changing interest rates over the period.

Constant interest rates

Figure 4.3 shows the evolution of bond price over time for constant interest rates. The price of par bonds remains the same as time elapses. The prices of discount bonds and premium bonds approach par as time elapses.

For the case of constant interest rates, the holding period return is the same for all bonds and equal to the yield to maturity. Discount bonds have a low current yield but have price appreciation, with the total return equalling the yield to maturity. Premium bonds have high current

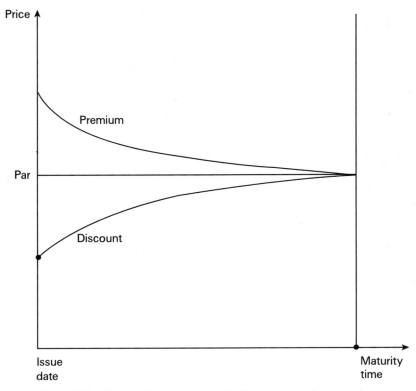

Figure 4.3   Bond price and maturity for constant interest rates

Table 4.4 Holding period returns with constant interest rates

Coupon ($)	Price at time 0 (P_0) ($)	Price at time 1 (P_1) ($)	Holding period return (%) $(P_1-P_0+c)/P_0$
8	96.5289	98.1818	10
10	100.00	100.00	10
12	103.4711	101.8182	10

Table 4.5 Holding period returns with interest rates rising to 12% at time 1

Coupon ($)	Price in $ at time 0 (P_0)	Price in $ at time 1 (P_1)	Percent capital gain (loss)	Current yield (%)	Holding period return $(P_1-P_0+c)/P_0$ (%)
8	96.5289	96.4286	(0.10)	8.29	8.18
10	100.00	98.2143	(1.79)	10	8.21
12	103.4711	100.00	(3.35)	11.60	8.24

yields, but the price declines, with a net return equal to the yield to maturity.

Using the information in table 4.3, the holding period returns are computed in table 4.4. If the interest rate is unchanged, the bond price at time 1 is $(c+par)/(1+y)$.

Changing interest rates

If interest rates change, the holding period return has two components – the percent capital gain plus the current yield. If interest rates rise, the percent capital gain is reduced and the holding period return is lower. The size of this impact depends upon the maturity of the bond and its coupon level and is discussed in chapter 6.

To illustrate the impact of changing interest rates on holding period returns, assume the same example except interest rates rise to 12 percent at time 1. The price of the bond at time 1 is $(c+par)/(1.12)$. See table 4.5. The rise in interest rates to 12 percent at time 1 causes capital losses that reduce the holding period rates below 10 percent, the rate that would prevail if interest rates remain unchanged at 10 percent.

Semiannual Interest

The typical bond in the United States pays interest twice per year or semiannually. The semiannual coupon is the annual coupon divided by two. The cash flows with semiannual coupons are shown in table 4.6 for a two-year bond with $9.00 annual coupon ($4.50 semiannually). With semiannual coupons, the interest rate is computed as a semiannual rate that we will denote as i. By convention, everyone in the market place uses the semiannual yield to maturity. The semiannual rate is the solution to the following equation:

$$P = \frac{c/2}{[1+i/2]^1} + \frac{c/2}{[1+i/2]^2} + \cdots + \frac{c/2+par}{[1+i/2]^{2n}}$$

$$= \begin{bmatrix} PV \\ c/2 \\ received \\ at\ time \\ 6\ months \end{bmatrix} + \begin{bmatrix} PV \\ c/2 \\ received \\ at\ time \\ 1\ year \end{bmatrix} + \cdots + \begin{bmatrix} PV \\ c/2+par \\ received \\ at\ time \\ n\ years \end{bmatrix} \qquad (28)$$

The exponent for each term in this expression is the number of semiannual periods until the cash flow is received. The first coupon of $c/2$ is received one six-month period from now and its exponent is one. The second coupon is received in two six-month periods and has an exponent of two. In the last term, the last coupon and par value are received in n years or $2n$ six-month periods.

Suppose there is a two-year bond with $100 par value, semiannual coupons of $4.50, and semiannual yield to maturity of 10 percent. Then the price is computed as follows:

$$P = \frac{\$4.50}{[1+0.10/2]^1} + \frac{\$4.50}{[1+0.10/2]^2} + \frac{\$4.50}{[1+0.10/2]^3} + \frac{\$4.50+\$100}{[1+0.10/2]^4}$$

$$= \$98.2270 \qquad (29)$$

Table 4.6 Bond cash flows for semiannual coupons

	Points in time (years)			
0	0.50	1.00	1.50	2.00
$-P$	+$4.50	+$4.50	$4.50	+$104.50

Accrued Interest

Coupon interest on bonds is paid semiannually. By convention, holders of bonds earn a proportion of the next coupon for the length of time the bond is held. Thus, if the six-month period from the last coupon to the next coupon contains 183 days (in general k days) and 20 days (in general j days) have elapsed since the last coupon payment, the holder for those twenty days is entitled to a proportion of the next coupon equal to 20/183 or 10.93 percent (in general j/k). Thus,

$$Accrued\ interest = \left[\frac{j}{k}\right]\left[\frac{c}{2}\right] = \left[\frac{days\ since\ last\ coupon}{days\ for\ 6\ month\ period}\right]\left[\begin{array}{c}semiannual\\coupon\end{array}\right] \quad (30)$$

When a bond is sold, the buyer pays the accrued interest to the seller.

If a person buys a bond in the middle of a period, the cash flows must be discounted for partial periods. If j days have elapsed and there are k days in a semiannual period, the proportion of a period that has elapsed is j/k. The price of a bond is the following:

$$P + \left[\frac{j}{k}\right]\left[\frac{c}{2}\right] = \frac{c/2}{[1+i/2]^{1-j/k}} + \frac{c/2}{[1+i/2]^{2-j/k}} + \cdots + \frac{c/2+par}{[1+i/2]^{2n-j/k}} \quad (31)$$

This simplifies to

$$P + \left[\frac{j}{k}\right]\left[\frac{c}{2}\right] = \left[1+\frac{i}{2}\right]^{j/k}\left[\frac{c/2}{[1+i/2]^{1}} + \frac{c/2}{[1+i/2]^{2}} + \cdots + \frac{c/2+par}{[1+i/2]^{2n}}\right] \quad (32)$$

To illustrate, assume a bond with \$100 par, semiannual coupon payments of \$4.50, and one and three-quarter years until maturity. In other words, the cash flows are as shown in table 4.7. Since one-half of a period has elapsed since the last coupon was paid, the accrued interest is one-half of \$4.50, or \$2.25. Suppose that i equals 10 percent:

$$P + \left[\frac{1}{2}\right](\$4.50) = \frac{\$4.50}{[1+0.10/2]^{1-1/2}} + \frac{\$4.50}{[1+0.10/2]^{2-1/2}}$$

$$+ \frac{\$4.50}{[1+0.10/2]^{3-1/2}} + \frac{\$4.50+\$100}{[1+0.10/2]^{4-1/2}}$$

$$= 100.65 \quad (33)$$

Table 4.7   Bond cash flows for bond buyer

	Points in time (years)			
0	0.25	0.75	1.25	1.75
$-P-accrued$ interest	$+\$4.50$	$+\$4.50$	$\$4.50$	$+\$104.50$

Solving for the price results in

$$P = \frac{\$4.50}{[1+0.10/2]^{1-1/2}} + \frac{\$4.50}{[1+0.10/2]^{2-1/2}}$$

$$+ \frac{\$4.50}{[1+0.10/2]^{3-1/2}} + \frac{\$4.50+\$100}{[1+0.10/2]^{4-1/2}} - \left[\frac{1}{2}\right](\$4.50)$$

$$= 98.40 \tag{34}$$

Newspaper Quotes

An example of newspaper quotes is given in figure 4.4. In the newspaper, bond prices are quoted per \$100 of par value, although trading units are typically \$10,000 or more. Coupons are quoted in eighths. Thus, $6\frac{1}{8}$'s means a semiannual coupon of \$6.125/2. The maturity date is the month and the last two digits of the year. Thus, Feb '10 means February 2010; the exact date in February has to be found from other sources, such as the *Monthly Statement of the Public Debt of the United States*. Prices are quoted in 32nds of a dollar. The semiannual yield to maturity is generally the yield in the newspaper.

Summary

Bonds involve cash inflows at future points in time. The price of the bond should be the present value discounted at the interest rate. Bonds have three types of yields. The current yield is the ratio of coupon over price. The stated yield (coupon rate) is the coupon as a percent of par. The yield to maturity is the internal rate of return. The relationship between these three yields is examined for discount bonds (selling below par), par bonds, and premium bonds (selling above par).

TREASURY BONDS, NOTES & BILLS

Monday, April 27, 1998

Representative and indicative Over-the-Counter quotations based on $1 million or more.

Treasury bond, note and bill quotes are as of mid-afternoon. Colons in bond and note bid-and-asked quotes represent 32nds; 101:01 means 101 1/32. Net changes in 32nds. Treasury bill quotes in hundredths, quoted in terms of a rate discount. Days to maturity calculated from settlement date. All yields are based on a one-day settlement and calculated on the offer quote. Current 13-week and 26-week bills are boldfaced. For bonds callable prior to maturity, yields are computed to the earliest call date for issues quoted above par and to the maturity date for issues quoted below par. n-Treasury note. i-Inflation-indexed. wi-When issued. iw-Inflation-indexed when issued; daily change is expressed in basis points.

Source: Dow Jones/Cantor Fitzgerald.

U.S. Treasury strips as of 3 p.m. Eastern time, also based on transactions of $1 million or more. Colons in bid-and-asked quotes represent 32nds; 99:01 means 99 1/32. Net changes in 32nds. Yields calculated on the asked quotation. ci-stripped coupon interest. bp-Treasury bond, stripped principal. np-Treasury note, stripped principal. For bonds callable prior to maturity, yields are computed to the earliest call date for issues quoted above par and to the maturity date for issues below par.

Source: Bear, Stearns & Co. via Street Software Technology Inc.

GOVT. BONDS & NOTES

Rate	Mo/Yr	Bid	Asked	Chg.	Ask Yld.

(tabular quotations of Treasury bonds and notes)

U.S. TREASURY STRIPS

Mat.	Type	Bid	Asked	Chg.	Ask Yld.

(tabular quotations of Treasury strips)

Figure 4.4 Newspaper quotations of US Treasury securities (from the *Wall Street Journal*). Reprinted by permission of the *Wall Street Journal*. © 1998 Dow Jones & Company, Inc. All Rights Reserved Worldwide

Appendix

Table A4.1 Present value of $1

	1%	2%	3%	4%	5%	6%	7%	8%	9%	10%	12%	14%
1	0.9901	0.9804	0.9709	0.9615	0.9524	0.9434	0.9346	0.9259	0.9174	0.9091	0.8929	0.8772
2	0.9803	0.9612	0.9426	0.9246	0.9070	0.8900	0.8734	0.8573	0.8417	0.8264	0.7972	0.7695
3	0.9706	0.9423	0.9151	0.8890	0.8638	0.8396	0.8163	0.7938	0.7722	0.7513	0.7118	0.6750
4	0.9610	0.9238	0.8885	0.8548	0.8227	0.7921	0.7629	0.7350	0.7084	0.6830	0.6355	0.5921
5	0.9515	0.9057	0.8626	0.8219	0.7835	0.7473	0.7130	0.6806	0.6499	0.6209	0.5674	0.5194
6	0.9420	0.8880	0.8375	0.7903	0.7462	0.7050	0.6663	0.6302	0.5963	0.5645	0.5066	0.4556
7	0.9327	0.8706	0.8131	0.7599	0.7107	0.6651	0.6227	0.5835	0.5470	0.5132	0.4523	0.3996
8	0.9235	0.8535	0.7894	0.7307	0.6768	0.6274	0.5820	0.5403	0.5019	0.4665	0.4039	0.3506
9	0.9143	0.8368	0.7664	0.7026	0.6446	0.5919	0.5439	0.5002	0.4604	0.4241	0.3606	0.3075
10	0.9053	0.8203	0.7441	0.6756	0.6139	0.5584	0.5083	0.4632	0.4224	0.3855	0.3220	0.2697
11	0.8963	0.8043	0.7224	0.6496	0.5847	0.5268	0.4751	0.4289	0.3875	0.3505	0.2875	0.2366
12	0.8874	0.7885	0.7014	0.6246	0.5568	0.4970	0.4440	0.3971	0.3555	0.3186	0.2567	0.2076
13	0.8787	0.7730	0.6810	0.6006	0.5303	0.4688	0.4150	0.3677	0.3262	0.2897	0.2292	0.1821
14	0.8700	0.7579	0.6611	0.5775	0.5051	0.4423	0.3878	0.3405	0.2992	0.2633	0.2046	0.1597
15	0.8613	0.7430	0.6419	0.5553	0.4810	0.4173	0.3624	0.3152	0.2745	0.2394	0.1827	0.1401

16	0.8528	0.7284	0.6232	0.5339	0.4581	0.3936	0.3387	0.2919	0.2519	0.2176	0.1631	0.1229
17	0.8444	0.7142	0.6050	0.5134	0.4363	0.3714	0.3166	0.2703	0.2311	0.1978	0.1456	0.1078
18	0.8360	0.7002	0.5874	0.4936	0.4155	0.3503	0.2959	0.2502	0.2120	0.1799	0.1300	0.0946
19	0.8277	0.6864	0.5703	0.4746	0.3957	0.3305	0.2765	0.2317	0.1945	0.1635	0.1161	0.0829
20	0.8195	0.6730	0.5537	0.4564	0.3769	0.3118	0.2584	0.2145	0.1784	0.1486	0.1037	0.0728
21	0.8114	0.6598	0.5375	0.4388	0.3589	0.2942	0.2415	0.1987	0.1637	0.1351	0.0926	0.0638
22	0.8034	0.6468	0.5219	0.4220	0.3418	0.2775	0.2257	0.1839	0.1502	0.1228	0.0826	0.0560
23	0.7954	0.6342	0.5067	0.4057	0.3256	0.2618	0.2109	0.1703	0.1378	0.1117	0.0738	0.0491
24	0.7876	0.6217	0.4919	0.3901	0.3101	0.2470	0.1971	0.1577	0.1264	0.1015	0.0659	0.0431
25	0.7798	0.6095	0.4776	0.3751	0.2953	0.2330	0.1842	0.1460	0.1160	0.0923	0.0588	0.0378
26	0.7720	0.5976	0.4637	0.3607	0.2812	0.2198	0.1722	0.1352	0.1064	0.0839	0.0525	0.0331
27	0.7644	0.5859	0.4502	0.3468	0.2678	0.2074	0.1609	0.1252	0.0976	0.0763	0.0469	0.0291
28	0.7568	0.5744	0.4371	0.3335	0.2551	0.1956	0.1504	0.1159	0.0895	0.0693	0.0419	0.0255
29	0.7493	0.5631	0.4243	0.3207	0.2429	0.1846	0.1406	0.1073	0.0822	0.0630	0.0374	0.0224
30	0.7419	0.5521	0.4120	0.3083	0.2314	0.1741	0.1314	0.0994	0.0754	0.0573	0.0334	0.0196

Table A4.2 Present value of an annuity of $1

	1%	2%	3%	4%	5%	6%	7%	8%	9%	10%	12%	14%
1	0.9901	0.9804	0.9709	0.9615	0.9524	0.9434	0.9346	0.9259	0.9174	0.9091	0.8929	0.8772
2	1.9704	1.9416	1.9135	1.8861	1.8594	1.8334	1.8080	1.7833	1.7591	1.7355	1.6901	1.6467
3	2.9410	2.8839	2.8286	2.7751	2.7232	2.6730	2.6243	2.5771	2.5313	2.4869	2.4018	2.3216
4	3.9020	3.8077	3.7171	3.6299	3.5460	3.4651	3.3872	3.3121	3.2397	3.1699	3.0373	2.9137
5	4.8534	4.7135	4.5797	4.4518	4.3295	4.2124	4.1002	3.9927	3.8897	3.7908	3.6048	3.4331
6	5.7955	5.6014	5.4172	5.2421	5.0757	4.9173	4.7665	4.6229	4.4859	4.3553	4.1114	3.8887
7	6.7282	6.4720	6.2303	6.0021	5.7864	5.5824	5.3893	5.2064	5.0330	4.8684	4.5638	4.2883
8	7.6517	7.3255	7.0197	6.7327	6.4632	6.2098	5.9713	5.7466	5.5348	5.3349	4.9676	4.6389
9	8.5660	8.1622	7.7861	7.4353	7.1078	6.8017	6.5152	6.2469	5.9952	5.7590	5.3282	4.9464
10	9.4713	8.9826	8.5302	8.1109	7.7217	7.3601	7.0236	6.7101	6.4177	6.1446	5.6502	5.2161
11	10.3676	9.7868	9.2526	8.7605	8.3064	7.8869	7.4987	7.1390	6.8052	6.4951	5.9377	5.4527
12	11.2551	10.5753	9.9540	9.3851	8.8633	8.3838	7.9427	7.5361	7.1607	6.8137	6.1944	5.6603
13	12.1337	11.3484	10.6350	9.9856	9.3936	8.8527	8.3577	7.9038	7.4869	7.1034	6.4235	5.8424
14	13.0037	12.1062	11.2961	10.5631	9.8986	9.2950	8.7455	8.2442	7.7862	7.3667	6.6282	6.0021
15	13.8651	12.8493	11.9379	11.1184	10.3797	9.7122	9.1079	8.5595	8.0607	7.6061	6.8109	6.1422

16	14.7179	13.5777	12.5611	11.6523	10.8378	10.1059	9.4466	8.8514	8.3126	7.8237	6.9740	6.2651
17	15.5623	14.2919	13.1661	12.1657	11.2741	10.4773	9.7632	9.1216	8.5436	8.0216	7.1196	6.3729
18	16.3983	14.9920	13.7535	12.6593	11.6896	10.8276	10.0591	9.3719	8.7556	8.2014	7.2497	6.4674
19	17.2260	15.6785	14.3238	13.1339	12.0853	11.1581	10.3356	9.6036	8.9501	8.3649	7.3658	6.5504
20	18.0456	16.3514	14.8775	13.5903	12.4622	11.4699	10.5940	9.8181	9.1285	8.5136	7.4694	6.6231
21	18.8570	17.0112	15.4150	14.0292	12.8212	11.7641	10.8355	10.0168	9.2922	8.6487	7.5620	6.6870
22	19.6604	17.6580	15.9369	14.4511	13.1630	12.0416	11.0612	10.2007	9.4424	8.7715	7.6446	6.7429
23	20.4558	18.2922	16.4436	14.8568	13.4886	12.3034	11.2722	10.3711	9.5802	8.8832	7.7184	6.7921
24	21.2434	18.9139	16.9355	15.2470	13.7986	12.5504	11.4693	10.5288	9.7066	8.9847	7.7843	6.8351
25	22.0232	19.5235	17.4131	15.6221	14.0939	12.7834	11.6536	10.6748	9.8226	9.0770	7.8431	6.8729
26	22.7952	20.1210	17.8768	15.9828	14.3752	13.0032	11.8258	10.8100	9.9290	9.1609	7.8957	6.9061
27	23.5596	20.7069	18.3270	16.3296	14.6430	13.2105	11.9867	10.9352	10.0266	9.2372	7.9426	6.9352
28	24.3164	21.2813	18.7641	16.6631	14.8981	13.4062	12.1371	11.0511	10.1161	9.3066	7.9844	6.9607
29	25.0658	21.8444	19.1885	16.9837	15.1411	13.5907	12.2777	11.1584	10.1983	9.3696	8.0218	6.9830
30	25.8077	22.3965	19.6004	17.2920	15.3725	13.7648	12.4090	11.2578	10.2737	9.4269	8.0552	7.0027

Notes

1 The yield to maturity is the internal rate of return on the bond.
2 An extensive literature addresses the linearity of this relationship. In the absence of market imperfections such as taxes, bond price is a linear function of coupon.

Questions and Problems

1 Suppose you have $20 and are going to invest it for one year at 8 percent. What is the future value? What is the future value if you invest for two years? Decompose the future value into original principal, simple interest, and compound interest.

2 Suppose you are going to receive $50 in two years. What is its present value at 8 percent interest. Compute the answer using the present value table and your calculator.

3 Suppose you will receive $50 one year from now and $80 two years from now. What is the present value at 8 percent?

4 Repeat problem 3 using a 10 percent interest rate. Is the present value higher or lower? Explain why.

5 You will receive an annuity of $12 per year for two years. For an 8 percent interest rate, compute the present value of this annuity three ways for an 8 percent interest rate. Use the tables, use your calculator, and use the formula for the present value of an annuity.

6 A two-year bond pays $12 coupons annually and has a $100 par value. Compute its price if the yield to maturity is 10 percent.

7 In problem 6, compute the stated yield and the current yield. What is the relationship between the current yield and the yield to maturity and why?

8 Using the information in problem 6, what is the holding period yield over the next year (a) if the yield to maturity remains at 10 percent, and (b) if the yield to maturity declines to 8 percent at time 1? In each case, decompose the holding period return into the current yield and the capital gain or loss.

9 A two-year bond with annual coupons of $12 and par value of $100 has a current price of $109.04.

   (a) What is its yield to maturity?
   (b) What is the current yield?
   (c) What would the yield to maturity be if the maturity of this bond is ten years?

10 In problem 9 (part (a)), suppose the holding period return over the next year is 8 percent. What would the yield to maturity at time 1 have to be for this to occur?

11 A Treasury strip with ten-year maturity and $100 par value has a current price of $55.84. Compute its yield to maturity.

12 In problem 11, suppose that the interest rate drops over the next year by 1 percent. What is the price of this strip in one year and what is the holding period return on this strip over the next year? What would the yield on this strip have to become in one year for the holding period return to be 5 percent higher than the initial yield to maturity in problem 11?

13 A two-year bond with a $12 annual coupon and $100 par value pays the coupon semiannually. The semiannual yield to maturity is 10 percent. Find the bond's price.

14 A two-year bond with an $8 annual coupon pays the coupon semiannually. Par value is $100 and the current price is $96.45. Compute the semiannual yield to maturity.

15 Suppose a bond has a semiannual coupon of $4 and par value of $100. Assume a semiannual period is 182 days and there are 100 days until the next coupon. Compute the accrued interest. Besides the next coupon in 100 days there will be three more semiannual coupons of $4 and a par value of $100 at final maturity. Compute the bond price if the semiannual yield to maturity is 9 percent.

16 A 20-year bond pays $8 coupons annually and has a $100 par value. Compute its price if the yield to maturity is 10 percent.

17 A 20-year bond pays $8 coupons annually and has a $100 par value. Compute its price if the yield to maturity is 6 percent.

18 Find the longest-maturity US Treasury bond in the newspaper. Compare its yield to maturity to its current yield. Are they close? Why?

5

Money Market Instruments and Rates

The most active market for securities as measured by daily volume of trading is the **money market,** which is defined as the market for securities with less than one year to maturity at the original issue date. Money market instruments include the following: Treasury bills, federal funds, repurchase agreements, certificates of deposit, commercial paper, and bankers' acceptances. Each of these instruments has slightly different characteristics, and thus each has a slightly different interest rate. Since many investors regard the individual money market instruments as close substitutes, changes in all the money market interest rates are highly correlated.

Money market instruments allow some issuers to raise funds for short periods of time at relatively low interest rates. These issuers include the US Treasury which issues Treasury bills; corporations that sell commercial paper; banks which issue certificates of deposit; and security dealers, who finance their holdings in the money market. Simultaneously, many investors find money market instruments to be highly liquid investments with relatively low default risk. An investment is liquid if it can be bought or sold rapidly without affecting the market price and if the risk of price fluctuation is small. These money market investors include individuals, corporations, banks, and other institutions with temporary excess funds, and money market mutual funds. The money market is largely a wholesale (as opposed to retail) market, with the denominations of most transactions in the millions of dollars. The primary participants are financial institutions and large nonfinancial businesses. Consumers play a limited role in the money market; they are buyers of some money market securities and investors in money market mutual funds.

Money Market Instruments

US Treasury bills

Treasury bills are issued by the US Treasury to finance government expenditures. For practical purposes, Treasury bills are default-free, since the Federal Reserve effectively has the power to provide sufficient funds to meet Treasury obligations. Treasury bills are highly liquid assets. They can be bought or sold rapidly without affecting the price, and the risk of price fluctuation is small. Consequently, Treasury bills have small bid–asked spreads.

Every Monday in its weekly auction, the Treasury issues large amounts of 13-week (91-day) and 26-week (182-day) Treasury bills. Every fourth week, the Treasury issues 52-week bills as well. Consequently, there are large numbers of Treasury bills outstanding. This large supply of securities increases trading volume and substantially enhances Treasury bill liquidity. Because Treasury bills are short-term securities, their price fluctuations are small when interest rates change. Thus, the risk of price decline is small for Treasury bills, as it is with the typical money market investment.

The interest earned on Treasury securities, including Treasury bills, is not subject to state and local income taxes. For this reason, Treasury bills may have a slightly lower interest than other money market instruments subject to these taxes. The default-free status of Treasury bills makes their yields lower than yields on otherwise identical money market instruments having some chance for default.

Federal funds

Commercial banks are required to keep reserves on deposit at the Federal Reserve. Banks with reserves in excess of required reserves can lend these funds to other banks. These interbank loans are called **federal funds** (abbreviated as **fed funds**) and are usually overnight loans. Through the fed funds market, commercial banks with excess funds are able to lend those funds to banks that are short of reserves. Large money center banks tend to be net buyers of fed funds, and small local banks tend to be net sellers.

Fed funds transactions are in large denominations, since otherwise the overnight interest would be insufficient to justify the transaction. The rate on these transactions is called the **federal funds rate**. This interest rate is the most volatile interest rate in the entire market. Daily fluctuations in the federal funds rate have sometimes been 4 or 5 percent. One reason for this rate volatility is that some banks may be suddenly forced to meet Federal Reserve requirements by borrowing fed funds. At the end of each quarter of the year, the federal funds rate has sometimes fluctuated dramatically. Annualized interest rates of 100 percent have been observed.

During the 1970s, the Federal Reserve Board monitored the federal funds rate very closely in implementing monetary policy. Until October 1979, the Federal Open Market Committee (FOMC) set fairly precise bands for the level of the federal funds rate. When market conditions pushed the rate outside of these bounds, the Federal Reserve took action to push the rate back within the bounds.

Since October 1979, the directives of the FOMC have put wider bounds upon the federal funds rate. The federal funds rate has experienced increased variability since October 1979. Most other money market interest rates are highly correlated with the federal funds rate and have had significantly greater variability since October 1979.

Repurchase agreements

Repurchase agreements (called **repos**, or **RPs**) are generally overnight sales of US government securities with an agreement to repurchase on the next business day. The volume of transactions in overnight repos is huge.

To illustrate repos, imagine a bond dealer closing operations for January 15 with an inventory of $450 million of Treasury securities. These securities are held by the dealer in its role as a market maker, with the dealer hoping to profit by the average bid–asked spread. The equity of the dealer is $50 million. An additional $400 million is required to pay for these securities since the terms of purchase require same-day payment. One possible source of dealer financing is a bank loan with the securities used as collateral for the loan. A second (and slightly less expensive) method of financing is a repo. That is, the dealer sells the securities to a lender for $400 (plus accrued interest) on the afternoon of January 15, agreeing to repurchase them the following morning of January 16 for $400 million plus one day's interest. Table 5.1 illustrates this sequence of events.

The price for the repurchase agreement is the current price plus interest. Since the loan is overnight, the interest rate on repos is typically slightly below the federal funds rate. Thus, repos allow nonbanks, which do not hold reserves at the Federal Reserve and consequently are unable to lend at the federal funds rate, to lend at a

Table 5.1 Financing needs of a bond dealer

Points in time		
2:00 p.m. January 15	5:00 p.m. January 15	9:00 a.m. January 16
Dealer buys $450 million of bonds	Dealer sells $400 million of bonds as repo	Dealer repurchases $400 million and pays overnight interest

rate slightly below the fed funds rate. Repos are confined to large dollar amounts per transaction. Otherwise, the cost of carrying out the transaction would outweigh the overnight interest. Repos for longer than overnight (called term repos) are possible, although they are not as common as overnight repos.

Repurchase agreements are extensively used as a means of short-term financing by government security dealers and by banks. In recent years, other money market securities (i.e. certificates of deposit, prime bankers' acceptances, and commercial paper) have been repoed. Dealers in these securities can now use repos as a source of financing.

From the viewpoint of the lender of funds, a repo is called a **reverse**. Reverses are quite attractive to a number of lenders, including nonfinancial corporations, banks, municipalities, and thrift institutions. These lenders can invest their temporarily excess funds in reverses for very short periods of time with minimal risk. Municipalities are typically restricted in their investments to federal government securities; reverses provide an attractive investment in these securities. Some reverses are used as a means of borrowing securities; that is, the lender of funds is also a borrower of securities. These borrowed securities may be used in a shortsale.

In general, the amount lent in a repo is slightly less than the market value of the bonds. This discount from market value is called a **haircut** and provides some protection to the lender if the dealer goes bankrupt and the securities are liquidated at the prevailing market price. The size of the haircut depends upon the underlying price risk of the security, with riskier securities having bigger haircuts.

The risk of a repo depends upon its legal status. Depending upon the wording, a repo may constitute a sale or a collateralized loan. If the repo is a sale, the lender owns the securities; in the event of borrower default, the lender can sell the securities and use the proceeds if the lender has physical possession of the securities. If a repo is a collateralized loan, the borrower owns the securities; in the event of borrower default, the lender merely has a general claim upon the borrower. With this latter type of arrangement, the lender is at greater risk, and the interest rate is higher.

Commercial paper

Commercial paper is a promissory note issued by firms as a source of short-term funds. The commercial paper market has existed because commercial paper can be a cheaper source of funds for financially sound firms than commercial bank loans. During recent years of high interest rates, the number of firms issuing commercial paper has increased significantly because the interest costs saved have increased substantially.

The majority of commercial paper is issued by financial companies, including bank holding companies, finance companies, and insurance companies. Financial companies tend to use commercial paper as a regular source of funds. Nonfinancial firms tend to issue commercial paper on an irregular basis to meet special financing needs.

Commercial paper is not secured by specific assets of the issuing firm. In a secured loan, specific assets are pledged as collateral behind the loan. In the event of default, the secured lender has first claim upon the pledged asset. If this specific asset is insufficient to pay off the lender's claim, the lender then has a general claim upon the other assets of the borrower. An "unsecured" loan does not have specific assets pledged as collateral. However, the lender has a general claim upon the assets of the borrower rather than on a specific asset. Thus, the term **unsecured** is a type of misnomer.

Although commercial paper is unsecured, it is typically backed by lines of credit at commercial banks. A line of credit is essentially a pre-arrangement between a commercial bank and a borrowing firm that allows the firm to borrow up to some prearranged limit during a stated time interval. Lines of credit are not legally binding on the bank. Except during periods of extremely tight money, banks honor these lines of credit. In order to obtain a line of credit, a firm may be required to maintain compensating deposit balances at the bank of perhaps 10 percent or to pay explicit fees to the bank for the line of credit. These costs are clearly part of the cost of issuing commercial paper.

Most commercial paper is issued with original maturities of less than 45 days. Commercial paper with maturities of less than nine months does not have to be registered with the Securities and Exchange Commission (SEC) as a public offering. This saves the considerable expense of SEC registration and may also avoid delays involved in the registration process.

Commercial paper may be sold directly by the issuer or may be sold to dealers who charge a placement fee of perhaps 1/8 percent. Firms regularly issuing commercial paper find it more economical to set up a department to issue commercial paper rather than use outside dealers. Since issues of commercial paper are heterogeneous, having many different issuers and many different maturity dates, there is no active secondary market for commercial paper. However, dealers may repurchase commercial paper for a fee.

Prime rate

The prime interest rate is often said to represent the rate at which commercial banks lend to their most creditworthy (and, therefore, lowest-risk) customers. In practice, many loans are made at rates below the prime; the prime rate is not the rate for the most creditworthy firms. Nevertheless, the prime interest rate is a benchmark indicator of the level of interest rates.

Since the market for bank loans is highly competitive, all commercial banks quote a single prime rate. The prime rate changes for all banks simultaneously.

Bankers' acceptances

Bankers' acceptances (BAs) are short-term debt obligations guaranteed by large commercial banks. Prime bankers' acceptances of the 10 largest banks trade anonymously. They are highly liquid, low-risk, and low-return investments.

Bankers' acceptances typically arise out of international trade. Consider the following example illustrated in figure 5.1. Assume an importer located in the United States and an exporter in Japan. The exporter would like to send goods to the US and receive payment in 90 days. In domestic transactions, trade credit is widely used to finance this transaction. With trade credit, the goods producer sends the merchandise and allows the purchaser some time before payment is made. During this period of time, the purchaser attempts to sell the merchandise and generate the cash to make payment. In international transactions, the parties are located in different countries, implying that suppliers may not know the financial status of buyers. Legal remedies are more difficult and expensive in international transactions.

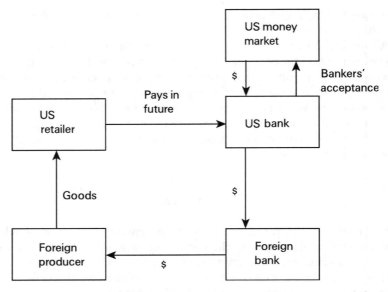

Figure 5.1 Bankers' acceptances

To reduce the risk of collecting payment in 90 days, a bankers' acceptance can be used.

In a bankers' acceptance, the importer obtains a commercial letter of credit from his bank in the US. Through this commercial letter of credit, the US bank guarantees payment for the imported goods in 90 days. The letter of credit is sent to the exporter's bank in Japan. The exporter ships the goods and endorses the shipping documents. The documents and a time draft for the amount to be paid are presented to the exporter's bank. The Japanese bank then sends the draft and documents to the US bank, which "accepts" them. We now have a bankers' acceptance.

Frequently, the US bank pays the exporter's bank the present value of the purchase price and in turn these funds are paid to the exporter. The US bank can hold on to the bankers' acceptance and earn interest or sell it in the market. If the acceptance is sold in the market, the US bank has not lent any net funds. However, the US bank does guarantee payment. If the importer is unable to make payment on the due date, the US bank guarantees payment. In addition to any interest earned, the US bank also receives a fee from the importer.

The Federal Reserve has a set of standards for designating BAs as collateral for loans from the Fed. A bank with eligible BAs can obtain loans from the Federal Reserve at the discount rate. Eligible BAs are much more liquid than noneligible BAs.

Bank certificates of deposit

Large certificates of deposit (CDs) at commercial banks represent a major source of funds for commercial banks. These large certificates (with face values of over $100,000) are a significant source of funds for money center and large regional commercial banks. There are four basic types of large certificates of deposit: domestic CDs, Eurodollar CDs, Yankee CDs, and thrift CDs.

Large domestic CDs were first issued by the First National City Bank of New York in 1961 in order to regain deposits lost during a period of rising interest rates because of restrictions on the interest rates allowed on deposits. With some interruptions, the domestic CD market continued to grow until the early 1980s when banks were allowed to issue Money Market Deposit Accounts (MMDAs) and Super Now accounts. These new accounts allow banks to pay interest on checking accounts, thus eliminating some of the advantage of domestic CDs.

Negotiable domestic CDs of major banks are highly liquid investments. An active resale market exists for these CDs. A number of foreign banks have branches in the United States. Dollar-denominated CDs of these foreign banks are called Yankee CDs. A small number of thrift institutions sell large-denomination thrift CDs.

Eurocurrency certificates of deposit

A Eurocurrency deposit is defined as a deposit denominated in terms of a foreign currency. Thus, a deposit in US dollar terms made in London, England, is considered a Eurodollar deposit. A deposit of Japanese yen in London is also called a Eurodollar deposit, although technically it is a "Euroyen" deposit. Large US banks frequently raise funds through Eurodeposits in branches of the banks located outside the United States. The interest rate on Eurodeposits is typically slightly higher than the rate on domestic US deposits, making these rates attractive to depositors. These subsidiaries are typically free of regulatory restrictions, thus reducing the net cost of deposits to the bank. Freedom from regulation tends to benefit both the depositors and the banks.

Eurodollar CDs are dollar-denominated certificates of deposit issued by banks located outside the United States, with London being the most common location. The most common issuers of Eurodollar CDs are branches of US, Canadian, Japanese, and European banks. A US bank may decide to issue Eurodollar CDs through its London branch if the interest rate on a Eurodollar CD compares favorably with the rate on a domestic CD. However, nonnegotiable Eurodollar time deposits are a more important source of funds for US banks than Eurodollar CDs.

The interest rates on Eurocurrency CDs are quoted as LIBOR plus some markup. LIBOR is the London Interbank Offered Rate, which is the interest rate at which Eurobanks in London offer to lend to one another. Eurocurrency CDs have higher interest rates than US domestic CDs, partially because the foreign countries involved may impose exchange controls, possibly forbidding repayment of the CD. This risk is called **sovereign risk**.

Money market funds

As interest rates rose markedly during the 1970s, many small investors found themselves cut off from high money market rates of return. Because most money market instruments are in large denominations, small investors were typically restricted to savings deposits at commercial banks and savings banks. These savings deposits paid rates several percent less than the rates available on money market instruments.

To fill this gap and provide access for small investors to the money market, money market mutual funds developed. These funds pooled the resources of small investors and invested those resources at attractive money market rates. Figure 5.2 shows the impact of money market funds on the flow of funds.

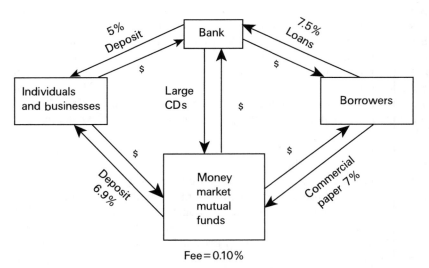

Figure 5.2 Money market funds

Money market funds have caused large outflows of funds into them from savings accounts. Many depository institutions lost funds in a process called **disintermediation**. In effect, money market funds bypassed banks and let investors put their money directly into the money market. To permit banks to compete with money market mutual funds, banks are now allowed to offer depository accounts with rates competitive with money market rates. These new accounts are called Money Market Deposit accounts and Super Now accounts.

The typical money market fund holds a portfolio of Treasury bills, bank certificates of deposit, commercial paper, and bankers' acceptances. Some money market funds specialize in particular instruments such as Treasury bills (for very-low-risk investors) or municipal notes, which are exempt from federal income taxes. Money market funds typically allow investors to write checks on their accounts with some restrictions. Thus, in many ways, large money market funds are like banks, although money market funds are not insured by the FDIC.

Money Market Rates

The *Wall Street Journal* publishes a daily table entitled Money Rates. An example is shown in figure 5.3. For example, the figure shows the previous day's federal funds rates – the high, the low, and the close.

One of the peculiarities of the money market is its way of quoting interest rates. Some money market instruments (Treasury bills, commercial paper, and bankers' acceptances) are quoted on a discount basis. Other rates (fed funds, Federal Reserve discount rate, and repo rates) are quoted on an add-on basis. Each of these rates is different from the yield to maturity, the rate generally used for comparing coupon-bearing bonds. The following discussion explains discount rates, add-on rates, and bond equivalent yields.

Quoting rates on a discount basis

Regardless what rate of interest is used to quote money market instruments, the cash flows are the same and are shown in table 5.2. The buyer pays the price P at time 0. When the money market instrument matures in t days, the par value is received.

The discount rate, d, is defined as the rate satisfying the following equation:

$$P = par\left[1 - \frac{dt}{360}\right] \tag{1}$$

MONEY RATES

Thursday, April 30 1998

The key U.S. and foreign annual interest rates below are a guide to general levels but don't always represent actual transactions.

PRIME RATE: 8.50% (effective 3/26/97). The base rate on corporate loans posted by at least 75% of the nation's 30 largest banks.

DISCOUNT RATE: 5.00%. The charge on loans to depository institutions by the Federal Reserve Banks.

FEDERAL FUNDS: 5 3/4% high, 5 1/2% low, 5 3/4% near closing bid, 6 % offered. Reserves traded among commercial banks for overnight use in amounts of $1 million or more. Source: Prebon Yamane (U.S.A.) Inc.

CALL MONEY: 7.25% (effective 3/27/97). The charge on loans to brokers on stock exchange collateral. Source: Dow Jones.

COMMERCIAL PAPER placed directly by General Electric Capital Corp.: 5.52% 30 to 50 days; 5.48% 51 to 64 days; 5.52% 65 to 89 days; 5.50% 90 to 270 days.

COMMERCIAL PAPER: High-grade unsecured notes sold through dealers by major corporations: 5.53% 30 days; 5.53% 60 days; 5.53% 90 days.

CERTIFICATES OF DEPOSIT: 5.21% one month; 5.22% two months; 5.27% three months; 5.59% six months; 5.76% one year. Average of top rates paid by major New York banks on primary new issues of negotiable C.D.s, usually on amounts of $1 million and more. The minimum unit is $100,000. Typical rates in the secondary market: 5.56% one month; 5.63% three months; 5.71% six months.

BANKERS ACCEPTANCES: 5.48% 30 days; 5.48% 60 days; 5.49% 90 days; 5.49% 120 days; 5.49% 150 days; 5.52% 180 days. Offered rates of negotiable, bank-backed business credit instruments typically financing an import order.

LONDON LATE EURODOLLARS: 5 5/8% - 5 1/2% one month; 5 21/32% - 5 17/32% two months; 5 11/16% - 5 9/16% three months; 5 23/32% - 5 19/32% four months; 5 3/4% - 5 5/8% five months; 5 25/32% - 5 21/32% six months.

LONDON INTERBANK OFFERED RATES (LIBOR): 5.65625% one month; 5.71875% three months; 5.81250% six months; 5.96875% one year. British Bankers' Association average of interbank offered rates for dollar deposits in the London market based on quotations at 16 major banks. Effective rate for contracts entered into two days from date appearing at top of this column.

FOREIGN PRIME RATES: Canada 6.50%; Germany 3.64%; Japan 1.625%; Switzerland 3.50%; Britain 7.25%. These rate indications aren't directly comparable; lending practices vary widely by location.

TREASURY BILLS: Results of the Monday, April 27, 1998, auction of short-term U.S. government bills, sold at a discount from face value in units of $10,000 to $1 million: 4.94% 13 weeks; 5.115% 26 weeks.

OVERNIGHT REPURCHASE RATE: 5.38%. Dealer financing rate for overnight sale and repurchase of Treasury securities. Source: Dow Jones.

FEDERAL HOME LOAN MORTGAGE CORP. (Freddie Mac): Posted yields on 30-year mortgage commitments. Delivery within 30 days 6.99%, 60 days 7.03%, standard conventional fixed-rate mortgages; 5.625%, 2% rate capped one-year adjustable rate mortgages. Source: Dow Jones.

FEDERAL NATIONAL MORTGAGE ASSOCIATION (Fannie Mae): Posted yields on 30 year mortgage commitments (priced at par) for delivery within 30 days 7.07%, 60 days 7.11%, standard conventional fixed rate-mortgages; 6.35%, 6/2 rate capped one-year adjustable rate mortgages. Source: Dow Jones.

MERRILL LYNCH READY ASSETS TRUST: 5.07%. Annualized average rate of return after expenses for the past 30 days; not a forecast of future returns.

Figure 5.3 Money market interest rates (from *Wall Street Journal*). Reprinted by permission of the *Wall Street Journal*. © 1998 Dow Jones & Company, Inc. All Rights Reserved Worldwide

Let us consider a simple example. A 90-day Treasury bill with a $100 par value has a discount rate of 8 percent. Its price is:

$$P = \$100\left[1 - \frac{(0.08)(90)}{360}\right] = \$98 \qquad (2)$$

Table 5.2 Money market cash flows

Points in time	
0	t days
$-P$	$+$par

The buyer of this Treasury bill pays $98 and, in 90 days, receives $100. The interest received is $2 which is 2 percent of the par value. Two percent for 90 days corresponds to an annualized rate of 8 percent for 360 days.

Several things are wrong with the discount rate. A 360-day year is used. Interest is computed as a percent of the par value, which tends to understate the interest rate compared to interest as a percent of the price. The apparent reason for this unusual way of quoting rates is the development of this market before hand-held calculators.

Add-on rate calculations

Federal funds, the Federal Reserve discount rate, and repos are quoted in terms of a rate called the add-on interest rate. Add-on interest rates relate the price and the par value in the following way:

$$P = \frac{par}{1 + (at/360)} \qquad (3)$$

The add-on rate is an improvement over the discount rate because the add-on rate computes the interest rate as a percent of the price. However, the add-on rate continues to use a 360-day year. The discount rate and the add-on rate are linked algebraicly as follows:

$$a = \frac{d}{1 - (dt/360)} \qquad (4)$$

The denominator of this expression is the price of the money market instrument per dollar of par. Since this price must be less than 1.0, the add-on rate, a, must be bigger than the discount rate, d.

As an illustration, continue the earlier example with a discount rate of 8 percent, maturity of 90 days, price of $98, and par value of $100.

Then:

$$a = \frac{0.08}{1 - ((0.08)(90)/360)} = 0.0816 = 8.16\% \qquad (5)$$

Bond equivalent yields

The bond equivalent yield is another money market rate that we will denote by r. The bond equivalent yield is the rate satisfying the following:

$$P = \frac{par}{1 + (rt/365)} \qquad (6)$$

The bond equivalent yield is better than the add-on rate because it uses a 365-day year. The bond equivalent yield, add-on rate, and discount rate are linked as follows:

$$r = a \left[\frac{365}{360} \right] = \left[\frac{d}{1 - (dt/360)} \right]\left[\frac{365}{360} \right] \qquad (7)$$

Since 365/360 is bigger than 1.0, the bond equivalent yield is bigger than the add-on rate (which is bigger than the discount rate). Continuing our earlier example with the discount rate equal to 8 percent, maturity in 90 days, a price of $98, and par value of $100, the bond equivalent yield is found as follows:

$$r = 0.0816 \left[\frac{365}{360} \right] = 0.0828 = 8.28\% \qquad (8)$$

The bond equivalent yield is widely used by market participants for comparing rates of return on Treasury bills with the yields to maturity available on coupon-bearing Treasury notes and bonds. The daily listings of the *Wall Street Journal* give bond equivalent yields for Treasury bills.

The bond equivalent yield, r, is an approximation of the yield to maturity for a bond. Although the two are fairly close, they are not identical. For short maturities, the difference can be considerable. As maturity approaches 182.5 days, the two converge.

Yield to maturity

The interest rate used for coupon-bearing bonds is the semiannual yield to maturity, i. For a money market instrument, the semiannual is defined as follows:

$$P = \frac{par}{[1+(i/2)]^{(2t/365)}} \tag{9}$$

The semiannual yield is larger than the bond equivalent if the maturity is less than 182.5 days. The two are equal at 182.5 days. The world would be a lot simpler if the semiannual yield to maturity were used for all debt obligations.

Some experts have advocated using the annual yield to maturity, y, defined as follows:

$$P = \frac{par}{[1+y]^{(t/365)}} \tag{10}$$

The annual yield to maturity compounds interest annually, while the semi-annual rate compounds interest twice per year. The annual yield to maturity equals the semiannual rate plus the semiannual rate squared divided by 4 (i.e. $y = i + i^2/4$).

Using our earlier example of a discount rate of 8 percent, maturity of 90 days, price of $98, and par value of $100, the semiannual yield to maturity and annual yield to maturity can be found using the formulas in table 5.3.

Table 5.3

Discount rate (d):

$$P = PAR\left[1 - \frac{dt}{360}\right] \qquad d = \left[\frac{360}{t}\right]\left[1 - \frac{P}{PAR}\right]$$

Add-on rate (a):

$$P = \frac{PAR}{1+(at/360)} \qquad a = \left[\frac{360}{t}\right]\left[\frac{PAR}{P} - 1\right]$$

Bond equivalent yield (r):

$$P = \frac{PAR}{1+(rt/365)} \qquad r = \left[\frac{365}{t}\right]\left[\frac{PAR}{P} - 1\right]$$

Semiannual yield to maturity (i):

$$P = \frac{PAR}{[1+i/2]^{(2t/365)}} \qquad i = 2[PAR/P]^{(365/2t)} - 2$$

Annual yield to maturity (y):

$$P = \frac{PAR}{[1+y]^{(t/365)}} \qquad y = [PAR/P]^{(365/t)} - 1$$

Comparing money market rates

There are at least five different money market rates: the discount rate, the add-on rate, the bond equivalent yield, the semiannual, and annual yields to maturity. Table 5.3 summarizes the previous results. The semiannual yield compounds every 6 months; the annual yield compounds every 12 months. The annual yield is bigger than the semiannual yield. Table 5.3 expresses price in terms of the five different rates and shows the five rates as a function of price.

To illustrate the relationships between the five rates, consider a case in which the discount rate, d, is 8 percent and the number of days, t, is 91.25. Since 91.25 days is one-quarter of a year, the calculation of the semiannual and annual yields is simple. First, compute the price, given these values of d and t and an assumed par value of $1:

$$P = PAR\left[1 - \frac{dt}{360}\right] = 1\left[1 - \frac{(0.08)(91.25)}{360}\right] = 0.979722 \qquad (11)$$

The price per dollar of par is $0.979722. In table 5.4, the formulas are used to compute the four remaining money market yields.

These money market yields for 91.25 days are shown graphically in figure 5.4. The relationship between the five money market rates is

Table 5.4

Add-on rate (a):	$a = \left[\dfrac{360}{t}\right]\left[\dfrac{PAR}{P} - 1\right]$
	$a = \left[\dfrac{360}{91.25}\right]\left[\dfrac{1}{0.979722} - 1\right] = 8.17\%$
Bond equivalent yield (r):	$r = \left[\dfrac{365}{t}\right]\left[\dfrac{PAR}{P} - 1\right]$
	$r = \left[\dfrac{365}{91.25}\right]\left[\dfrac{1}{0.979722} - 1\right] = 8.28\%$
Semiannual yield to maturity (i):	$i = 2[PAR/P]^{(365/2t)} - 2$
	$i = 2[1/0.979722]^{(365/182.5)} - 2 = 8.36\%$
Annual yield to maturity (y):	$y = [PAR/P]^{(365/t)} - 1$
	$y = [1/0.979722]^{(365/91.25)} - 1 = 8.54\%$

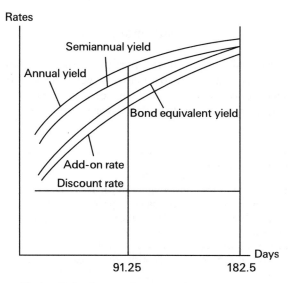

Figure 5.4 Comparing money market rates

shown in figure 5.4 for maturities up to one-half year, that is, 182.5 days. Several tendencies are apparent from figure 5.4. First, the biggest rate is the annual yield, followed by the semiannual yield, the bond equivalent yield, the add-on rate, and the discount rate. Second, the bond equivalent yield approaches the semiannual yield to maturity as maturity approaches one-half year. Third, the differences between the bond equivalent yield and the semiannual yield are sizable for shorter maturities. Bond equivalent yield is a poor approximation of semiannual yield for the shorter maturities. Fourth, the differences between the discount rate and the other rates increase for longer maturities, suggesting that the discount rate is quite misleading for maturities close to one-half year.

Figure 5.4 has a lesson for investors in the money market. Express all money market investments in terms of the same type of rate before selecting investments. Choosing between investments quoted in terms of different rates could lead to poor investment choices.

A more important implication of figure 5.4 and the discussion of money market rates is that all money market institutions should quote rates by the same method. Money market institutions should confer and select one single rate for quoting all varieties of money market instruments. The semiannual yield to maturity is the logical choice for a uniform rate because this rate is used for coupon-bearing bonds with maturities exceeding one-half year.

Summary

Money market instruments have maturities of less than one year. Trading in money market instruments is very active, and the total volume of transactions is huge. A variety of money market instruments exist. Each meets a special need of borrowers and lenders.

Questions and Problems

1 Explain why each of the following money market instruments exists: commercial paper, bankers' acceptances, repurchase agreements, certificates of deposit, and federal funds. Why does each of these have an advantage over competing methods of financing?
2 Why did the market for Eurodeposits develop? What is the advantage of a Eurodeposit over a domestic deposit from a bank's viewpoint as well as a depositor's?
3 Find the prices of the following Treasury bills per dollar of par:

   (a) 40 days, discount rate of 6 percent
   (b) 90 days, discount rate of 12 percent
   (c) 80 days, discount rate of 8 percent
   (d) 92 days, discount rate of 7 percent.

4 In problem 3, find the add-on interest rates, bond equivalent yields, semiannual, and annual yields to maturity.
5 Determine Treasury bill discount rates, assuming the following information. Assume $1 par values:

   (a) $P=0.96$, $t=91$ days
   (b) $P=0.94$, $t=91$ days
   (c) $P=0.98$, $t=91$ days
   (d) $P=0.98$, $t=90$ days.

6 Assume a discount rate of 6 percent. Compute the add-on interest rate, the bond equivalent yield, the semiannual, and annual yield to maturity for 30, 60, 90, 180 days. Graph these results.
7 Suppose that you are considering investing in two 91-day money market instruments – Treasury bills with a discount rate of 5 percent or commercial paper with a bond equivalent yield of 5.20 percent. Which investment is better?
8 Look in the *Wall Street Journal* for the column entitled "Money Rates." Compare the prime rate, the federal funds rate, the discount rate, the commercial paper rate, the bankers' acceptance rate, and the Treasury bill rate. For the federal funds rate, note the difference between the high and the low.

6

The Risk of Changing Interest Rates

Risk-averse investors are concerned about the possibility of bond prices going down as interest rates rise. Macaulay's duration is a widely used measure of the sensitivity of bond prices to changing interest rates and leads to two important conclusions. First, the prices of low-coupon bonds are more sensitive to changes in interest rates than the prices of high-coupon bonds. Second, longer-maturity bonds are more sensitive to changing interest rates than shorter-maturity bonds. Thus, long-maturity and low-coupon bonds are the riskiest to hold. The lowest-risk bonds are short-maturity and high-coupon bonds.

Duration

Macaulay's duration (DUR) is the most common measure of bond price volatility and equals the percentage change in bond price for a change in interest rates.

$$DUR = \frac{percent\ price\ change}{yield\ change} \tag{1}$$

$$DUR = \frac{1c/(1+y)^1 + 2c/(1+y)^2 + \cdots + n(c+par)/(1+y)^n}{price} \tag{2}$$

The numerator of duration is (minus) the derivative of bond price with respect to yield to maturity times $(1+y)$. The derivative divided by the price is equal to the instantaneous percentage change in price as interest rates change. Each term in the numerator is the present value of the cash flows in a particular period times the number of periods until those cash flows are received. This represents a weighted average maturity of the cash flows.

Computing DUR using the preceding formula can be time-consuming, especially if n is large. To make the computations faster, it is convenient to take the sum in the numerator analytically, resulting in:

$$DUR = \frac{[c(1+y)/y][(1-(1+y)^{-n})/y] + n(par - c/y)/(1+y)^n}{price} \quad (3)$$

Since $[1-(1+y)^{-n}]/y$ represents the present value of an n-period annuity discounted at the rate y, DUR can easily be computed using the preceding formula and a hand-held calculator.

The duration calculations can be illustrated by the following example. Assume a 10-year bond with $6 annual coupon, $100 par value, and yield to maturity of 8 percent. The price of this bond is $86.58. Table 6.1 shows the computations of the numerator using equation (2).

Adding these ten numbers results in a numerator of 659.31. Dividing the numerator by the price results in 659.31/86.58 or a duration of 7.62. The number 7.62 represents a weighted average maturity of the cash flows.

Using the duration formula in equation (3) gives the same result but with far fewer calculations:

$$DUR = \frac{[6(1.08)/0.08][(1-(1.08)^{-10})/0.08] + [10(100-6/0.08)/(1.08)^{10}]}{86.58}$$

$$= 7.62 \quad (4)$$

Table 6.1 Duration calculations

Maturity	$jc/(1+y)^j$	$n(c+PAR)/(1+y)^n$
1	5.56	
2	10.29	
3	14.29	
4	17.64	
5	20.42	
6	22.69	
7	24.51	
8	25.93	
9	27.01	
10		490.98

Some practitioners use modified duration, defined as Macaulay's duration divided by one plus the interest rate $(1+y)$. Modified duration is slightly smaller than Macaulay's duration.

An intuitive interpretation of duration

Since duration represents the percentage change in bond prices as interest rates change, the change in bond price must be approximately equal to the duration of a bond times the change in interest rates:

$$Price\ Change \approx [Price][Duration][Yield\ Change] \qquad (5)$$

where the symbol $\approx$ indicates approximately equal to. Dividing both sides by price results in:

$$Precent\ Price\ Change \approx [Duration][Yield\ Change] \qquad (6)$$

Consider the following example, shown in figure 6.1. The yield to maturity, y, is 10 percent and the interest rate changes from 10 percent to 11 percent. A perpetual bond's duration equals $(1+y)/y = 1.10/0.10 = 11$. If the perpetual bond initially has a yield of 10 percent and a coupon of \$10, the price is \$100.

$$P_0 = \frac{c}{y} = \frac{10}{0.10} = 100 \qquad (7)$$

If the interest rate increases to 11 percent, the bond's price declines to \$90.91:

$$P_1 = \frac{c}{y} = \frac{10}{0.11} = 90.91 \qquad (8)$$

The percentage change in price is:

$$\%\Delta P = \frac{P_1 - P_0}{P_0} = \frac{90.91 - 100}{100} = -9.09\% \qquad (9)$$

where Δ indicates the change in a variable. The duration approximation is:

$$\%\Delta P \approx (Duration)(\Delta y)$$

$$\approx (11)(0.01) = 0.11 \qquad (10)$$

The duration approximation suggests a price decline by approximately 11 percent (i.e. [11][0.01]) to \$89. Thus, the duration approximation has an error of about 2 percent. If the changes in interest rates are smaller, the duration approximation is more accurate. In fact, for

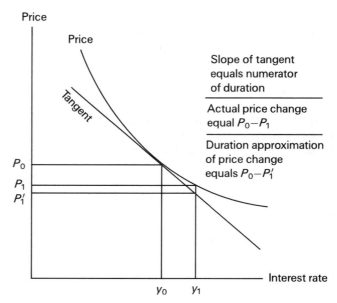

Figure 6.1   Duration as an approximation of price change

infinitesimal changes in interest rates, the duration approximation is highly accurate.

Durations for zero-coupon, par, and perpetual bonds, and mortgages

Durations for zero-coupon bonds, par bonds, perpetual bonds, and mortgages are of special interest and are shown in table 6.2. See the Appendix to this chapter for the derivations.

Duration can also be expressed as follows:

$$DUR = n - [n - DUR_{par}]\left[\frac{c/P}{y}\right] \qquad (11)$$

where DUR_{par} is the duration of a par bond and c/P is the current yield. For a zero-coupon bond, c in the last term is zero and the duration is simply the maturity, n. As the coupon increases, the last term gets bigger and the duration gets smaller since this term is negative.

Table 6.2 Bond price volatilities for special types of bonds

Type of bond	Duration
Zero-coupon	n
Par	$\dfrac{(1+y)[1-(1+y)^{-n}]}{y}$
Perpetual	$(1+y)/y$
Mortgage	$\dfrac{1+y}{y}-\dfrac{n}{(1+y)^{n}-1}$

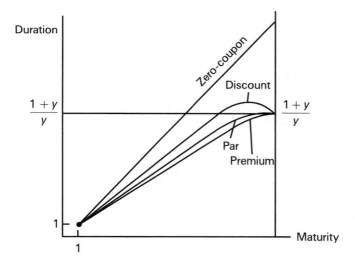

Figure 6.2 Duration versus maturity

Properties of duration

The relationship between duration, maturity, and coupon level is shown in figure 6.2, which assumes the same yield, y, for all bonds. The duration for premium and par bonds increases as maturity gets larger, eventually reaching the duration of a perpetual bond of $(1+y)/y$. For discount bonds, the duration increases as maturity gets larger until, at a long maturity, it reaches a maximum value; then the duration declines until it reaches the duration of a perpetual bond.

Table 6.3 Duration for various coupons and maturities yield to maturity of 8%

Maturity	Coupon					
	0	0.04	0.06	0.08	0.10	0.12
1	1	1	1	1	1	1
5	5	4.59	4.44	4.31	4.20	4.11
10	10	8.12	7.62	7.25	6.97	6.74
15	15	10.62	9.79	9.24	8.86	8.57
20	20	12.26	11.23	10.60	10.18	9.88
25	25	13.25	12.15	11.53	11.12	10.84
30	30	13.77	12.73	12.16	11.80	11.55

Note: Perpetual bond has duration of $1.08/0.08 = 13.50$.

Table 6.3 illustrates the relationship between duration and maturity assuming an 8 percent interest rate. Moving across the rows, coupon gets bigger and duration decreases. Moving down the columns, maturity increases and the duration gets bigger.

The riskiest bonds are long-maturity, deep discount (i.e. low-coupon) bonds, with zero-coupon bonds having the greatest price volatilities. High-coupon, short-maturity bonds have low volatilities. The greater price sensitivity of long-maturity bonds has important implications for term structure theories. In the liquidity preference theory, the greater price volatility of long-term bonds causes investors to require higher yields as maturity increases to compensate for higher risk.

Duration of portfolios

The duration of a portfolio of bonds is the price-weighted average of the durations of the bonds in the portfolio. To illustrate the calculation of the duration of a portfolio, suppose two bonds with prices P_1 and P_2 and durations DUR_1 and DUR_2. Then the portfolio duration is

$$DURATION_{portfolio} = \frac{(P_1)(DUR_1) + (P_2)(DUR_2)}{P_1 + P_2} \qquad (12)$$

As example, consider the duration of a portfolio composed of two ten-year bonds: a 6 percent coupon bond with a price of $86.58 per $100 of par and an 8 percent coupon bond with a price of par.

The portfolio duration is calculated as follows.

$$DURATION_{portfolio} = \frac{(86.58)(7.62) + (100)(7.25)}{86.58 + 100}$$

$$= 7.42 \qquad (13)$$

Immunization at a Horizon Date

Some investors are faced with a very specialized type of problem. The investor has money to invest today and must achieve a specific investment goal at a future date. Severe penalties are incurred if the investment goal is not attained; any excess beyond the desired goal brings no rewards. This type of investor is called an immunizer, because such investors would like to protect themselves against the chance of attaining less than the desired goal.

Pension funds and life insurance companies are investors with this type of problem. Using actuarial tables, the pension fund can predict with considerable accuracy its obligations to the pensioners in a defined benefit plan. The pension fund manager has no direct incentive to attain more than the contractually-bound retirement benefits and a big incentive to avoid defaulting on these obligations. Several strategies have been advocated for immunizers. We will discuss the pros and cons of each.

Zero coupon strategy

One simple strategy to lock in a dollar target is to buy zero coupon bonds. Since these bonds have no coupons, the risk of uncertain returns from investing the coupons is solved. The only cash flows occur at time 0 and at final maturity. See figure 6.3.

The US Treasury allows a number of Treasury securities to be stripped of their coupons. That is, the individual coupons and par value are sold separately. The resulting securities are called **strips** and are actively traded.

With the growth of the market for strips, the need for more complicated strategies to immunize has been reduced. Nevertheless, an extensive literature has developed on procedures for immunizing with coupon-bearing bonds. In effect, these strategies try to create the equivalent of a zero coupon bond position from a portfolio of coupon-bearing bonds.

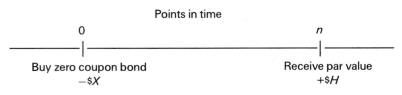

Figure 6.3 The zero coupon strategy

Maturity strategy

Some investigators use the so-called maturity strategy as a benchmark. In this strategy, an investor purchases a coupon-bearing bond with maturity equal to the investor's horizon. The cash flows are shown in figure 6.4.

An investor following this strategy is faced with the problem of reinvesting the coupons received in the future. For example, the coupon received at time 1 must be invested. If this coupon is invested in coupon-bearing bonds, then subsequent coupons must be reinvested. Since the reinvestment rates are not known at time 0, the total value of the bond portfolio is not known for certain. If interest rates at times 1 through $n-1$ are lower than the initial interest rate at time 0, the total portfolio value is less than the amount required.

Duration strategy

Another investment strategy is to invest in coupon-bearing bonds with maturity greater than the horizon date. This is shown in figure 6.5. The value of the bond portfolio using this strategy is uncertain for two reasons. First, the coupons from time 1 until time $n-1$ have to be reinvested at uncertain future interest rates. Second, the bond portfolio is sold at the horizon date n. Since the bonds will have $m-n$ periods left until maturity, the market value of the portfolio at this horizon date is uncertain.

Two different adverse events could upset this strategy and make the liquidating value of the portfolio less than the required goal. First, interest rates might decline. Then, the reinvestment rate on the coupons is low, but the market value of the bonds at the horizon date is high; these two factors affect the liquidating value of the portfolio at the horizon date in opposite directions. A second possibility is a rise in interest rates. This would raise the reinvestment rate on coupons but lower the market value of the bonds on the horizon date. The higher

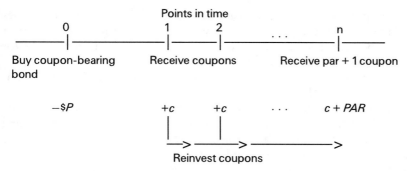

Figure 6.4   Maturity strategy

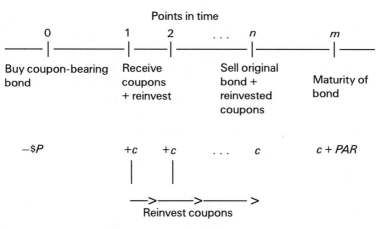

Figure 6.5   Duration strategy

reinvestment rate and the lower market value have opposite impacts upon the liquidating value of the portfolio. The net impact is not clear.

Investors can lock-in the liquidating value of their portfolio on the horizon date by setting the duration of the portfolio equal to the number of periods until the horizon date. This duration strategy is completely effective if two assumptions are met: (1) yield curves are flat, and (2) only one small change in interest rates occurs immediately after the portfolio is chosen.

Under the duration immunization strategy, if interest rates rise and the market value of the bonds in the portfolio goes down, the bond coupons are reinvested at high rates of interest, exactly offsetting the decline in the bond's market value. If interest rates decline, offsetting effects occur in the opposite direction. The market value of the bond portfolio rises and the coupons are reinvested at lower rates of interest. The immunizer would be certain of the value of the portfolio at the horizon date for increases and decreases in interest rates.

The duration strategy assumes one change in interest rates and a flat term structure. Now, consider immunization strategies if these two assumptions are relaxed. If multiple changes in interest rates occur, the portfolio can be approximately immunized if portfolio rebalancing occurs after each small change in interest rates. After each change, the duration is set equal to the number of periods until the horizon date. If yield curves are not flat, the duration strategy works approximately if the portfolio is rebalanced each time a small change in interest rates occurs.

In practice, two major drawbacks limit the use of duration immunization strategies employing coupon-bearing bonds. First, the need to rebalance the portfolio frequently results in expensive transactions costs. Second, the biggest advantage of immunization occurs for long horizons. Since the maturity of a bond is larger than its duration, a portfolio with a long duration has a much longer maturity. The lack of long-term bonds limits the use of the strategy. For example, a portfolio with a 20-year duration might require bonds with maturities of 40 years, depending upon the level of interest rates. Since bonds with maturities more than 30 years are rare, immunization is not practical in this case.

Dedicated portfolio strategy

Another strategy used by bond investors to lock-in a terminal value at their horizon date is called a dedicated portfolio strategy. This strategy assumes a very low reinvestment rate on coupons. In order to achieve the same terminal value with a lower reinvestment rate, the investor must initially invest more money. This will guarantee the minimum goal even under the worst-case scenario. However, the initial cost of the dedicated strategy is higher than a duration strategy. With a duration strategy, there are costs for rebalancing after the initial investment. If the strategy falls short of its goals, additional funds will have to be contributed.

Other bond portfolio strategies

Some bond investors are concerned with the risk of short-term fluctuations in the value of their portfolio. In particular, if interest rates rise, the market value of the portfolio falls.

Several strategies are available for these investors. The simplest strategy is to invest in very-short-term securities. Then, the value of the portfolio is very stable. The disadvantage is the relatively low returns available on short-term bonds.

Two riskier strategies (with higher expected returns) are available. The so-called ladder strategy invests approximately equal proportions of the portfolio in a wide variety of maturities. If interest rates rise, the shorter-maturity part of the portfolio has only small price declines. When the shortest-maturity bond matures, the proceeds can be reinvested at the higher prevailing interest rate. The total portfolio risk is much lower than investing in a long-term bond exclusively.

The barbell strategy invests equal proportions of the portfolio in short-term and long-term bonds. A rise in interest rates causes the prices of long-term bonds to drop considerably, but those of short-term bonds to remain relatively stable. When the short-term bond matures, reinvestment at the new higher interest rate is available. The barbell strategy is higher-risk than the ladder strategy, but much lower-risk than 100 percent investment in long-term bonds.

Immunizing Assets and Liabilities

Some financial institutions such as banks may have assets and liabilities that are sensitive to changes in interest rates. For example, as interest rates increase, the value of the assets goes down, but so does the value of the liabilities. The interest rate risk is the net risk of assets and liabilities.

The net position of the institution can be protected from the risk of changing interest rates by matching the maturities of assets and liabilities. Assets and liabilities can be divided into maturity classes. If the total assets in each class equal the total liabilities in each class, the total position of the institution is protected against changing interest rates.

Summary

Bond investors are interested in the sensitivity of their bond holdings to changes in interest rates. Duration shows that interest rate sensitivity declines as bond coupon gets larger and increases as maturity increases, except for some very-long-maturity discount bonds. Shorter-maturity, higher-coupon bonds are low-risk; and longer-maturity, lower-coupon bonds are high risk.

Some investors are immunizers who want to lock-in a terminal value at a particular horizon date. These investors can select from the zero coupon bond, maturity, duration, and dedicated strategies. Buying zero coupon bonds (strips) is an excellent strategy, if available.

Questions and Problems

1   Assume a yield to maturity of 8 percent. Compute the duration for the following bonds. Assume $100 par values. For the 12% coupon bond, compute the duration using the three duration formulas. Which formula is easiest to compute?

    (a)   10 years, zero coupon
    (b)   10 years, 8 percent coupon
    (c)   10 years, 12 percent coupon

2   In problem 1, assume that yields change from 8 to 9 percent. Work out the exact change in price and compare it with the change in price predicted by duration. Explain the difference. Assume $100 par values.

3   Compute the duration of a portfolio composed of a ten-year, zero coupon bond and a ten-year, 8 percent coupon bond. For simplicity assume each bond has a par value of $100. Suppose that equal dollar amounts are invested in the two bonds. How does the portfolio duration change? Which portfolio is riskier?

4   A perpetual bond has a coupon of $6 and a yield to maturity of 6 percent. Work out the actual percentage change in price and the duration approximation in the following three cases:

    (a)   The yield decreases by 1 percent
    (b)   The yield increases by 1 percent
    (c)   The yield increases by 8 percent.

5   For an investor who desires to immunize a portfolio, compare the advantages and disadvantages of a duration strategy versus a dedicated strategy in a real-world situation. How does the zero coupon bond strategy compare with each of these other strategies?

6   Compute the duration of the longest-maturity Treasury bond and longest-maturity Treasury note listed in the *Wall Street Journal*.

7   Suppose that the interest rate on all bonds is 8%. You compute the duration on a particular bond and find it to be greater than 13.50. What can you say about the coupon on this bond? (Hint: draw a diagram showing duration versus maturity.)

Appendix
Maximum Value of Duration for Discount Bonds

For discount bonds, duration reaches its maximum for a maturity of:

$$\frac{1+y}{y-c/PAR} + \frac{1}{ln(1+y)} + \frac{y[PAR/c-1/y]}{(1+y)^n \, ln(1+y)} \tag{14}$$

This maximum value is:

$$\frac{1+y}{y} + \frac{y[PAR/c - 1/y]}{(1+y)^{n^*}(1+y)} \tag{15}$$

where n^* is the maturity where duration has attained a maximum. Notice that this maximum value is only slightly larger than the duration of a perpetual bond. The first term is the duration of a perpetual bond; for large values of n^*, the second term is close to zero.

More Accurate Approximations

While duration provides reasonably accurate approximations of the change in bond price as interest rates change, the accuracy of the approximation can be improved by considering higher derivatives. Using a Taylor expansion, the total percentage change in bond price as yield changes can be expressed in terms of all the derivatives:

$$\frac{\%\Delta P}{P} = \left[\frac{dP}{dy}\right]\left[\frac{1}{P}\right]\Delta y + \left[\frac{d^2P}{dy^2}\right]\left[\frac{1}{P}\right]\left[\frac{(\Delta y)^2}{2!}\right]$$

$$+ \left[\frac{d^3P}{dy^3}\right]\left[\frac{1}{P}\right]\left[\frac{(\Delta y)^3}{3!}\right] + \cdots \tag{16}$$

where:

$$\frac{dP}{dy} = \text{first derivative}$$

$$\frac{d^2P}{dy^2} = \text{second derivative}$$

$$\frac{d^3P}{dy^3} = \text{third derivative}$$

The Taylor expansion expresses the percentage change in bond price ($\Delta P/P$) in terms of the first, second, and higher derivatives. The first derivative term incorporates minus duration divided by $1 + y$.[1] That is,

$$\frac{-duration}{(1+y)} = \left[\frac{dP}{dy}\right]\left[\frac{1}{P}\right] \tag{17}$$

The second derivative term incorporates what has been called convexity.

$$Convexity = \left[\frac{d^2P}{dy^2}\right]\left[\frac{1}{P}\right]\left[\frac{1}{2}\right] \tag{18}$$

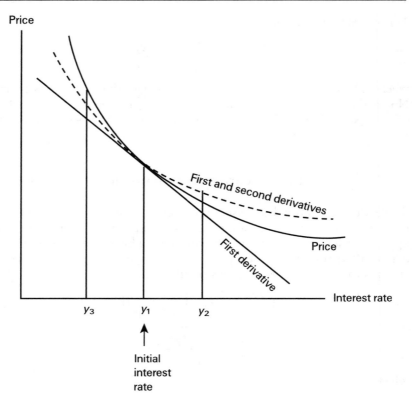

Figure 6A.1 Duration and convexity

In the Taylor expansion, the convexity is multiplied by the change in the change in yield squared (i.e. $(\Delta y)^2$). The impact of the second derivative or convexity term is shown in figure 6A.1 as the dotted line.

The second derivative makes the approximation more accurate. For increases in interest rates to y_2 the duration plus convexity approximation gives a high estimate of the bond price. For decreases in interest rates to y_3, the duration and convexity approximation give a low estimate of the price. To see why an increase in yields gives high estimates, note that the odd-numbered derivatives (i.e. dP/dy) are negative. If the interest rate increases (decreases), then the odd-numbered derivatives are multiplied by a positive (negative) Δy, implying that the odd-numbered derivative terms are negative (positive). The second derivative is positive and multiplied by Δy squared, which is always positive. Consequently, the second derivative term is always positive.

As each derivative is added to the Taylor expansion, the approximation converges to the true value. When interest rates increase, the signs of the terms in the Taylor expansion are negative, positive, negative, and so on. The only way for the approximation to converge to the true value is for the approximation with the first term to lie below the true value, with the second term included to lie above, with the third term included to lie below, and so on. When interest rates decline, all the terms in the Taylor expansion are positive. The first term gives a low estimate and as additional terms are added, the approximation gets closer, but never higher than the true value.

In the case of a perpetual bond, the Taylor expansion is:[2]

$$\frac{\%\Delta P}{P} = \frac{-\Delta y}{y} + \frac{(\Delta y)^2}{y^2} - \frac{(\Delta y)^3}{y^3} + \cdots = \frac{-\Delta y}{y + \Delta y} \tag{19}$$

In this equation, the first derivative term is $-\Delta y/y$, which is duration divided by $(1+y)(\Delta y)$. The second derivative term is $(\Delta y)^2/y^2$, which is the convexity (i.e. $1/y^2$) times $(\Delta y)^2$. The Taylor series has a simple sum for perpetual bonds, namely $-\Delta y/(y + \Delta y)$.

From the Taylor series, each term equals the previous term times $\Delta y/y$. As long as Δy is small relative to y, the additional derivatives add progressively smaller amounts to the total change. The example in table 6A.1 illustrates the importance of the terms in the Taylor expansion. Assume a perpetual bond with an $8 annual coupon and an interest rate of 8 percent, implying a price of $100 (i.e. $8/0.08 = 100$). If the interest rate increases to 9 percent, the price becomes $88.89 (i.e. $8/0.09 = 88.89$). The decline in price is $11.11, or 11.11 percent. Compare this actual change with the individual terms in the Taylor expansion.

Table 6A.1 Taylor expansion for a perpetual bond

First derivative $-\Delta y/y$	Second derivative $(\Delta y/y)^2$	Third derivative $-(\Delta y/y)^3$	Total change $-\Delta y/(y+\Delta y)$
$-0.01/0.08$ $= -0.125$	$(0.01/0.08)^2$ $= +0.0156$	$-(0.01/0.08)^3$ $= -0.0020$	$-0.01/(0.08+0.01)$ $= -0.1111$
First term	Sum of first two terms	Sum of first three terms	Total change
-0.125	-0.1094	-0.1114	-0.1111

Errors = Approximation − Total change

0.0139	−0.0017	0.0003	

The errors in table 6A.1 get closer to zero as more terms are added. The estimated change from the first term is too large by 0.0139, or 1.39 percent. The estimated change from the sum of the first two terms is too small by 0.0017, or 0.17 percent, but the absolute size of the error is reduced. Using the sum of the first three terms, the estimated change is again too large, although the absolute value of the error has become even smaller.

For perpetual bonds, the higher derivative terms are less important as the change in yield becomes smaller because each term in the Taylor expansion equals the previous term times $\Delta y/y$. The higher derivatives are also less important as the yield increases because the yield is in the denominator of each term of the Taylor expansion.

The percent error for perpetual bonds is:

$$\%_e = \frac{-\Delta y/(y+\Delta y)-(-\Delta y/y)}{-\Delta y/(y+\Delta y)}$$

$$= \frac{-\Delta y}{y} \tag{20}$$

If the absolute value of the change in yield is small relative to the level of yield, the percent error from the duration (i.e. first derivative) approximation is close to zero. Adding the higher derivatives does not add much accuracy.

The preceding discussion of the Taylor expansion has been for perpetual bonds. Similar results apply for shorter-maturity bonds. In addition, for shorter maturities, the higher derivative terms are less important. Thus, for shorter maturities the duration approximation is quite accurate.

Notes

1 Duration divided by $1+y$ is called modified duration and is a better measure of price sensitivity than duration by itself.
2 M. Livingston, "Measuring bond price volatility," *Journal of Financial and Quantitative Analysis*, 14 (June 1979), pp. 343–9.

7

Time Value with Nonflat Term Structure

The term structure of interest rates is the relationship between maturity (or term) and interest rates. Typically, longer-maturity debt has higher interest rates, although the relationship between maturity and interest rates varies widely. Figure 7.1 shows several patterns as reported in the *Treasury Bulletin*. Sometimes interest rates decline for longer maturities. Sometimes interest rates rise as maturity increases and then decline (a humped curve). Sometimes they have a dish shape. This chapter discusses present value computations with nonflat term structures.

Spot Interest Rates

An interest rate that begins today and continues until some future date is frequently called a spot interest rate. We will denote spot interest rates by capital R.

Each spot interest rate has two subscripts. The first subscript denotes the point in time when the interest rate is observed. The second denotes how long the interest rate lasts. Recall that time 0 is now. Future points in time are denoted by time 1, time 2, etc. Thus, $R_{0,1}$ is observed now and runs for one period. $R_{0,2}$ is observed now and lasts two periods. $R_{0,n}$ is observed now and lasts n periods. Figure 7.2 illustrates.

In this chapter, we will stick to interest rates that are observed now, with a first subscript of 0. In later chapters, other cases are considered. As one example, $R_{1,1}$ is the interest rate observed one period into the future and lasting one period until time 2.

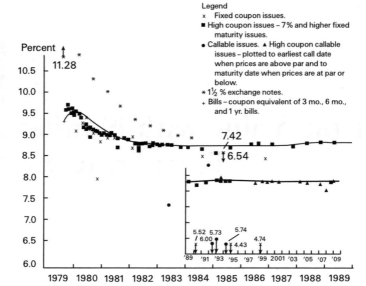

(a) Yields on Treasury securities on June 29, 1979

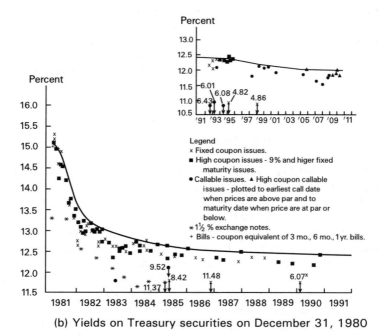

(b) Yields on Treasury securities on December 31, 1980

Figure 7.1 Various term structures (from US Department of Treasury, *Treasury Bulletin*)

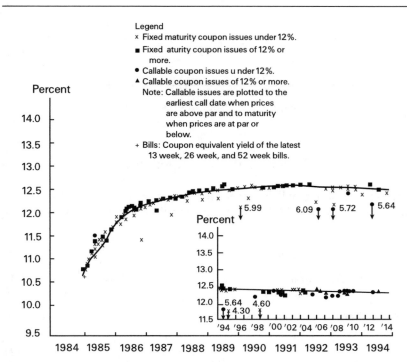

(c) Yields on Treasury securities on September 28, 1984

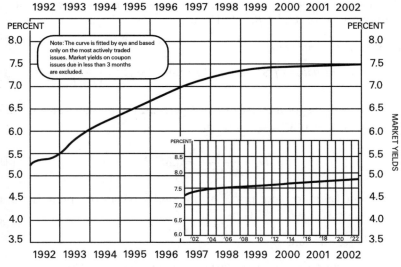

(d) Yields of Treasury securities on September 30, 1991

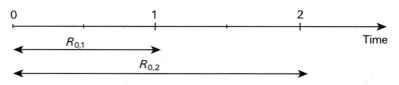

Figure 7.2   Spot interest rates

Present Values or Spot Prices

Suppose one dollar will be received one period from now. Its present value or spot price is $1/(1+R_{0,1})$. To simplify the notation, we call this D_1. Thus,

One-period present value

$$\text{Present value of \$1 received at time } 1 = D_1 = \frac{1}{1+R_{0,1}} \qquad (1)$$

Suppose that the one-period spot interest rate $R_{0,1}$ is 4 percent. Then,

$$D_1 = \frac{1}{1.04} = 0.9615 \qquad (2)$$

One dollar received at time 1 has a present value of \$0.9615.

The present value (or spot price) of one dollar received two periods from now is D_2 or $1/(1+R_{0,2})^2$. Thus,

Two-period present value

$$\text{Present value of \$1 received at time } 2 = D_2 = \frac{1}{(1+R_{0,2})^2} \qquad (3)$$

If the two-period spot interest rate is 8 percent, the present value of one dollar received at time 2 is \$0.8573.

$$D_2 = \frac{1}{(1.08)^2} = 0.8573 \qquad (4)$$

The present value (or spot price) of one dollar received n periods from now is D_n or $1/(1+R_{0,n})^n$. Thus,

n-period present value

$$\text{Present value of \$1 received at time } n = D_n = \frac{1}{(1+R_{0,n})^n} \qquad (5)$$

If n is 8 periods and $R_{0,8}$ is 10 percent, then,

$$D_8 = \frac{1}{(1.10)^8} = 0.4665 \qquad (6)$$

The reader should practice present value calculations on a financial calculator.

The present value of one dollar received in the more distant future is smaller than the present value of a dollar in the nearer future. That is,

$$D_1 \geqslant D_2 \geqslant \cdots \geqslant D_n$$

$$\begin{bmatrix} Present\ value \\ of\ \$1\ received \\ at\ time\ 1 \end{bmatrix} \geqslant \begin{bmatrix} Present\ value \\ of\ \$1\ received \\ at\ time\ 2 \end{bmatrix} \geqslant \ldots \geqslant \begin{bmatrix} Present\ value \\ of\ \$1\ received \\ at\ time\ n \end{bmatrix} \qquad (7)$$

In terms of the spot interest rates, we have

$$\frac{1}{(1+R_1)} \geqslant \frac{1}{(1+R_2)^2} \geqslant \cdots \geqslant \frac{1}{(1-R_n)^n} \qquad (8)$$

Notice that the present values or spot prices decrease for longer maturities in our examples.

$$D_1 \geqslant D_2 \geqslant D_8$$
$$0.9615 \geqslant 0.8573 \geqslant 0.4665 \qquad (9)$$

Treasury Strips

Treasury strips are zero-coupon bonds. The buyer purchases these for a price P_n and receives the par value at maturity n. The cash flows are shown in table 7.1.

The price of a strip should be the par value discounted at the appropriate spot interest rate. The prices of strips are quoted per $100 of par value. Using our earlier term structure of interest rates,

One-period strip

$$\begin{array}{c} Price\ of \\ one\text{-}period \\ strip \end{array} = P_1 = [D_1][PAR] = \frac{PAR}{1+R_{0,1}} = \left[\frac{1}{1.04}\right]100 = 96.15 \qquad (10)$$

Table 7.1 Cash flows for treasury strip

	Points in time			
	0	1	⋯	n
Cash flows	$-P_n$	0	0	$+PAR$

Two-period strip

$$\begin{array}{l}\text{Price of}\\ \text{two-period}\\ \text{strip}\end{array} = P_2 = [D_2][PAR] = \frac{PAR}{(1+R_{0,2})^2} = \left[\frac{1}{(1.08)^2}\right]100 = 85.73 \quad (11)$$

Check the newspaper listings for prices of Treasury strips. The price of a more distant strip is always smaller.

Finding spot interest rates from strip prices

The spot interest rates can be found from the spot prices for Treasury strips. Suppose the prices of one-period and two-period strips are \$96.15 and \$85.73 per \$100 of par. The spot interest rates can be found as follows:

One-period strip

$$\text{Since } P_1 = \frac{PAR}{1+R_{0,1}} \quad (12)$$

$$1+R_{0,1} = \frac{PAR}{P_1} = \frac{100}{96.15} = 1.04 \quad (13)$$

$$R_{0,1} = 0.04 = 4\%$$

Two-period strip

$$\text{Since } P_2 = \frac{PAR}{(1+R_{0,2})^2} \quad (14)$$

$$(1+R_{0,2})^2 = \frac{PAR}{P_2} = \frac{100}{85.73} = 1.1665 \quad (15)$$

$$R_{0,2} = 0.08 = 8\%$$

For an n-period Treasury strip, the n-period spot interest rate can be found as follows:

n-period strip

$$\text{Since } P_n = \frac{PAR}{(1+R_{0,n})^n} \quad (16)$$

$$(1+R_{0,n})^n = \frac{PAR}{P_n} \quad (17)$$

$$R_{0,n} = \sqrt[n]{\frac{PAR}{P_n}} - 1 \quad (18)$$

Forward Interest Rates

In many financial transactions, borrowers and lenders agree right now to make a loan in the future. The conditions of the loan are set at time 0, but the transaction does not occur until a future date. These are called forward loans. Table 7.2 shows the timing.

Individual consumers typically do not engage in forward transactions, but restrict themselves primarily to spot transactions, that is, transactions where the goods or services are received and payment made immediately. A lease is an example of a forward contract. At time 0, a lease agreement is reached to provide some service in the future and make payments in the future.

Forward loans and interest rates are important to consider because forward loans are substitutes for spot loans and compete with spot loans. Consequently, the determinants of forward interest rates are also the determinants of spot interest rates.

Suppose we have a loan in which the cash flows to the lender (bond buyer) are shown in table 7.3. Although the loan agreement is signed at time 0, there are no cash flows at time 0. The cash flows do not occur until the delivery date.

Let the forward interest rate for period 2 be denoted by $f_{0,2}$. The first subscript indicates that the rate is observed at time 0. The second denotes an interest rate for period 2. We will consider forward loans

Table 7.2 Timing of a forward contract

	Points in time	
	0	Delivery date
Transaction	Sign contract and set price	Pay $ and receive commodity or Deliver commodity and receive $

Table 7.3 Forward contract cash flows for lender (bond buyer)

	Points in time		
	0	1 Delivery date	2 Maturity date
Cash flows	0	$-F$ (Lend $F)	$+PAR$ (Receive PAR)

lasting one period; if loan maturities exceed one period, an additional subscript is needed to indicate when the loan begins and when it ends.

The forward interest rate discounts money from time 2 until time 1. Suppose \$1 will be received at time 2. Its time 1 value is \$1 discounted at the forward interest rate. The time 1 value of a dollar received at time 2 is:

$$Time\ 1\ value = \frac{1}{1 + f_{0,2}} \qquad (19)$$

Suppose $f_{0,2}$ is 12.15 percent. Then \$1 received at time 2 has a time 1 value of \$0.8917 (see table 7.4).

$$Time\ 1\ value = \frac{1}{1.1215} = 0.8917 \qquad (20)$$

The time 2 value of \$1 received at time 3 is:

$$Time\ 2\ value = \frac{1}{1 + f_{0,3}} \qquad (21)$$

See table 7.5.

In general, the time $n-1$ value of \$1 received at time n is:

$$Time\ n-1\ value = \frac{1}{1 + f_{0,n}} \qquad (22)$$

Table 7.4 Forward contract cash flows for lender (bond buyer)

		Points in time	
	0	1 Delivery date	2 Maturity date
Cash flows	0	$-1/(1 + f_{0,2})$ -0.8917	$+1.00$

Table 7.5 Forward contract cash flows for lender (bond buyer)

			Points in time	
	0	1	2 Delivery date	3 Maturity date
Cash flows	0	0	$-1/(1 + f_{0,3})$	$+1.00$

Forward interest rates allow discounting for several periods. Thus the time 1 value of $1 received at time 3 is:

$$\text{Time 1 value} = \frac{1}{(1 + f_{0,2})(1 + f_{0,3})} \tag{23}$$

Suppose that $f_{0,2}$ is 12.15 percent and $f_{0,3}$ is 10 percent. The time 1 value of $1 received at time 3 is as follows:

$$\text{Time 1 value} = \frac{1}{(1.1215)(1.10)} = \left[\frac{1}{1.1215}\right]\left[\frac{1}{1.10}\right]$$
$$= [0.8917][0.9091] = 0.8106 \tag{24}$$

The present (time 0) value of $1 received at time 3 is:

$$\text{Time 0 value} = \frac{1}{(1 + R_{0,1})(1 + f_{0,2})(1 + f_{0,3})} \tag{25}$$

Link between spot and forward interest rates

Since the present value can be expressed in terms of both spot and forward interest rates, the two are linked. In particular,

Two periods

$$\frac{1}{(1 + R_{0,2})^2} = \frac{1}{(1 + R_{0,1})(1 + f_{0,2})} \tag{26}$$

Take the reciprocal:

$$(1 + R_{0,2})^2 = (1 + R_{0,1})(1 + f_{0,2}) \tag{27}$$

In words, the two-period spot interest rate is the geometric mean of the one-period spot interest rate and the forward interest $f_{0,2}$. Using our earlier numerical example,

$$(1.08)^2 = (1.04)(1.1215) = 1.1664 \tag{28}$$

This equation indicates that an investor with $1 to invest at time 0 should end up with the same value at time 2 ($1.1664) if the money is invested at 8 percent for two periods or invested for one period at 4 percent and then reinvested forward at 12.15 percent. Since the forward interest rate is known at time 0, the investor can lock-in a return of 12.15 percent for the second period. The time 2 value ($1.1664) is known for certain in each case.

Equation (27) says that the two-period spot interest rate is the geometric mean of the one-period spot interest rate and the forward interest rate. Equation (27) is approximately the same as saying that the two-period spot interest rate is the arithmetic mean of the one-period spot rate and the forward interest rate. To see this point, expand equation (27):

$$1 + 2R_{0,2} + R_{0,2}^2 = 1 + R_{0,1} + f_{0,2} + R_{0,1}f_{0,2} \tag{29}$$

Omit the squared term and the product term, resulting in the following approximation:

$$1 + 2R_{0,2} \approx 1 + R_{0,1} + f_{0,2} \tag{30}$$

This is rearranged to:

$$R_{0,2} \approx \frac{R_{0,1} + f_{0,2}}{2} \tag{31}$$

If the one-period spot interest rate is 4 percent and the forward interest rate is 12.15 percent, the arithmetic approximation of the two-period spot interest rate is 8.08 percent, whereas the actual interest rate (geometric mean) is 8 percent.

Three periods

$$\frac{1}{(1 + R_{0,3})^3} = \frac{1}{(1 + R_{0,1})(1 + f_{0,2})(1 + f_{0,3})} \tag{32}$$

Take the reciprocal:

$$(1 + R_{0,3})^3 = (1 + R_{0,1})(1 + f_{0,2})(1 + f_{0,3}) = (1 + R_{0,2})^2(1 + f_{0,3}) \tag{33}$$

The three-period spot interest rate is the geometric mean of the one-period spot interest rate and the two forward rates, $f_{0,2}$ and $f_{0,3}$. An investor with \$1 to invest at time 0 should end up with the same wealth at time 3 if the investment is at the spot rate $R_{0,3}$ for three periods or at $R_{0,1}$ for the first period, $f_{0,2}$ for the second period, and $f_{0,3}$ for the third period.

n periods

$$\frac{1}{(1 + R_{0,n})^n} = \frac{1}{(1 + R_{0,1})(1 + f_{0,2}) \cdots (1 + f_{0,n})} \tag{34}$$

Take the reciprocal:

$$(1 + R_{0,n})^n = (1 + R_{0,1})(1 + f_{0,2}) \cdots (1 + f_{0,n}) = (1 + R_{0,n-1})^{n-1}(1 + f_n) \tag{35}$$

The n-period spot interest rate is the geometric mean of the one-period spot interest rate and the forward rates until period n. Someone can invest for n periods at the spot rate $R_{0,n}$ or invest for n periods at the sequence of rates $R_{0,1}, f_{0,2}, \ldots, f_{0,n}$. In either case, the value after n periods is the same.

Shape of the Term Structure

A rising (falling) term structure occurs when spot interest rates increase (decrease) for longer maturities. The shape of the spot rates is related to the forward rates. The case of two periods illustrates the link. If the two-period spot interest rate ($R_{0,2}$) is greater (less) than the one-period spot rate ($R_{0,1}$), the forward rate ($f_{0,2}$) must be greater (less) than the two-period spot interest rate. Figure 7.3 illustrates these cases.

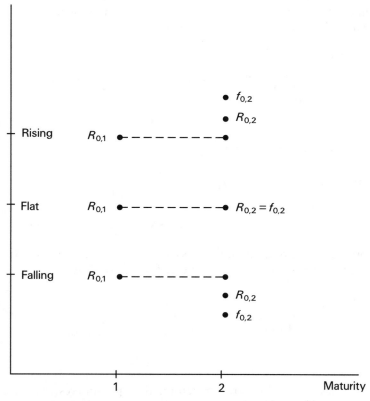

Figure 7.3 Rising, flat, and falling term structures

The important lesson is that rising (falling) spot interests imply rising (falling) forward interest rates. The reason is that $R_{0,2}$ is the geometric mean of $R_{0,1}$ and $f_{0,2}$. Since $R_{0,2}$ is the average of $R_{0,1}$ and $f_{0,2}$, $R_{0,2}$ must lie between them. For rising term structures, $R_{0,1} < R_{0,2} < f_{0,2}$. For falling term structures, $R_{0,1} > R_{0,2} > f_{0,2}$.

Annuities

Frequently, debt instruments involve constant cash flows over several periods. These constant cash flows are called annuities. For bonds, coupons are annuities, since the coupon payment is the same over a number of periods. For mortgages, the periodic payment is the same every period and is an annuity.

The present value of an annuity is simply the sum of the present values of the individual components of the annuity. The present value of an annuity of $1 at time 1 and $1 at time 2 is the sum of the present values. We will call this present value A_2. That is,

Two periods

$$\frac{Present\ Value}{of\ Annuity} = A_2 = \frac{1}{1+R_{0,1}} + \frac{1}{(1+R_{0,2})^2}$$

$$= D_1 + D_2 \tag{36}$$

Using our earlier numerical example,

$$Present\ Value\ of\ Annuity = A_2 = \frac{1}{1.04} + \frac{1}{(1.08)^2}$$

$$= 0.9615 + 0.8573 = 1.8188 \tag{37}$$

The present value of an annuity of $1 for two periods is $1.8188.

The present value of a dollar annuity for n periods is

n periods

$$\frac{Present\ Value}{of\ Annuity} = A_n = \frac{1}{1+R_{0,1}} + \cdots + \frac{1}{(1+R_{0,n})^n}$$

$$= D_1 + \cdots + D_n \tag{38}$$

In the case of a flat term structure, the spot interest rate for all periods is R. Then the formula for the present value of an annuity simplifies:

n periods flat term structure

$$Present\ Value\ of\ Annuity = A_n = \frac{1}{1+R} + \cdots + \frac{1}{(1+R)^n}$$

(39)

$$= \left[\frac{1}{R}\right]\left[1 - \frac{1}{(1+R)^n}\right]$$

If the term structure is flat and the spot interest rates equal 10 percent, the present value of a ten-period annuity is computed as follows:

$$Present\ Value\ of\ Annuity = A_{10} = \left[\frac{1}{R}\right]\left[1 - \frac{1}{(1+R)^n}\right]$$

(40)

$$A_{10} = \left[\frac{1}{0.10}\right]\left[1 - \frac{1}{(1.10)^{10}}\right] = \frac{0.61446}{0.10} = 6.1446$$

Prices of Coupon-Bearing Bonds

An n-period coupon-bearing bond pays periodic coupons and par at maturity. The pattern of cash flows is shown in table 7.6.

A coupon-bearing bond is essentially a portfolio of zero-coupon bonds or strips. Consider one-period, two-period, and n-period coupon-bearing bonds. The price of each bond is the present value of each of the coupons (c) and the par value.

One-period bond

$$P_1 = \frac{c + PAR}{1 + R_{0,1}}$$

(41)

$$= [c + PAR]D_1$$

Table 7.6 Cash flows for coupon-bearing bond

		Points in time	
	0	1	2 through $n-1$	n
Cash flows	$-P_n$	c	c	$c + PAR$

To illustrate, suppose the one-period spot interest rate $(R_{0,1})$ is 4 percent, and a bond has a coupon of $6 and par value of $100:

$$P_1 = \frac{6+100}{1.04} = 101.92 \tag{42}$$

Two-period bond

$$P_2 = \frac{c}{1+R_{0,1}} + \frac{c+PAR}{(1+R_{0,2})^2}$$

$$= [c][D_1] + [c+PAR]D_2 \tag{43}$$

$$= [c][D_1] + [c][D_2] + [PAR][D_2]$$

$$= [c][A_2] + [PAR][D_2]$$

To illustrate, suppose the one-period spot interest rate $(R_{0,1})$ is 4 percent, the two-period spot interest rate $(R_{0,2})$ is 8 percent, and a bond has a coupon of $6 and par value of $100:

$$P_2 = \frac{6}{1.04} + \frac{6+100}{(1.08)^2} = 96.65 \tag{44}$$

n-period bond

$$P_n = \frac{c}{1+R_{0,1}} + \cdots + \frac{c+PAR}{(1+R_{0,n})^n}$$

$$= [c][D_1] + \cdots + [c+PAR][D_n] \tag{45}$$

$$= [c][A_n] + [PAR][D_n]$$

Yield to Maturity and Spot Rates

The yield to maturity on a coupon-bearing bond is a polynomial average of the spot interest rates. To see this point, consider the case of two-period bonds.

$$P_2 = \frac{c}{1+y} + \frac{c+PAR}{(1+y)^2} = \frac{c}{1+R_{0,1}} + \frac{c+PAR}{(1+R_{0,2})^2} \tag{46}$$

The yield to maturity is an average of $R_{0,1}$ and $R_{0,2}$. The precise average depends upon the size of the bond coupon and the maturity in the general case. For short maturities, the yield to maturity is close to the n-period spot interest rate. For longer-maturities, the yield to maturity is heavily influenced by all the spot interest rates.

In the case of a bond with a price of par, the yield to maturity can be explicitly expressed as a function of the spot interest rates. In the two-period case, we have:

$$ypar_2 = \frac{1 - (1/(1 + R_{0,2})^2)}{1/(1 + R_{0,1}) + 1/(1 + R_{0,2})^2} \tag{47}$$

If the one-period spot interest rate is 4 percent and the two-period spot rate is 8 percent,

$$ypar_2 = \frac{1 - (1/(1.08)^2)}{(1/1.04) + 1/(1.08)^2} = 7.84\% \tag{48}$$

In practice, coupons are units of 1/8 of a dollar.

In the case of n-period par bonds,

$$ypar_n = \frac{1 - (1/(1 + R_{0,n})^n}{1/(1 + R_{0,1}) + \cdots + 1/(1 + R_{0,n})^n} \tag{49}$$

Summary

In general, interest rates vary by maturity. Usually, longer-term interest rates are higher. This chapter examines future value and present value calculations for a nonflat term structure. With a nonflat term structure, forward interest rates are important to consider. A forward interest rate is set at time zero for a loan that commences at a future date. Spot and forward interest rates are closely linked.

Questions and Problems

1 Assume that the one-period spot interest rate is 3 percent and the two-period spot interest rate is 6 percent. Answer the following questions:

   (a) What is the present value of $100 received one year from now?
   (b) What is the present value of $100 received two years from now?
   (c) You are going to receive $100 two years from now. What is its time 1 value? What is the forward interest rate?
   (d) Suppose you invest $1 today at the two-period spot interest rate; what is its value at time 2? Alternatively you invest $1 at the one-period spot rate and reinvest at the forward interest rate; what is the value at time 2? How do these two investments compare?

2 Treasury strips with $100 par values have the following prices: one-period, $90; two-period, $80. Answer the following questions:

   (a) What are the one-period and two-period spot interest rates?
   (b) What is the forward interest rate?

(c) If you invest $1 in one-period strips, what is the value after one period?

(d) If you invest $1 in two-period strips, what is the value after two periods?

(e) If you invest $1 at time 1 at the forward interest rate implied by the strips, what is the value of this dollar at time 2?

3 Treasury strips with $100 par values have the following prices: one-period, $94; two-period, $87. You are going to receive an annuity of $100 for the next two periods. What is the present value of this annuity? What is the time 1 value of this annuity? What is the time 2 value of this annuity?

4 An annuity of $100 per period for two periods has a present value of $178.33. If the term structure of interest rates is flat, compute the interest rate.

5 Suppose the term structure in problem 1 applies. A two-period coupon-bearing bond has an annual coupon of $5.00 and par value of $100. Answer the following questions:

(a) What is the bond's price?

(b) What is the bond's yield to maturity?

(c) Suppose you arrange (at time 0) to buy this bond in the forward market for delivery at time 1 immediately after the coupon is paid. What should the forward price be?

6 As a reward for reading this book, you are given a choice between $100 received one year from now and $115 received two years from now. How should you go about deciding which of these choices is better?

7 Suppose that the prices of one- through four-period strips per $100 of par are $95, $90, $85, $80. Compute the spot and forward interest rates and show these on a graph.

8 Compute the spot and forward interest rates if the prices of one-period and two-period strips are each $92 per $100 of par value.

9 Using the information in problem 7, compute the yield to maturity on a two-period par bond.

10 A one-period par bond has a price of $100, par value of $100, and coupon of $6. A two-period par bond has a price of $100, par value of $100, and coupon of $8. What is the two-period spot interest rate?

11 Suppose that the one-period spot interest rate is 10 percent. What is the minimum value for the two-period spot interest rate? (Hint: Express the two-period spot rate in terms of the one-period spot rate and the forward rate.)

8

Arbitrage

One of the most important concepts in finance is the concept of **arbitrage**, also called the **law of one price**. In frictionless markets, the same asset must have one price at a particular instant in time, no matter where it is traded. As a simple example, consider a common stock traded on both the New York Stock Exchange and the Pacific Stock Exchange. If the stock has a price of $50 in New York and $53 on the Pacific Exchange, an arbitrager can simultaneously buy the stock at $50 and sell (shortsell) it at $53, for an immediate and risk-free profit of $3. The purchase at $50 and the sale at $53 drive the prices together. An arbitrager does not need any capital to make arbitrage profits. Therefore, one small arbitrager who repeatedly and rationally exploits price differences is able to drive the prices together.

Arbitrage is clearest in a world of frictionless financial markets, when the following assumptions will hold: (1) no taxes, (2) no default risk, (3) no transactions costs, and (4) unrestricted shortselling (defined below) is allowed. In practice, markets are not frictionless. Frictions can create differences between the prices of the same thing in different markets. Thus, a stock trading in New York and on the West Coast may have slightly different prices because of the transactions costs of buying in the lower-priced market and selling in the higher-priced market.

This chapter presents several examples of arbitrage linking the prices in different markets. Other examples occur throughout the book. One of the important aspects of arbitrage is shortselling, selling something that you don't own. We discuss this topic next.

Shortselling

In a **shortsale**, an investor (the shortseller) sells a security that he does not own. One intent of a shortsale is to sell the security at current prices,

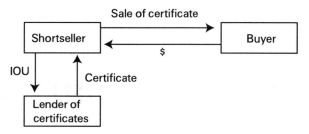

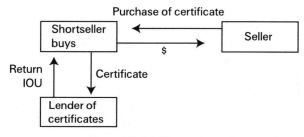

Figure 8.1 Shortsales

expecting to buy the security back at a lower price in the future. To carry out the shortsale, the shortseller borrows certificates of ownership from another investor who owns the security (see figure 8.1). The shortseller must pay the lender of the certificates any dividends due on the securities. When the shortseller closes out the shortsale by buying the security in the market, the new certificates are returned to the individual who lent the securities to the shortseller. The shortseller makes a profit (loss) if the securities are repurchased at a lower (higher) price. A shortsale has no time limit. Short positions can remain in effect indefinitely as long as collateral requirements (discussed below) are met.

In an **unrestricted shortsale**, the shortseller can use the proceeds from the sale. In practice, most shortsellers are not able to use the proceeds because of the possibility of a shortseller absconding with the funds. In addition, shortsellers usually have to post **collateral** to guarantee against default. For example, if someone shortsold a security at $100 and the price moved up to $120, the shortseller has an unrealized loss of $20. Unless collateral of at least $20 has been posted, the shortseller might be tempted to default by simply walking away from the transaction. The lender of the securities has legal recourse, but at considerable expense.

Table 8.1 Shortselling a bond equals borrowing

	Points in time		
	0	1	2
Cash flows	+ $82.64	0	− $100

Shortsales of common stocks are restricted by the downtick rule. Shortsales are not allowed after declines in prices. This rule prevents someone from inundating the market with shortsale orders and possibly creating a selling panic among owners of the stock. In the past, some speculators have shortsold large quantities of a stock and then spread rumors of bad news. After panicked owners sold their stock and drove prices down, the shortsellers covered their positions for huge profits. With a downtick rule this type of manipulation is more difficult.

Shortselling a bond is the equivalent of borrowing money. Table 8.1 illustrates the case when a two-period strip is shortsold. The shortseller receives $82.64 immediately and pays back $100 two years later. The interest is $17.36 at the interest rate of 10 percent. The opposite of shortselling is buying. Buying a bond is the equivalent of lending money.

Conditions for Arbitrage

In the case where a security sells for different prices in two markets, the arbitrage is straightforward. Buy in the underpriced market and simultaneously sell in the overpriced market. In cases of multi-period cash flows, the existence of a profitable arbitrage is not as clearcut. The following rule identifies an arbitrage opportunity: **If the cumulative net cash flows from a position are never negative and are positive in at least one period, an arbitrage opportunity exists.**

The cumulative net cash flows are found by adding the cash flows starting from the present until the future date. Thus, the cumulative cash flows for time 1 are the sum of the time 0 and time 1 cash flows. The cumulative cash flows for time 2 are the sum of the time 0, time 1, and time 2 cash flows. Several examples are presented below to illustrate this rule about cumulative cash flows.

Arbitrage and Present Values

Arbitrage has many important implications in financial markets. In the following example, arbitrage is shown to constrain present values.

Table 8.2 Arbitrage cash flows

Action	Points in time		
	0	1	2
Buy one-period strip	− $70	+ $100	–
Shortsell two-period strip	+ $80	–	− $100
Net cash flows	+ $10	+ $100	− $100
Cumulative net cash flows	+ $10	+ $110	+ $10

Arbitrage guarantees that the present value of a dollar received later cannot have a value greater than a dollar received sooner. To prove this result by arbitrage, consider the following counter-example. Suppose a one-period strip with $100 par value has a price of $70 and a two-period strip with $100 par value has a price of $80. That is, the present value of $100 received at time 1 is $70 and the present value of $100 received at time 2 is $80.

The following arbitrage opportunity is available. Buy the one-period strip at a price of $70 and shortsell the two-period strip at a price of $80. The cash flows are shown in table 8.2.

The arbitrager makes a sure profit of $10 immediately; the $100 net cash inflow at time 1 can be used to pay off the cash outflow of $100 at time 2; conceivably, interest might be earned from time 1 to time 2.

The cumulative net cash flows are found by adding net cash flows as we move from the present to the future. In table 8.2, the cumulative net cash flows are always positive, indicating a sure profit. The sure profit from arbitrage is immediate and requires no collateral. Therefore, one arbitrager without any collateral can repeatedly engage in this arbitrage transaction until the profits from arbitrage disappear.

Arbitrage operations drive prices toward their equilibrium values. That is, purchase of the one-period strip by the arbitrager drives its price up; sale of the two-period strip forces its price down. Arbitrage profits cease to exist when the price of the one-period strip is greater than or equal to the price of the two-period strip, or when the present value of $1 received in one period is greater than or equal to the present value of $1 received in two periods.

In contrast, suppose that the price of a one-period strip is higher than the price of the two-period strip as shown in table 8.3. Buying the two-period and shortselling the one-period, does not result in an arbitrage opportunity since the cumulative net cash flows are not always positive.

Table 8.3 A non-arbitrage position

Action	Points in time		
	0	1	2
Shortsell one-period strip	+ $88	− $100	−
Buy two-period strip	− $80	−	+ $100
Net cash flows	+ $8	− $100	+ $100
Cumulative net cash flows	+ $8	− $92	+ $8

Arbitrage and Bond Coupons

Arbitrage guarantees that a bond with a higher coupon (and the same maturity) must have a higher price. Consider the counter-example in table 8.4. Bonds G and H are two-period bonds with par values of $100 and prices of $100. Bond G has a coupon of $6 and bond H has a coupon of $8. The higher-coupon bond has the same price as the lower-coupon bond.

These prices present an arbitrage opportunity: shortsell bond G and buy bond H. The cash flows are shown in table 8.5. At time 0, the net cash flow is zero; the net cash flows at times 1 and 2 are + $2. The cumulative net cash flow is always zero or positive, resulting in a risk-free arbitrage profit. The actions of arbitragers push the price of bond H higher relative to bond G.

The arbitrage no longer results in a risk-free profit when the price of the higher-coupon bond exceeds the price of the lower-coupon bond. For example, if bond H has a price of $102, the cash flows from shortselling bond G and buying bond H are shown in table 8.6. There is a cash outflow of $2 at time 0 and cash inflows of $2 at times 1 and 2. This position is not a risk-free arbitrage, since the cumulative net cash flows are negative in one period.

The discussion can be generalized. Let the prices of bonds G and H be P_G and P_H and their coupons be c_G and c_H. As long as c_H exceeds c_G and P_H is less than or equal to P_G, an arbitrage opportunity exists. Consequently, in order to have no arbitrage, a bond with a higher coupon (and the same maturity) must have a higher price.

An Example of a Replicating Portfolio

Arbitrage occurs if a particular security can be created from a portfolio of other securities at a lower price (the replicating portfolio). Assume a

Table 8.4 Two-period bonds

	Points in time		
	0	1	2
Bond G	−$100	+$6	+$106
Bond H	−$100	+$8	+$108

Table 8.5 Arbitrage for two-period bonds

	Points in time		
	0	1	2
Shortsell bond G	+$100	−$6	−$106
Buy bond H	−$100	+$8	+$108
Net cash flows	0	+$2.00	+$2.00
Cumulative net cash flows	0	+$2.00	+$4.00

Table 8.6 Two-period bonds: no arbitrage profit

	Points in time		
	0	1	2
Shortsell bond G	+$100	−$6	−$106
Buy bond H	−$102	+$8	+$108
Net cash flows	−$2	+$2.00	+$2.00
Cumulative net cash flows	−$2	0	+$2.00

particular investment with price of P_0 has a set of future cash inflows. A replicating portfolio (or combination of securities) has the same future cash flows and current value of P_R. The prices of the investment and the replicating portfolio should be the same (i.e. $P_0 = P_R$). Otherwise there will be arbitrage opportunities.

The concept of replicating portfolios can be illustrated by a counter-example, a case where arbitrage opportunities exist. Assume a two-period bond with price of $100, annual coupon of $6, and par value of $100. There are Treasury strips with $100 par values. The one-period strip has a price of $94.34 and the two-period strip has a price of $85.73. Strips are assumed to be divisible; part of a strip can be

Table 8.7 Arbitrage between coupon-bearing bond and strips

	Points in time		
	0	1	2
Short two-period bond	+ $100	− $6	− $106
Buy 6% of a one-period strip	− $5.66	+ $6	−
Buy 106% of a two-period strip	− $90.87	−	+ $106
Net cash flows	+ $3.47	0	0
Cumulative net cash flows	+ $3.47	+ $3.47	+ $3.47

purchased. Because a two-period coupon-bearing bond can be created from a portfolio of strips, the following arbitrage opportunity is available.

Table 8.7 shows the cash flows from shorting the two-period coupon-bearing bond: $100 is received at time 0; $6 is paid at time 1; $106 is paid at time 2. Suppose we try to duplicate the time 1 and time 2 cash flows (with the opposite sign) from a portfolio of strips. In order to get a cash inflow of $6 at time 1, 6 percent of a one-period strip can be purchased for a time 0 cost of (0.06)($94.34), but with a cash inflow of (0.06)($100) at time 1. To receive + $106 at time 2, 106 percent of a two-period strip must be purchased, resulting in a cash inflow of (1.06)($100) at time 1 and a cash outflow of (1.06)($85.73) at time 0. Thus, by buying 6 percent of a one-period strip and 106 percent of a two-period strip, the time 1 and time 2 cash flows on the coupon-bearing bond are replicated, but the total purchase price of the strips is $3.47 less than the sale price of the coupon-bearing bond.

Thus, there is an arbitrage profit because the prices of strips are too low relative to the price of the coupon-bearing bond. The actions of arbitragers will force the prices to adjust until there is no arbitrage opportunity. There is no arbitrage profit if the price of the two-period strip becomes $89.00. If the same strategy is followed, the cash flows will be as shown in table 8.8.

In practice, bond dealers look for arbitrage opportunities by comparing the prices of strips and strippable coupon-bearing bonds. If a bond is worth more as strips, bond dealers will purchase coupon-bearing bonds and strip them, selling off the individual strips. If a coupon-bearing bond has a greater value than individual strips, bond dealers purchase a portfolio of strips and reconstitute it into a coupon-bearing bond. When a bond is stripped, it is decomposed into coupon strips and par strips, which are not interchangeable. Coupon strips are generally more liquid than par strips and typically sell at slightly higher prices. Since coupons and par values are not interchangeable, there is no risk-free arbitrage

Table 8.8 Cash flows in equilibrium when price of two-period strip is $89.00

	Points in time		
	0	1	2
Short two-period bond	+ $100	− $6	− $106
Buy 6% of a one-period strip	− $5.66	+ $6	–
Buy 106% of a two-period strip	− $94.34	–	+ $106
Net cash flows	0	0	0
Cumulative net cash flows	0	0	0

between them and the prices of principal strips and coupon strips do not have to be identical.

Creating Forward Contracts from Spot Securities

This section discusses the link between spot and forward markets, laying the groundwork for the link between spot and futures markets. The primary lesson of this section is: **arbitrage provides the fundamental link between the spot and forward markets.**[1]

An investor can create a forward position from spot securities in a frictionless market. The two-period case provides the basic insight. A long forward position has a zero cash flow at time 0, an outflow at time 1, and an inflow at time 2 (see table 8.9).

Creating a forward position requires finding some combination of one-period and two-period spot securities having the same cash flows as a forward position in table 8.8. The necessary positions are shown in table 8.10. Go long (buy) a single two-period strip and simultaneously shortsell x percent of a one-period strip, with the constraint that the net cash flows at time 0 are zero. Algebraically, find a value of x such that $xS_1 = S_2$, implying that x must equal S_2/S_1. The time 0 net cash flows have a sum of zero; the time 1 net cash flows are an outflow equal to S_2/S_1, which is the forward price; at time 2 there is a cash inflow of $1. This set of cash flows is defined as a long forward position, that is, a loan of funds in the forward market.

The amount S_2/S_1 is a forward price; it represents the time 1 value of $100 received at time 2. Denoting this forward price as F_2, the definitions of forward price, forward rate, and of S_1 and S_2 imply that:

$$F_2 = \frac{S_2}{S_1} = \frac{par}{1 + f_{0,2}} \tag{1}$$

Table 8.9 Long forward position

	Points in time		
	0	1	2
Long forward	0	− Forward price	+ Par

Table 8.10 Creating a long forward position

Actions (at time 0)	Points in time		
	0	1	2
Long 1 two-period strip	$-S_2$	−	+ $100
Short S_2/S_1 one-period bonds	$+S_1[S_2/S_1]$	$-1[S_2/S_1]$	−
Net = long forward	0	$-[S_2/S_1]$	+ $100

Table 8.11 Creating a long forward position

Actions (at time 0)	Points in time		
	0	1	2
Long 1 two-period strip	− $85.73	−	+ $100
Short 0.8573/0.9615 one-period bonds	+ $85.73	− $89.16	−
Net = long forward	0	− $89.16	+ $100

Table 8.12 Creating a short forward (borrowing) position

Actions (at time 0)	Points in time		
	0	1	2
Short 1 two-period strip	+ $85.73	−	− $100
Long 0.8573/0.9615 one-period bonds	− $85.73	+ $89.16	−
Net = Short forward	0	+ $89.16	− $100

To illustrate the relationship between spot and forward interest rates, consider the following example. Assume $R_{0,1}=0.04$, $D_1=0.9615$, $R_{0,2}=0.08$, $D_2=0.8573$, $f_{0,2}=0.1215$, $F_2=0.8916$. The price of a one-period strip is $96.15 and two-period is $85.73. Then, the operations shown in table 8.11 create a long (lend) forward position from a spot position. Table 8.12 shows the operations to create a short forward position, which is the equivalent of borrowing in the forward market.

The forward interest rate is the discount rate for which $100 at time 2 has a value of $89.16 at time 1. That is, the forward rate $f_{0,2}$ satisfies the following equation: $89.16 = 100/(1 + f_{0,2})$. The resulting forward interest rate is 12.15 percent. The two-period spot interest rate of 8 percent is the geometric average of the one-period interest rate of 4 percent and the forward rate of 12.15 percent. That is, $(1.08)^2 = (1.04)(1.1215)$.

Arbitrage and Forward Interest Rates

Arbitrage forces a precise relationship between actual forward interest rates and the forward interest rates implied by the spot interest rates. In our example, the implied forward rate is 12.15 percent. If the actual forward interest rate is different, arbitragers will enter the market and force the actual interest rate and the implied interest rate to become equal.

What happens if the market for actual forward loans has an interest rate of 15 percent, at the same time that the implied forward interest rate is 12.15 percent? Arbitragers are able to profit and, by their exploitation of profit opportunities, drive all interest rates toward equilibrium values. The arbitrage operation to profit from the price disparity is to borrow at 12.15 percent and lend at 15 percent. To borrow at the implied forward rate of 12.15 percent requires the short forward position in Treasury strips shown in table 8.12. The arbitrage is shown in table 8.13. This arbitrage is completely risk-free, since the investor taking this position

Table 8.13 Arbitrage position: lend at 15 percent and borrow (short forward) at 12.15 percent

Actions (at time 0)	Points in time		
	0	1	2
Lend forward at 15%	0	$-$100/1.15 $= -$86.96	$+$100
Short 1 two-period strip	$+$85.73	–	$-$100
Long 0.8573/0.9615 one-period strips	$-$85.73	$+$89.16	–
Net	0	$+$2.20	0

Table 8.14 Arbitrage position: lend at 12.15 percent and borrow (short forward) at 5 percent

Actions (at time 0)	Points in time		
	0	1	2
Borrow forward at 5%	0	+ $100/1.05 = + $95.24	− $100
Long 1 two-period strip	− $85.73	–	+ $100
Short 0.8573/0.9615 one-period strips	+ $85.73	− $89.16	–
Net	0	+ $6.08	0

has a certain profit at time 1. The arbitrage operations force the interest rates toward their equilibrium values. That is, lending at 15% forces this rate down; borrowing at 12.15 percent forces this rate up. Arbitrage ceases to be profitable when the two rates are identical.

Suppose the market for actual forward loans has an interest rate of 5 percent, at the same time that the implied forward interest rate is 12.15 percent. The arbitrage operation is to borrow at 5 percent and lend (long forward) at 12.15 percent. The arbitrage is shown in table 8.14. Borrowing at the 5 percent actual forward interest rate forces this rate up; lending at 12.15 percent forces this rate down until the two rates are identical.

Summary

Arbitrage is the simultaneous purchase and sale of identical items for different prices. The arbitrager buys at the lower price and sells at the higher price. These actions force the prices to be in equilibrium. A replicating portfolio has the same future cash flows as a particular security. If the future cash flows are the same, the prices should be the same. If not, arbitrage opportunities are available. These drive prices together. Arbitrage links the prices of equivalent positions.

Note

1 The development of financial futures markets has had a dramatic impact upon spot financial markets. Futures markets are very similar to forward markets.

Questions and Problems

1   A one-period strip has a price of $86 and par value of $100. A two-period strip has a price of $88 and par value of $100. Show the arbitrage opportunity.

2   A two-period bond has an annual coupon of $7, par value of $100, and price of $98. Another two-period bond has an annual coupon of $8, par value of $100, and price of $98. Are there any arbitrage opportunities?

3   In problem 2, is there an arbitrage opportunity if the $8-coupon bond has a price of $98.25?

4   In problem 2, suppose the $8-coupon bond has a price of $101, are there arbitrage opportunities?

5   The coupon on a two-period par bond is $9. A one-period strip has a price of $93.46 and a two-period strip has a price of $87.34. Are there arbitrage opportunities? Explain.

6   Suppose that $R_{0,1}$ is 3 percent and $R_{0,2}$ is 6 percent. For one-period and two-period strips with $100 par values, show the operations to create: (a) a long forward position, (b) a short forward position.

7   Assuming the term structure in the preceding problem, show the arbitrage operations if the actual forward interest rate is: (a) 15 percent, (b) 5 percent.

9
Term Structure of Interest Rates

This chapter focuses upon the reasons why interest rates differ by maturity, or **term**. A schedule of spot interest rates by maturity is called the **term structure of interest rates**. The term structure can be rising, flat, declining, or humped.

The term structure is not directly observable, since no tax-free, default-free zero-coupon bonds exist. Analysts generally try to estimate the term structure from the yields for coupon-bearing bonds. A **yield curve** shows the relationship between interest rates and maturity for coupon-bearing bonds. Every quarter, the *Treasury Bulletin* constructs yield curves from US Treasury bills, notes, and bonds, differing in coupon level, call features, and some other characteristics. The *Wall Street Journal* also constructs yield curves from bonds with a wide variety of characteristics. Chapter 7 contains several common shapes of the yield curve and the dates when these shapes occurred (figure 7.1).

Historical Patterns in Yield Curves

The most frequent shape for yield curves is upward-sloping. Downward-sloping yield curves have occurred at the end of the expansion phase of business cycles. At these business cycle peaks, heavy demand for credit, inflationary pressures, and tight money tend to push all interest rates to high levels. This business cycle pattern for the term structure is illustrated in figure 9.1. This pattern implies the following three empirical

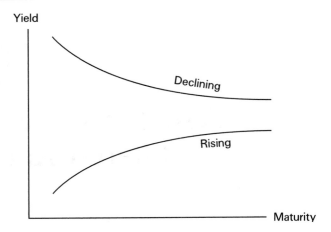

Figure 9.1 Business cycle patterns for the term structure

regularities for term structures:

1   The most common yield curve shape is upward-sloping.
2   Declining yield curves occur when interest rates are historically high.
3   Short-term interest rates are more variable than long-term interest rates.

Historical evidence indicates two other empirical regularities of the term structure:

4   For maturities of six months and less, the yield curve has an upward slope most of the time.
5   The prices of long-term bonds are more variable than the prices of short-term bonds.

Although the prices of long-term bonds are more variable than those of short-term bonds, the yields on short-term bonds are more variable. These are not contradictory statements, as is shown by the following simple example. Consider a 1-year bond and a 30-year bond, each with a price and par value of $100 and coupons of $8, implying yields to maturity of 8 percent on each of the bonds. Suppose the yield on the 1-year bond increases by 2 percent to 10 percent and the yield on the 30-year bond increases by 1 percent to 9 percent. Then, the new prices are:

One-year bond

$$P = \frac{\$108}{1.10} = \$98.18 \tag{1}$$

Thirty-year bond

$$P = \$8\left[\frac{1-(1.09)^{-30}}{0.09}\right] + \frac{\$100}{(1.09)^{30}} = \$89.69 \qquad (2)$$

Although the change in the interest rate on the 30-year bond is one-half the change in rate on the 1-year bond, the change in price for the 30-year bond is five times as large. For the longer-term bond, the change in interest rates compounded over 30 periods causes a large price reaction.

In general, the percentage change in bond price is approximately equal to the Duration times the change in yield. Formally,

$$\%\Delta Price = [Duration][\Delta y] \qquad (3)$$

For long-term bonds, the Duration is very large. Although the change in yield is relatively small for long-term bonds, the Duration effect is big enough to dominate. Thus, the total change in price for long-term bonds is bigger than for short-term bonds.

Any complete theory of the term structure should predict all of the preceding regularities. None of the theories described below predicts all of the empirical regularities. Thus, no single theory is a complete explanation of the term structure. However, each theory provides some interesting insight into the term structure.

Segmented Markets Theory

In the segmented markets theory, a separate market exists for each maturity. Interest rates for each maturity are set by demand and supply for funds for that maturity. While in other theories investors shift between maturities, investors do not shift between different maturities in this theory, according to which, some investors – for example, commercial banks – confine their holdings of bonds to short maturities, whereas other investors – such as life insurance companies – purchase long-term bonds exclusively and hold these to maturity. Thus, short-term and long-term markets exist independent of the other market.

To illustrate the segmented markets hypothesis, consider commercial banks. These typically confine their bond holdings to short-maturity bonds, because the prices of these bonds do not change much as interest rates change. These low-risk short-term bonds earn modest rates of return and appeal to low-risk investors. Consequently, short-term bond holdings serve banks as low-risk, low-return, highly liquid reserves, available to meet sudden and unexpected needs for immediate funds.

A proponent of the segmented markets hypothesis might argue as follows. When demand for bank loans is low, banks have excess funds, which they invest in short-term bonds. Increased demand by banks drives bond prices up and interest rates down. When demand for bank loans is high, banks reduce their holdings of short-term bonds and use the proceeds to make commercial loans. Sales of bonds lower bond prices and increase short-term interest rates. Thus, the actions of commercial banks affect short-term interest rates, but longer-maturity interest rates are not affected.

The segmented markets theory is consistent with any shape of yield curve, but it does not predict any of the empirical regularities of the term structure. In this theory, bonds with different maturities are not perfect substitutes for investors. Perfect substitutes should have the same holding period returns. If bonds with different maturities have different holding period returns, they are imperfect substitutes and markets are segmented by maturity. Empirically, holding period returns differ by maturity, consistent with segmented markets. Researchers have found that the supply of bonds of different maturities affects the yields for those maturities – a bigger supply tends to lower prices and increase interest rates.

Increasing Liquidity Premiums

In the theory of increasing liquidity premiums, yields increase as maturity increases for two reasons. First, bond investors are risk-averse (i.e. they prefer lower variability of return). Second, bond prices for longer-term bonds are more variable. Bond investors require higher yields to maturity on longer-term bonds to compensate for the higher risk.

If all investors are risk-neutral, the expected rate of return on all investments equals the risk-free interest rate, implying a flat term structure. If investors are risk-averse, the higher-risk (longer-maturity) securities have higher expected returns.

To illustrate the basic idea of the increasing liquidity premium theory, assume an initially flat term structure, a 10 percent interest rate, a 1-year bond and a perpetual bond with annual coupons of $10 and selling at par of $100. If interest rates increase to 11 percent, the price of the 1-year bond becomes $110/1.11 = \$99.099$, a small percentage change of 0.9 percent. The price of the perpetual bond becomes $10/.11 = \$90.909$, a large percentage change of approximately 9.1 percent. In the liquidity preference theory, the larger price declines for longer-maturity bonds cause buyers of long-term bonds to require higher interest rates as compensation for the greater risk of declining prices. Therefore, the initial yields on the one-period and the perpetual bonds cannot be 10 percent. The perpetual bond sells at a higher yield to compensate for the larger risk of price declines.

The liquidity preference theory overlooks bond issuers. Some issuers prefer long-term funds, locking-in a fixed interest rate. Other bond issuers prefer short-term, or intermediate-term funds. A complete term structure theory should account for the maturity needs of all borrowers.

The theory of increasing liquidity premiums implies yield curves that are always rising. The empirical evidence contradicts this implication. Yield curves usually slope upward, but sometimes they slope downward. Declining yield curves and humped yield curves contradict the theory.

Preferred Habitat

In the preferred habitat theory, investors prefer to purchase bonds of particular maturities – not necessarily short- or long-term – and require higher yields to buy bonds of other maturities. The preferred habitat theory is effectively a combination of the segmentation theory and the liquidity preference theory. Instead of always preferring short maturities, as in the liquidity preference theory, investors may prefer other maturities, depending upon their individual investment objectives. Instead of being totally unwilling to shift from the preferred maturity as in the segmentation theory, the preferred habitat theory suggests a willingness to purchase nearby maturities, but only at higher interest rates. For a maturity farther from the preferred habitat, the required interest rate is higher to compensate the buyer for the risks involved.

In the liquidity preference theory, longer maturity implies greater risk to the buyer of a bond. The preferred habitat theory allows for the possibility that shorter-maturity bonds might be riskier. For example, assume an investor who wants to invest for 10 periods and is concerned exclusively with the value of the portfolio at the end of the 10-year period and not with the value on intervening dates. For this individual, investing in 1-year securities and then reinvesting repeatedly in other 1-year securities is riskier than locking-in a fixed return by buying a 10-year zero-coupon bond. If such investors are common in the market, short-term interest rates are higher than longer-term rates because of risk aversion.

The preferred habitat theory is consistent with any shape of the term structure. But the theory does not, by itself, predict any of the five empirical regularities.

Money Substitute

In the money substitute theory of Kessel, very-short-term bonds are close substitutes for holding cash. According to this view, many investors restrict their purchases to short-term money market instruments because the risks associated with these are very small. Consequently, the prices of money market instruments are driven up and their rates down relative to longer-maturity rates.

The money substitute theory assumes a large number of investors in short-term bonds relative to the supply. That is, buyers of bonds have a stronger preference for very short maturities than issuers. This drives bond prices up and interest rates down.

The main justification for this belief is the restricted choices available to these short-term investors. A corporation with temporarily excess funds does not want to take on much risk of loss. This constraint eliminates most other investments from consideration. For example, corporations with temporarily excess cash for two weeks want no risk of loss and minimal transactions costs. A two-week money market instrument is a very attractive investment.

An additional justification for the money substitute theory is the preference of issuers for somewhat longer maturities. In order to minimize the costs of issuing securities, issuers attempt to reduce the frequency of issue by issuing longer-maturity instruments less frequently.

The money substitute theory predicts the tendency of the yield curve to have upward slopes for very short maturities. The money substitute theory does not, by itself, predict any of the other empirical regularities.

Expectations Hypothesis

The most widely discussed theory of the term structure of interest rates is the expectations hypothesis. In the expectations hypothesis, the current forward interest rates are determined by the market's anticipations of future spot interest rates. For the two-period case, the forward rate for period 2 is a predictor of the one-period spot interest rate one period into the future. In mathematical terms:

$$f_{0,2} = E[R_{1,1}] \qquad (4)$$

where:

$f_{0,2} =$ forward interest rate for period 2
$E[R_{1,1}] =$ the expected one-period spot interest rate observed one period from now

In other words, the forward interest rate is determined by people's anticipation of the average spot interest rate next period. If the market believes the spot interest rate next period will be high relative to the current spot rate, then the forward interest rate is higher than the current spot rate; the current yield curve is rising. Thus, the shape of the current yield curve is linked to anticipations of interest rates in the future. Some concrete examples are presented below.

In the general case:

$$f_{0,j} = E[R_{j-1,1}] \tag{5}$$

where:

E = the expectation

$f_{0,j}$ = the forward rate observed at time 0 (presubscript) for period j (postsubscript)

$R_{j-1,1}$ = the spot rate observed at time $j-1$ (presubscript) and lasting one period (postsubscript)

This notation is illustrated in figure 9.2.

According to the unbiased expectations hypothesis, the forward interest, $f_{0,2}$, is an unbiased predictor of the spot rate, $R_{1,1}$, observed one period later; on average, the forward rate equals the subsequent spot rate. The forward rate $f_{0,3}$ is an unbiased predictor of the spot rate $R_{2,1}$ observed two periods later, and so on. See figure 9.3.

The unbiased expectations hypothesis links the forward rates observed today to expectations of future spot interest rates. Since today's spot rates are the geometric mean of today's forward rates, this hypothesis ties today's spot interest rates to spot interest rates expected to prevail in the future.

The unbiased expectations hypothesis is consistent with any yield curve shape. Under this hypothesis, a flat yield curve occurs if the market

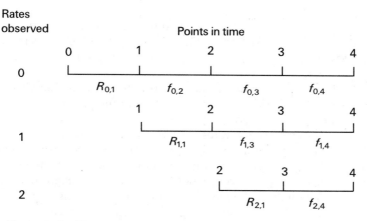

Figure 9.2 Elapsed time and spot and forward interest rates

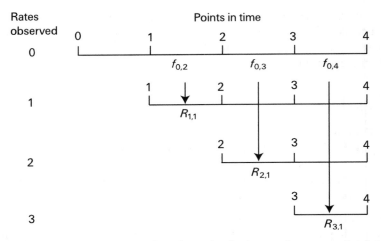

Figure 9.3 Unbiased expectations hypothesis: forward rates predict future spot interest rates

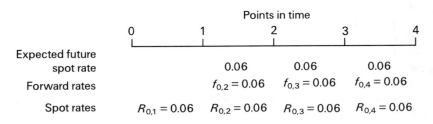

Figure 9.4 Example of a flat term structure

expects all future interest rates to equal the current one-period spot rate. For example, if the current spot rate is 6 percent and all expected future spot rates are 6 percent, all current forward and spot rates are 6 percent. See figure 9.4.

If the market anticipates higher future interest rates, the yield curve rises. In figure 9.5, the market expects rising future interest rates, and the current spot rates also rise.[1]

If the forward interest rates decline monotonically, the spot rates decline also. Figure 9.6 illustrates how a declining yield curve can occur.

One of the empirical regularities mentioned above is the tendency for declining yield curves to occur when interest rates are high by historical standards. The unbiased expectations hypothesis is consistent with this pattern if the market is forecasting interest rates to decline from their current levels.

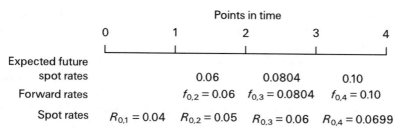

Figure 9.5 Example of a rising term structure

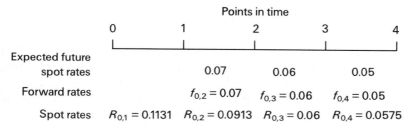

Figure 9.6 Example of a declining term structure

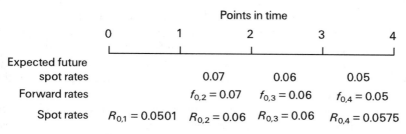

Figure 9.7 Humped term structure

An unusual and interesting yield curve shape is the humped (or humpbacked) yield curve. Humped yield curves occur when interest rates are high by historical standards. Under the unbiased expectations hypothesis, humped yield curves occur if the market expects interest rates to rise for a while and then to decline. Figure 9.7 presents an example where the current spot rate is 5.01 percent, and the forward rate rises to 7 percent and then declines to 6 percent and 5 percent.

The unbiased expectations hypothesis has been faulted by some observers for making the unrealistic behavioral assumption that investors can forecast very distant future interest rates. These distant forecasts are essential for setting the forward interest rates. How can investors forecast interest rates 10, 15, 20, or 25 years into the future when there is so much uncertainty about events over these long horizons?

The unbiased expectations hypothesis does not, by itself, predict any of the empirical regularities of yield curves. However, if the unbiased expectations hypothesis is combined with the additional hypothesis of greater variability of nearer-term expectations of future rates, the combined theory predicts the tendency for short-term interest rates to be more variable than long-term rates.

Combined Theory

Combining the unbiased expectations hypothesis with the liquidity premium theory results in a more powerful theory. This combined theory is consistent with any shape of the yield curve and predicts upward-sloping yield curves most of the time. In the combined theory, the forward rate equals the expected future spot rate plus a liquidity premium:

$$f_{0,j} = E[R_{j-1,1}] + L_j \qquad (6)$$

where L_j is the liquidity premium for maturity j. Liquidity premiums may increase with maturity (that is, L_j is greater than or equal to L_{j-1}). For example, suppose an expected future spot interest rate of 5 percent, and a liquidity premium of 1 percent for period 2, 1.5 percent for period 3, and 2.0 percent for period 4. Then, the forward and spot rates are as shown in figure 9.8. The spot interest rates increase with maturity, although the market expects future spot rates to be unchanged from the current one-period spot rate.

With the combined theory, a declining term structure is possible even though liquidity premiums increase with maturity. For example, suppose

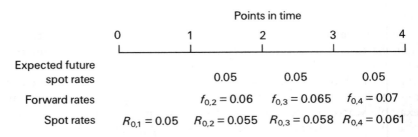

Figure 9.8 Rising term structure and constant expected future interest rates

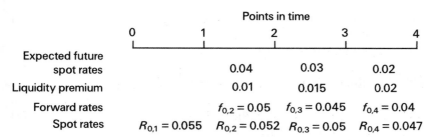

Figure 9.9   Rising liquidity premiums and a declining term structure

there is a liquidity premium of 1 percent for period 2, 1.5 percent for period 3, and 2.0 percent for period 4, but with the declining expected future spot interest rates as shown in figure 9.9. The spot rates decline because the fall in the expected future spot rate is greater than the increase in the liquidity premium.

Humpbacked Curves

The most unusual yield curve is the hump(back)ed curve. This curve occurs when interest rates are high by historical standards. An actual example of a humped yield curve from the *Treasury Bulletin* was presented in chapter 7.

There are several explanations of humped curves. First, according to the unbiased expectations hypothesis, a humped curve occurs if interest rates are expected to rise over the next several periods and then decline. An example was given earlier in this chapter (see figure 9.7). Second, humped curves can result from skewed expectations of future interest rates. That is, the market may believe constant future interest rates are likely, but a small probability exists for considerably lower interest rates in the future; then the yield curve is humped. Humped yield curves might also occur in a segmented market, with a particular segment of the yield curve having higher rates than shorter- and longer-maturities.

Holding Period Returns

The holding period return (or realized return) depends upon the current spot interest rate and changes in forward rates over time. Let:

$P_{0,n}$ = the price observed at time 0 of a strip (zero-coupon bond) maturing at time n.

$P_{1,n}$ = the price observed at time 1 of a strip (zero-coupon bond) maturing at time n.

HPR = holding period return

The holding period return is defined as follows:

$$HPR = \frac{P_{1,n}}{P_{0,n}} - 1 \tag{7}$$

By substituting the prices expressed in terms of forward interest rates, we have:

$$HPR = \frac{(1+R_{0,1})(1+f_{0,2})(1+f_{0,3})\cdots(1+f_{0,n})}{(1+R_{1,1})(1+f_{1,3})\cdots(1+f_{1,n})} - 1 \tag{8}$$

The holding period return equals the one-period spot rate $(R_{0,1})$ if the forward rates come true, that is if:

$$f_{0,2} = R_{1,1}$$

$$f_{0,3} = f_{1,3} \tag{9}$$

through

$$f_{0,n} = f_{1,n}$$

Equation (8) is approximately the same as

$$HPR = R_{0,1} + [f_{0,2} - R_{1,1}] + [f_{0,3} - f_{1,3}] + \cdots + [f_{0,n} - f_{1,n}] \tag{10}$$

Thus, the holding period return is approximately the one-period spot interest rate plus the sum of the differences between the forward rates and the subsequent forward rates. For example, if all interest rates fall, the holding period return is approximately equal to the one-period spot rates plus the sum of the declines in the forward interest rates.

The expected holding period return is

$$E(HPR) = R_{0,1} + [f_{0,2} - E(R_{1,1})] + [f_{0,3} - E(f_{1,3})]$$
$$+ \cdots + [f_{0,n} - E(f_{1,n})] \tag{11}$$

The expected holding period return equals the current spot interest rate if the forward rate for period 2 equals the expected spot rate next period, and the more distant forward rates equal the expected forward rates next period. The terms with the differences between the forward rates and the expected future rates represent risk premiums. If these terms are positive, there are risk premiums and the expected holding period return is higher than the current spot rate. In the expectations hypothesis, the forward rates equal the expected future rates, the expected holding period return equals the one-period spot interest rate $(R_{0,1})$ for all bonds, and there are no risk premiums. In contrast, in the increasing liquidity premium theory, longer-term bonds have forward rates higher than the expected future rates, and the expected return exceeds the current spot interest rate.

Two-period example

In the case of two periods, the holding period return is approximately:

$$HPR = R_{0,1} + [f_{0,2} - R_{1,1}] \qquad (12)$$

The holding period return is the one-period spot rate plus the difference between the forward rate and the spot rate next period. This difference is often called the forecast error.

The expected holding period return is:

$$E(HPR) = R_{0,1} + [f_{0,2} - E(R_{1,1})] \qquad (13)$$

The expected holding period return is the one-period spot rate plus the difference between the forward rate and the expected future spot rate. This difference is called the liquidity premium, L_2. If the expectations hypothesis holds, the forward rate equals the expected future spot rate and the liquidity premium is zero. If the combined theory applies, the forward rate equals the expected future spot rate plus a liquidity premium.

Summary

Yield curves exhibit five empirical regularities: (1) the most common yield curve shape is upward-sloping; (2) declining yield curves occur when interest rates are historically high; (3) short-term interest rates are more variable than long-term interest rates; (4) for maturities of six months and less, the yield curve has an upward slope most of the time; (5) long-term bond prices are more variable than short-term bond prices.

Three types of theories of the term structure are the segmented markets theory, liquidity theories, and expectations theories. Each of these theories provides some insights, but none provides a complete

Table 9.1 Predictions of the theories

Theory	Consistent with	
	Yield curve shapes	Empirical regularity number
Segmented markets	Any	
Increasing liquidity premiums	Rising	1,5
Preferred habitat	Any	
Money substitute	Rising	4,5
Unbiased expectations	Any	
Combined	Any	1,2,5

explanation of yield curves and their empirical regularities. Table 9.1 summarizes the predictive value of the various theories.

Note

1 The spot rates are computed from the following formula:

$$(1 + R_{0,n})^n = (1 + R_{0,1})(1 + f_{0,2}) \cdots (1 + f_{0,n})$$

For example, for the four-period case:

$$(1 + R_{0,4})^4 = (1 + R_{0,1})(1 + f_{0,2})(1 + f_{0,3})(1 + f_{0,4})$$

Questions and Problems

1 Describe the major empirical regularities of the term structure of interest rates.
2 Explain each of the major term structure theories.
3 To what extent are the theories consistent with the empirical regularities?
4 Which of the term structure theories are consistent with rising, flat, declining, or humped yield curves?
5 Suppose an initially flat term structure with all interest rates equal to 6 percent. Compute the price change for a one-year par bond if the interest rate increases by 2 percent. Then compute the price change on a perpetual par bond if the interest rate on this bond increases by 1 percent. Compute the Durations of each bond. Which bond has a greater percentage price change and why?
6 Suppose the one-period spot interest rate is 4 percent and the forward interest rate is 8 percent. Compute the holding period return over the next period for a two-period zero-coupon bond for each of the following values for next period's spot interest rate: 5 percent, 8 percent, 12 percent.

7 You observe the following term structure. What term structure theories are consistent with it?

Maturity (years)	Spot rate
1	.12
2	.14
3	.05
4	.04

8 Assume the combined theory explains the term structure. The one-period spot rate is 5 percent, the expected spot rate next period is 7 percent and the liquidity premium is 2 percent. Compute the forward interest rate.

9 Suppose that we observe the following prices on strips with $100 par values: $S_1 = \$97.09$; $S_2 = \$92.46$; $S_3 = \$86.38$; $S_4 = \$79.21$. Which term structure theories are consistent with these strips prices?

10 Suppose that we observe the following prices on strips with $100 par values: $S_1 = \$97.09$; $S_2 = \$92.46$; $S_3 = \$86.38$; $S_4 = \$85.48$. Which term structure theories are consistent with these strips prices?

10
Default Risk

For any bond, default by the issuer is always a possibility. The word default means violation of any of the terms of the agreement between the borrower and lender. The most serious violations are nonpayment of coupon and principal, but other violations of the agreement can occur. If the violation of the agreement is minor, the parties may renegotiate the contract. But if the agreement violations are significant, the debtholders may force the issuer into bankruptcy. Bankruptcy is a formal legal proceeding administered by special bankruptcy courts.

For the US Treasury, default on Treasury debt obligations is unlikely. The reason is simply that the Treasury can always borrow more money from the Federal Reserve, which has the power to create money. However, default on municipal bonds, mortgages, corporate bonds, and bank debt is always a possibility.

Default on Municipal Bonds

For municipal bonds issued by state and local governments, default is possible. Municipal bonds are of two types – general obligation bonds and revenue bonds. General obligation (GO) bonds are backed by the full taxing authority of a municipality and have relatively low probabilities of default. Revenue bonds are backed by the proceeds from a specific project, such as a toll highway, and have a much higher default probability. There are many varieties of revenue bonds and the default risks can vary widely. Many municipal bonds carry insurance against default. In the event of default by the issuer, the insurer pays off the bonds.

Default on Mortgages

For mortgages, individual borrowers may default. Marketable mortgages carry default insurance, the insurer guaranteeing payment. Marketable mortgages trade as essentially default-free obligations. Mortgages are discussed in chapter 12.

Corporate Bonds

Bond indentures

Every corporate bond issue has an **indenture** – a formalized contract between the issuing firm, the bondholders, and a trustee. The indenture specifies the obligations of the firm to the bondholders, including the coupon payments, the maturity, the call feature, call prices, and sinking fund requirements. The bond trustee is appointed to act on behalf of the bondholders, who might otherwise find it difficult to protect their own interests. Consequently, the trustee must be independent of the issuing firm. Typically, the trustee will be the trust department of a large bank. The firm pays the trustee a fee as stated in the bond indenture.

A bond indenture contains protective covenants, which are prohibitions on the actions of the firm. The basic idea of protective covenants is to protect the bondholders from possible firm or stockholder actions that might be harmful to the bondholder. As a simple example, suppose a firm issues a mortgage bond which has specific assets pledged as collateral. To protect this pledged collateral, the indenture includes protective covenants, prohibiting the sale of the pledged asset or the use of this collateral for some other loan, and requiring proper upkeep. Protective covenants restricting dividend payments to stockholders are common. A dividend restriction prevents the firm from liquidating assets and paying the proceeds to stockholders, or from underinvesting in new assets. Many other protective covenants are included in bond indentures as standard practice.

The term **default** means a violation of any part of the bond indenture including nonpayment of interest and/or violation of a protective covenant. For example, if a protective covenant in the indenture requires the firm's current ratio (i.e. current assets divided by current liabilities) to be above 2.0, the firm is in default if the ratio falls below 2.0. A default requires the trustee to act on behalf of the bondholders. After default, one possibility is a renegotiation of the contract; this is likely to occur if the default is a minor violation of the indenture. A second possibility is to file for bankruptcy.

Bankruptcy

A bankruptcy is a legal proceeding administered by special bankruptcy courts. The firm itself or the creditors can file to begin a bankruptcy proceeding. During this proceeding, the court protects the firm's assets and appoints someone to run the firm's operations to avoid poor management practices and/or disappearance of the firm's assets.

Bankruptcy courts perform a special and important function for the legal system. To see the value of the bankruptcy courts, consider a situation of default without any bankruptcy courts. Imagine a firm that has defaulted on its financial obligations to its ten creditors. Without bankruptcy courts, the ten creditors of the firm seek legal redress by suing the defaulting firm individually. Legally, the priorities of creditors are determined by the time when suits are begun. The creditor who initiates legal action first has first claim; the second one has second claim; and so on. This type of competitive priority system forces the creditors to act in their own interest at the expense of the other creditors. The problem with this system is that the total amount available to creditors may be reduced by their acting in their self-interest. This has been called the **common pool problem**, described below.

The common pool problem is illustrated by the following example. Imagine a lake that has a fish population worth $100,000 if caught and sold immediately to consumers. If one-third of the fish are caught each year, reproduction is sufficient to maintain the fish population at a constant level, and a constant fish harvest of $33,000 can occur year after year. If there is only one fisherman, that fisherman is faced with the following choice: harvest $100,000 of fish in the current year or harvest $33,000 of fish indefinitely. If the discount rate for finding the present value of the perpetual harvest is less than 33.33 percent, then the present value of the perpetual harvest exceeds $100,000, the amount available from the single big harvest. For example, if the discount rate is 10 percent, the present value of the harvest is $330,000, and the single fisherman chooses to have a small annual harvest.

If there are many fishermen in this one lake, individual fishermen can maximize the present value of their own income by fishing as much as possible, as quickly as possible. The fishermen have incentives to catch all the fish immediately. The total amount received by all the fishermen is $100,000. If the fishermen could design a system for them to harvest fish in concert, they would increase the present value of their catch.

The purpose of bankruptcy courts is to solve the common pool problem. Without bankruptcy courts, individual creditors have incentives to sue a defaulting firm and try to rapidly seize as many assets for themselves as possible. The actions of these competing creditors can easily destroy a sizable part of the value of a firm. Bankruptcy courts are a system for settling creditors' claims jointly so that the creditors can act in concert for their mutual benefit. Instead of individual creditors acting in ways to harm each other, the bankruptcy courts allow the settlement of their claims jointly.

Liquidation versus reorganization

There are two possible resolutions of bankruptcy. First, a firm may be liquidated by the court. In a liquidation, the individual assets of the firm are sold. Second, and more frequently, the firm may be reorganized by the court. In a reorganization, the claimants against the firm agree to surrender their old claims in exchange for a new set of scaled-down claims. The reorganized firm continues to operate during and after the bankruptcy. Firms are reorganized because a going concern may have more value than a liquidation of individual assets. A reorganization and liquidation do not have to be mutually exclusive, since a reorganization can involve liquidation of some assets.

From a theoretical financial viewpoint, bankruptcy should occur when the value of equity is zero, or, equivalently, when the firm's fixed obligations exceed the value of the firm. This implies that stockholders should receive nothing from the resolution of bankruptcy. In practice, stockholders frequently receive positive payoffs from bankruptcy. The explanation for this is not entirely clear. Possibly, bankruptcy proceedings themselves are biased in favor of equity-holders. The bankruptcy procedure involves negotiations between the claimants. Stockholders may be able to out-negotiate the others.

Costs of bankruptcy

A bankruptcy proceeding involves costs. The most obvious costs are payments to the courts and to attorneys. Court costs are a small percentage of assets for large bankrupt firms. The largest costs of bankruptcy are probably lost profit opportunities. Because opportunity costs are hard to measure, the size of total bankruptcy costs is difficult to estimate. Firms in bankruptcy may be unable to undertake profitable investment opportunities for two reasons. First, the court (which has the responsibility for running the firm) has protection of creditors' interest as its primary goal. Second, raising funds by issuing stocks and bonds is constrained during bankruptcy. In addition, sales from existing product lines may falter because customers may hesitate to buy from a bankrupt firm. Imagine the second thoughts of an individual considering the purchase of a car from a firm in bankruptcy. What value is a warrantee from a firm in bankruptcy?

Will replacement parts be available? What will the future trade-in value be?

Types of corporate debt

Mortgage bonds are backed by specific assets. If there is default on mortgage bonds, the mortgage bondholders have the first claim on the pledged asset.

Corporate debentures are unsecured debt. Unsecured debt has a general claim on the assets of the firm rather than a claim on specific assets. A firm may sell several different issues of debentures. These may be ordered in terms of priority of claims. Senior (or unsubordinated) debt has prior claim compared to junior (or subordinated) debt.

Income bonds arise out of a bankruptcy proceeding. They pay interest only if sufficient income is earned. The exact conditions when interest must be paid are specified in the bond indenture. Any interest not paid is owed for future payment.

Income bonds give a firm that has gone through bankruptcy more "breathing room" compared to a straight bond. Nonpayment of interest on straight bonds constitutes default and most likely will precipitate bankruptcy. An income bond is similar to a preferred stock, except that interest is a tax-deductible expense and preferred dividends are not.

Protective covenants

The management of a corporation is the agent for the stockholders and is supposed to act in their best interest. In this agent role, the management can be expected to seek out ways to benefit the stockholders at the expense of the bondholders. Consequently, there is a natural conflict between the stockholders and the bondholders. One way for the bondholders to protect themselves against the stockholders is to require the inclusion of protective covenants in the bond indenture. Protective covenants make it difficult for the stockholders to expropriate the wealth of bondholders.

The American Bar Association has prepared a document entitled *Commentaries on Model Debenture Indenture Provisions*. This book lists standard bond indenture provisions. These protective covenants are written by legal experts and are based upon previous case law, i.e. cases in which bondholders sued firms that had acted against the interests of the bondholders. These model indentures are specifically designed to prevent repetition of these actions. The indenture provisions in the *Commentaries on Model Debenture Indenture Provisions* are widely used by corporate bonds and are often called **boilerplate**.

Four types of protective covenants are quite common: restrictions on (1) the issuance of additional debt, (2) dividend payments, (3) mergers, and (4) disposition of assets. Clearly, the stockholders benefit at the expense of the bondholders if the firm sells additional debt with a higher priority than existing debt, if the firm pays large cash dividends or repurchases large amounts of its stock in the market, if the firm merges and bondholders receive a riskier post-merger claim, or if the working assets of the firm are not properly maintained. Protective covenants try to prevent the stockholders from reducing the value of bonds.

Bond Ratings

The chance of default is an important consideration to bond buyers. Since there are many thousands of different bond issues, gathering information to assess the chances of default of individual issues is a difficult process. Bond rating agencies have been developed to help provide this information to the market. Moody's and Standard & Poor's (S&P) are the two largest rating agencies. Their ratings categories are shown in table 10.1. Bonds with higher default risk should have higher yields. Several studies have documented the link between bond yields, ratings, and subsequent defaults.

Ratings are good relative predictors of default. The highest rating category has the smallest frequency of default. The second-highest rating category has a slightly larger frequency of default, and so on. Since the ratings are good predictors of default frequency, the next logical question is what determines the ratings. The ratings agencies do not reveal the exact procedure used to derive ratings.

Default predictors for corporate bonds

Ratings are a measure of ability to pay. For corporate bonds, ability to pay depends upon debt levels, profitability, and firm risk levels. A bond will tend to have a higher rating if the following are true:

1 The firm has lower debt ratios (debt/assets, debt/equity).
2 The firm has higher interest coverage ratios (earnings before interest and taxes divided by interest).
3 The firm has higher rates of return of assets (profit/assets, profit/ equity).
4 The firm has lower relative variation in earnings over time.
5 The firm is of larger size.
6 The bond issue is unsubordinated.

Table 10.1 Bond ratings

Moody's	Fitch; Duff & Phelps; and S&P	Interpretation
Aaa	AAA	Highest quality
Aa1	AA +	
Aa2	AA	High quality
Aa3	AA −	
A1	A +	
A2	A	Strong payment capacity
A3	A −	
Baa1	BBB +	
Baa2	BBB	Adequate payment capacity
Baa3	BBB −	
Ba1	BB +	Likely to fulfill obligations; ongoing
Ba2	BB	uncertainty
Ba3	BB −	
B1	B +	
B2	B	High risk obligations
B3	B −	
Caa	⎧ CCC + ⎫ ⎨ CCC ⎬ ⎩ CCC − ⎭	Current vulnerability to default
Ca	CC	In bankruptcy or default or other
C	C	marked shortcomings
D	D	

Default predictors for municipal bonds

For revenue bonds, the likelihood of default depends upon the reliability of the revenues from the project. For general obligation bonds, default depends upon the taxing power, wealth, and total debt burden of the municipality.

Default predictors for mortgages

The most important predictor of default for mortgages is the loan-to-value ratio, defined as the value of the loan as a percent of the value of the property. The higher this ratio, the greater is the likelihood of default. A high ratio of loan to property value indicates relatively low equity for the homeowner. Default risk is also higher if the ratio of loan payments to income is high, because small declines in income may force default.

The default cycle

Default rates have a life cycle. Immediately following the issue, the default rate is relatively low. The default rate increases until the issue has been outstanding for eight or nine years. Then, the default rate decreases. Predictors of bankruptcy have considerable interest to bondholders, corporate management, and stockholders. The same financial ratios that determine ratings tend to deteriorate before bankruptcy occurs. Several years before actual bankruptcy, deterioration of these ratios is an early warning sign.

In an informationally efficient market, ratings changes by Moody's and Standard & Poor's should not have any incremental informational value. That is, prices should not adjust after a rating change because the market has already reacted to the same information as the rating agency. Overall, the evidence seems to be consistent with efficiency, although in some circumstances a rating change may affect prices.

In a small percentage (about 15%) of circumstances, a particular bond issue may have a split rating – namely, different ratings by Standard & Poor's and by Moody's. Standard & Poor's might rate an issue at its highest rating, AAA. At exactly the same time, Moody's might rate the same issue at its second-highest rating, Aa. Split ratings reflect a divergence of opinion about the riskiness of an issue. The bond market prices issues with split ratings between bonds with the higher and the lower ratings.

The raters have introduced subratings. For example, A-rated bonds are broken down into the categories of A-1, A-2, and A-3. The subratings are finer gradations, and they allow for gradual changes in ratings.

Smaller rating agencies

Moody's and S&P are the largest rating agencies. Other, smaller rating agencies exist and provide so-called third ratings. The best known are Fitch and Duff & Phelps. While Moody's and S&P automatically rate most public issues of debt, Fitch and Duff & Phelps rate issues only when approached. In the typical case, an issuer approaching Fitch or Duff & Phelps feels that Moody's and S&P under-rate their issue. The issuer pays Fitch or Duff & Phelps a rating fee. The issuer has the option to have the rating released or suppressed. Obviously, released ratings tend to be higher than those of Moody's and S&P. The market tends to value Fitch or Duff & Phelps ratings. A higher rating from a smaller rater tends to lower the yield on a bond issue.

The smaller raters seem to perform a useful economic function. First, issuers voluntarily pay for their ratings and would only do so if the issuers perceive value from the ratings. Second, the market yields are affected by a third rating. Therefore, bond investors value these ratings. Third, the smaller raters can follow more flexible rating methodologies than bigger raters, which must efficiently rate very large numbers of issues.

High-Yield (Junk) Bonds

Bonds with lower ratings (i.e. BB and below) are called high-yield (junk) bonds. There are two types of high-yield bonds; "fallen angels" and "original-issue." "Fallen angels" are bonds originally issued with higher ratings, which have declined as the firm has fallen on hard times. Until recently, most high-yield bonds were fallen angels.

Since 1977, many "original-issue" high-yield bonds have appeared. Original-issue high-yield bonds are of two varieties. Some are issued by firms with very high business (operating) risk. Others are issued by highly levered firms. Some highly levered mergers have been financed with high-yield bonds. Because these mergers had a very small proportion of equity financing, the bonds carried a high risk of default and high yields.

The role of original issue high-yield bonds has been controversial. Traditionally, the market for investment-grade public debt has been restricted to larger firms. Smaller firms have been forced to finance with bank debt, or possibly private placements of debt with insurance companies. Original issue high-yield debt has opened up a new source of funds to many smaller and high-risk firms. In one view, high-yield debt has been a stimulus to economic expansion because firms were removed from the straitjacket of highly restrictive bank loans. In the opposing view, high-yield debt issuers escaped the important monitoring function provided by commercial banks and consequently suffered from unwise financing and investment decisions.

Several authors have argued that the junk bond market was monopolized by the underwriter firm of Drexel, Burnham, Lambert under the direction of Michael Milken. In this view, Milken was able to sell junk bonds at unfair yields and at high underwriter fees. The evidence shows the bond yields and underwriter fees on Drexel's junk bonds were in line with those of other issuers.

A sizable number of corporate bond issues now contain covenants to protect the bondholders against possible bondholder losses from mergers.

One such covenant is a due-on-sale clause or **poison put**, requiring existing bonds to be repaid before a merger can occur. Corporate bonds without such protective covenants may have a premium added to the yield to compensate the bondholders for the possibility of merger.

The securities of firms actually in bankruptcy continue to trade in the market at depressed prices. Investing in the bonds of a bankrupt firm is a high-risk, potentially high-return strategy. The majority of the bonds of bankrupt firms are not very good performers, but some of them will turn out to be very lucrative investments, if the fortunes of the firm turn around sharply.

Investing in high-yield bonds is a specialized field. It requires a detailed knowledge of bankruptcy law as well as knowledge about individual firms. A number of high-yield bond mutual funds have been established. Besides allowing investors to diversify, these mutual funds allow investment in high-yield bonds by those who do not have the knowledge and time to evaluate each particular high-yield bond issue.

Default rates increase as bond rating decreases. High-yield bonds (rated Ba, B, Caa) have much higher default rates than investment-grade bonds (Aaa, Aa, A, Baa).

Summary

A bond represents a contractual agreement between an issuer, bondholders, and a trustee. The obligations of the parties are spelled out in the bond indenture, which contains protective covenants. Violation of this contractual agreement constitutes default. Bankruptcy is a legal proceeding, administered by special bankruptcy courts. In a bankruptcy, the assets of the firm are liquidated or the firm is reorganized.

Bankruptcy is costly. Besides legal costs, there are lost sales and investment opportunities. Ratings of bonds provide valuable information about default probabilities. For corporations, ratings are a function of debt levels, firm profitability, the riskiness of the firm's assets, and firm size.

Questions and Problems

1 Describe the functions of a corporate bond indenture. What role does the bond trustee play?
2 Why do bond indentures include protective covenants? Give some examples of protective covenants and the reasons why they might be included.

3 Why do special bankruptcy courts exist?
4 Define financial distress. What alternatives are available to firms in financial distress instead of defaulting? Describe the pros and cons of each alternative.
5 Describe the costs associated with bankruptcy.
6 What does the term *secured debt* mean?
7 Describe the financial characteristics that determine bond ratings.
8 Are high-yield bonds good investments? Why or why not?

11

Put and Call Options

Options are interesting for two reasons. Puts and calls on underlying securities are widely traded and allow investors to transfer risk. In addition, many types of bonds have options embedded in the underlying security, including callable bonds and putable bonds.

There are two types of options: European and American. European options can be exercised only at expiration. American options can be exercised at any time. Most options traded in the United States are American options.

Call Options

A call option is the right to purchase the underlying asset for a specified exercise price until the expiration date. The following notation is used:

C = market value of the call option
P = market value of underlying asset
E = exercise price (strike price)

If the price of the underlying asset (P) is less than the exercise price (E), the call is described as being out-of-the-money. If P equals E, the call option is described as being at-the-money. If the price of the underlying asset exceeds the exercise price ($P > E$), the call option is described as being in-the-money.

Value of call at expiration

At expiration, the value of the call must be zero if the market value of the underlying asset is less than or equal to the exercise price.

No rational investor would exercise a call option if the underlying asset sells for the exercise price or less, since buying the underlying security in the open market is cheaper than exercising the call option. For example, in table 11.1, if a bond sells for $90 in the open market, a call option with an exercise price of $100 is valueless at expiration. Instead of exercising the call and paying the $100 exercise price, it is preferable to buy the bond directly for $90.

In table 11.1, if the price of the underlying asset exceeds the exercise price, the call option is worth the price of the underlying asset minus the exercise price, that is, $P - E$. The amount $P - E$ has often been called the intrinsic value of the option. If the call sells for less than $P - E$, an arbitrager would buy the call, exercise it, and make an arbitrage profit. At expiration, buying the call option for C and exercising it is equivalent to buying the underlying security directly for P. Thus, $P = C + E$, or $C = P - E$.

At expiration, the value of a call option is:

$$C = 0 \qquad \text{if } P \leqslant E \quad \text{at- or out-of-the-money} \qquad (1)$$

$$C = P - E \qquad \text{if } P > E \quad \text{in-the-money} \qquad (2)$$

Value of call option before expiration

With time left until expiration, an American call option has a value greater than an otherwise identical expiring call option. Table 11.2 illustrates the possibilities. Before expiration:

$$C > 0 \qquad \text{if } P \leqslant E \quad \text{at- or out-of-the-money} \qquad (3)$$

$$C > P - E \qquad \text{if } P > E \quad \text{in-the-money} \qquad (4)$$

If a call option is currently at- or out-of-the-money, equation (3) indicates that the option still has value. At some future point in time, the option may be in-the-money and worth at least $P - E$. The present value of this possibility must be positive. Thus, $C > 0$.

Table 11.1 Value of call option at expiration, $E = \$100$

$P < E$ e.g. $P = 90$	$P = E$ $P = 100$	$P > E$ $P = 110$
$C = 0$	$C = 0$	$C = P - E$ e.g. $C = 10$
out-of-the-money	at-the-money	in-the-money

Table 11.2 Value of call option before expiration, $E = \$100$

$P < E$ e.g. $P = 90$	$P = E$ $P = 100$	$P > E$ $P = 110$
$C > 0$	$C > 0$	$C > P - E$ e.g. $C > 10$

If the call option is in-the-money, the option can be exercised immediately for E, receiving a security worth P. The net value of immediate exercise is $P - E$. However, in the future the option may be more in-the-money and have a greater value. The present value of this possibility makes the option worth more than the immediate exercise value of $P - E$. Thus, equation (4) must hold.

If these conditions do not hold, arbitrage opportunities are available to investors. For out-of-the-money call options, a zero price allows an arbitrager to buy the call for nothing. If the call expires worthless, the arbitrager loses nothing; if the call ends up in-the-money, the arbitrager has a net profit. For a zero investment, the arbitrager can never lose and may have a profit. To eliminate profitable arbitrage, the market value of the call option must be positive.

For in-the-money call options, a price less than the underlying asset price minus the exercise price $(P - E)$ allows an arbitrager to buy the call option for C and exercise it for E, for a total cost of $C + E$. The acquired security is then sold for its market value P, which, by assumption, is greater than $C + E$ for an arbitrage profit of $P - (C + E)$. To eliminate arbitrage profit opportunities, $C + E$ must be equal to or exceed P, meaning that C must be greater than or equal to $P - E$. For example, if a bond sells for \$110 and if a call option with \$100 exercise price sells for \$5, anyone could buy the call for \$5, exercise it for \$100, and sell the resulting bond for \$110 for a sure profit of \$5.

The greater-than ($>$) symbol in equations (3) and (4) shows exercise of a call option before expiration to be an inferior choice. The possibility of a large value for the call option at some future date makes early exercise of an option a poor choice in most circumstances. For this reason, call options are generally described as being worth more "alive than dead," that is, if not exercised immediately.

The price of the underlying security is a logical upper bound for the price of a call option. No one should logically pay more for an option to buy a security than the price to purchase the security outright. If a bond is selling for \$100, a logical person would never pay more than \$100 for a call option. The investor is better off to buy the underlying

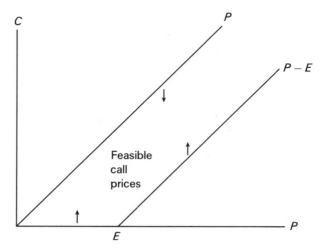

Figure 11.1 Call option bounds

asset itself. These bounds on the value of a call option are shown in figure 11.1, which relates the value of a call option to the value of the underlying security.

Profit profile for call

The possible value of a call option can be seen from a profit profile. As a reference point, consider someone who buys a bond (for which options trade) currently selling at its exercise price of $100, and holds this bond for three months until the option expires. The possible profits and losses, overlooking coupon interest, are shown as a solid line in figure 11.2.

Consider the purchase of a call option for $4 with exercise price of $100. The investor holds this call option for three months until expiration. The profit profile is shown as the dotted line in figure 11.2. The first step in drawing the profit profile is to compute the profit or loss on the position for several levels of the price of the underlying asset at expiration. These prices should include the option's exercise price and several points on either side of the exercise price. The procedure is illustrated in table 11.3.

The call buyer suffers a loss of $4, the entire purchase, if the bond price is below the exercise price of $100. This $4 is the maximum loss for the buyer of a call option. If the bond price at expiration is above the exercise, the profit equals $P - E - \$4$. A net loss is incurred if the bond price is below $104 and a net profit if the bond price is above $104. The profit profile indicates that call buyers are anticipating a rising price for the underlying asset.

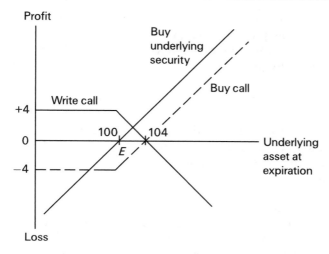

Figure 11.2 Profit profiles for call option

Table 11.3 Profits or losses for call buyer

	Price of underlying at expiration			
	98	100	102	104
Buy call	−4	−4	−4	−4
Exercise call at expiration			−100	−100
Sell underlying acquired from exercise			+102	+104
Net profit = −C−E+P	−4	−4	−2	0

If the bond price is at or below the exercise price, the profit profile shows the call buyer's maximum loss to be the purchase price, C. Since this call purchase price is a small percentage of the bond price, the loss from buying a call is small in absolute dollars compared to the loss from purchasing the bond outright. On the other hand, the call buyer gains substantially if the bond does well.

For everyone who buys a call option, someone sells or writes a call. The call writer agrees to sell the underlying asset at the exercise price if the option is exercised by the call buyer. Call options are a **zero-sum game,** meaning that the call buyer's gains are the call writer's losses and vice versa. In effect, the buyer and the writer are betting against each other. The profits or losses for a call writer in the earlier example are shown in table 11.4.

The profit profile for the call writer is shown in figure 11.2. If the call is out-of-the-money at expiration, the call writer benefits by the original sale price of the call. For every dollar that the underlying asset rises above the exercise price, the call writer's profit is reduced by $1.

Writing a covered call option

The previous section discussed writing a naked call option. This is a risky position because the potential for loss is unbounded. Notice in the profit profile for writing a call in figure 11.2 that the losses become very large as the price of the underlying security increases.

Another, less risky, procedure is to write a covered call. This involves the purchase of the underlying security and the writing of a call option on that security. To illustrate the writing of a covered call option, assume that an investor buys the underlying security at its current price of $100 and simultaneously writes a 3-month call option at an exercise price of $100. The profits and losses at expiration are shown in table 11.5.

Table 11.4 Profits or losses for call writer

	Price of underlying at expiration			
	98	100	102	104
Write call	+4	+4	+4	+4
Sell underlying at call price at expiration			+100	+100
Buy underlying in the open market			−102	−104
Net profit $= +C+E-P$	+4	+4	+2	0

Table 11.5 Profits or losses from writing a covered call

	Price of underlying at expiration			
	98	100	102	104
Buy underlying	−100	−100	−100	−100
Write call	+4	+4	+4	+4
Sell underlying at exercise price when call is exercised			+100	+100
Sell underlying at market price	+98	+100		
Net profit	+2	+4	+4	+4

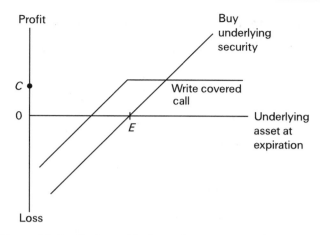

Figure 11.3 Profit profile for writing a covered call option

The profit profile for writing a covered call option is shown in figure 11.3. If the call option is in-the-money, the option is exercised and the covered call writer must sell the underlying security at the exercise price of $100. The maximum gain is $4, the original sale price of the call option. If the call option is out-of-the-money, the covered call option writer receives $4 for writing the call, and this reduces the loss from owning the underlying security.

Put Options

A put option is a right to sell a security at a stated exercise price E during a stated time interval.

Value of put option at expiration

To see the value of a put option, consider the possible payoffs at expiration for a buyer of a put (see table 11.6). The price of a put is denoted by *Put*. At expiration, if the price of the underlying security equals or exceeds the exercise price $(P > E)$, the put has no value, since no investor would choose to sell the underlying asset at E when the higher market price of P is available. If a bond sells at $110 and if there is a put option with $100 exercise price, exercising the put option involves selling the bond at the exercise price of $100. For any rational investor, selling the bond at its current market price of $110 is preferable. No one would exercise the put option. At expiration, the put option expires worthless.

Table 11.6 Value of put option at expiration, $E = \$100$

$P < E$ e.g. $P = 90$	$P = E$ $P = 100$	$P > E$ $P = 110$
$Put = E - P$ e.g. $Put = 10$ in-the-money	$Put = 0$ at-the-money	$Put = 0$ out-of-money

At expiration, if the underlying asset price is less than the exercise price, the put has value, since it represents the right to sell the underlying asset at E, which is above the current market price. Clearly, the put is worth the difference $E - P$. For example, if a bond sells for $80, a put option with a $100 exercise price is worth $20 at expiration. If the put sells for $15, an arbitrager can buy the put for $15, buy the bond for $80, and sell the bond for $100 by exercising the put. There is a sure profit of $5.

At expiration, the value of a put, *Put*, must be:

$$Put = 0 \qquad \text{if } P \geqslant E \quad \text{at- or out-of-the-money} \qquad (5)$$

$$Put = E - P \qquad \text{if } P < E \quad \text{in-the-money} \qquad (6)$$

Value of put option before expiration

Before expiration, the value of a put option is as shown in table 11.7. Before expiration:

$$Put > 0 \qquad \text{if } P \geqslant E \quad \text{at- or out-of-the-money} \qquad (7)$$

$$Put > E - P \qquad \text{if } P < E \quad \text{in-the-money} \qquad (8)$$

Put option profit profile

The example in table 11.8 illustrates a put option profit profile. Three months before expiration an investor buys a put option for a price (*Put*) of $3 with exercise price ($E$) of $100.

The profit profile is shown in figure 11.4. The put buyer makes a net profit if the price of the underlying security is less than the exercise price minus the purchase price of the put (that is, if $P < E - Put$). The profit profile clearly indicates that the put option purchaser expects falling prices for the underlying asset.

Table 11.7 Value of put option before expiration, $E = \$100$

$P < E$ e.g. $P = 90$	$P = E$ $P = 100$	$P > E$ $P = 110$
$Put > E - P$ e.g. $Put = 10$ in-the-money	$Put > 0$ at-the-money	$Put > 0$ out-of-the-money

Table 11.8 Profits or losses for buying a put option

	Price of underlying at expiration			
	96	98	100	104
Buy put	-3	-3	-3	-3
Buy underlying at expiration	-96	-98		
Exercise put by selling underlying at $100	$+100$	$+100$		
Net profit $= -Put + E - P$	$+1$	-1	-3	-3

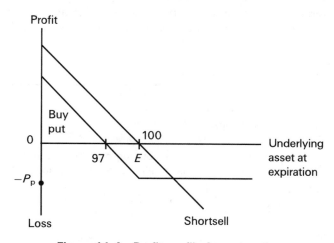

Figure 11.4 Profit profile for put option

Figure 11.4 also shows the profits and losses from shortselling the asset. Buying the put is similar to shortselling, since for both positions profits are earned if the underlying asset declines. If the underlying asset rises, the results are quite different. Purchase of the put has a maximum loss of the original purchase price. In contrast, shortselling of the asset results in a loss of $1 for every dollar that the asset's price rises; the potential loss on shortselling is unlimited.

The put writer (seller) enters into a contract to buy the underlying asset at the exercise price if the buyer of the put option chooses to exercise. The put writer is playing directly against the put buyer. The cash inflows to one are cash outflows to the other.

Put–Call Parity

There is a relationship between the price of a put option, the price of a call option with the same exercise price, the price of the underlying security, and the interest rate. This relationship is called **put–call parity**.

For European[1] options on nondividend-paying or noninterest-bearing assets, the put-call parity relationship is:

$$Price\ of\ a\ call = Price\ of\ a\ put + Price\ of\ underlying\ asset$$
$$+ Borrowing\ the\ present\ value\ of\ the$$
$$exercise\ price \qquad (9)$$

Table 11.9 shows that purchase of a European call option results in the same cash flows at expiration as purchase of a European put option plus purchase of the underlying asset plus borrowing the present value of the exercise price. Positions with the same value at expiration have the same value before expiration, assuming no intervening cash flows.

Table 11.9 Put–call parity

	$P < E$	$P = E$	$P > E$
Cash flows at expiration from buying call			
Call	0	0	$P - E$
Cash flows at expiration from buying put, buying underlying and borrowing present value of exercise price			
Put	$E - P$	0	0
Underlying	$+ P$	$+ P$	$+ P$
Loan	$- E$	$- E$	$- E$
Net	0	0	$P - E$

Table 11.10 Example of put–call parity

	$P=90$	$P=100$	$P=110$
Cash flows at expiration from buying call			
Call	0	0	10
Cash flows at expiration from buying put, buying underlying and borrowing present value of exercise price			
Put	10	0	0
Underlying	+90	+100	+110
Loan	−100	−100	−100
Net	0	0	+10

Put–call parity is illustrated by the example in table 11.10. An investor buys a call option with an exercise price of $100. Alternatively, the investor buys a put with exercise price of $100, buys the underlying security for $100, and borrows the present value of the exercise price, $90. This put–call parity result can be written as:

$$C = Put + P - ED \qquad (10)$$

where D is the present value of $1 received at the expiration date of the options. This can be rearranged to:

$$P = C - Put + ED \qquad (11)$$

Purchase of underlying asset = Purchase of call option
+ Sale of put option
+ Lending PV of exercise price

Similarly:

Shortsale of underlying asset = Sale of call option
+ Purchase of put option
+ Borrowing PV of exercise price (12)

The volatility of a call option

From put–call parity, a call option has greater volatility than the underlying asset. That is, the percentage change in the price of a call option is greater than the percentage change in the price of the underlying asset.

Put–call parity provides an intuitive explanation for the greater volatility of the call option. The buyer of a call option has a position that is equivalent to buying a put, buying the underlying asset, and borrowing the present value of the exercise price. The call buyer effectively is able to borrow the present value of the exercise price and create the equivalent of a type of levered or margined position in the underlying security. Any levered position must have greater percentage price changes than the underlying asset because the holder of the levered position (that is, the call buyer) invests a smaller amount than an investor who buys the underlying asset for cash. For every dollar change in price of the underlying, the levered position has to change by a greater percent, because the levered investor has invested fewer dollars.

Determinants of the Value of a Call Option

The value of a call option is determined by the following six factors.

1 *The price of the underlying asset*: the value of a call option is a positive function of the price of the underlying security. The higher the value of the underlying asset, the greater the value of the call option.
2 *The exercise price*: the value of a call option is inversely related to the exercise price. The lower the exercise price, the higher the value of the call option. Other things being equal, a lower exercise price means that the call option is more in-the-money.
3 *The time until expiration*: the value of a call option is a positive function of time until expiration. The longer the time until expiration, the greater the value of the call option. Clearly, a longer-lived call option equals a shorter-lived option plus some additional value. For example, an option with 6 months to run is equal to a 3-month option plus something additional. The impact of longer remaining life is shown graphically in figure 11.5.

These first three determinants of call option value are illustrated by table 11.11 of call option prices. Look across any row of the table; the value of the call option decreases as the exercise price increases. Look down any column; time to maturity increases and the value of the call option also increases.

4 *The price volatility of the underlying asset*: the greater the volatility of the underlying asset, the higher the value of the call option, since payoffs to a call buyer are asymmetric. If the underlying asset does poorly, the call buyer loses everything. If the underlying asset does well, the call buyer does very well. Greater dispersion in the possible value of the underlying asset implies bigger call option payoffs on the upside but the same payoff (loss of everything) on the downside, making a call option more valuable.

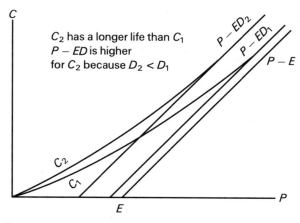

Figure 11.5 Impact of longer remaining life on the value of a call option

Table 11.11 The impact of maturity and exercise price upon call options

Maturity (months)	Price of underlying = $110 Exercise price		
	$90	$100	$110
3	$30	$16	$4
6	$34	$19	$6.50
9	$37	$21.50	$8.50

The impact of volatility upon call option value is illustrated by the two-security example in table 11.12. Assume two securities with the possible prices at expiration as shown. Each of these securities has the same mean of 100, but security 2 has greater dispersion of outcomes. An option on security 2 is more valuable because of this dispersion. To see the point, consider the case of call options with exercise prices of $100 on each security. The call option on security 2 clearly has a greater value. If the options are out-of-the-money or at-the-money, both options expire worthless. If the options are in-the-money, the second option has a higher payoff and, therefore, must be worth more. The impact of volatility upon the value of a call option is shown in figure 11.6.

5   *The risk-free interest rate*: the higher the interest rate, the greater the value of a call option.[2]

Table 11.12 Value of a call

Call option on security 1			
Prices of underlying	90	100	110
Value of call option	0	0	10
Probability	1/3	1/3	1/3
Mean value = (0)(1/3) + (0)(1/3) + (10)(1/3) = 3.33			
Call option on security 2			
Prices of underlying	80	100	120
Value of call option	0	0	20
Probability	1/3	1/3	1/3
Mean value = (0)(1/3) + (0)(1/3) + (20)(1/3) = 6.67			

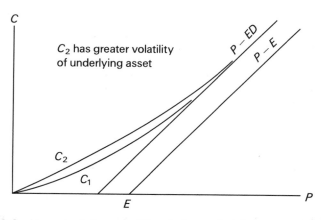

Figure 11.6 Impact of the volatility of the underlying asset on the value of a call option

6 *Dividends or interest on the underlying asset*: the higher the cash payments, the lower the value of a call option. The total return on an asset is the cash payment (dividends or coupon interest) plus price appreciation. For a given total rate of return, higher cash payments on an asset imply lower returns from price increases. Since the call buyer gains only if the price of the underlying asset increases, higher cash payments on the underlying asset tend to reduce the capital gains and the value of the call option.

From put–call parity, the price of a put can be shown to depend upon the call price, the price of the underlying asset, and the present value of the exercise price. It follows that the preceding six determinants of call prices also affect put prices. There are two major differences for puts. First, as the price of the underlying security increases, the value of the put goes down. That is, the value of a put is inversely related to the price of the underlying security. Second, higher exercise price increases the value of the put. The value of a put option is directly related to the exercise price.

Embedded Options

Debt instruments often have options embedded. The large majority of corporate debt and municipal debt instruments and all mortgages contain a call option, which allows the borrower to repay the principal of the loan. Since borrowing corresponds to shortselling a bond, borrowing with an embedded call option is equivalent to shortselling a debt instrument and buying a call option with exercise price equal to the remaining principal. The price of the call option is included in the higher coupon payment for the callable debt.

Suppose there is a perpetual *non*callable debt with par value of $100 and annual coupon of $8 and also a perpetual debt callable at par of $100 with coupon of $10. The borrower pays $2 more per year for the call option. Thus, a callable bond has a higher coupon and yield to maturity than an otherwise identical noncallable bond.

If the callable debt suddenly lost its call feature, its value would become $125, that is, $10 discounted at 8 percent, 10/0.08. Therefore, the value of the call option is $25. In general, the value of a noncallable debt equals the value of a callable debt plus the value of the call option.

$$\text{Noncallable bond} = \text{Callable bond} + \text{Call option}$$
$$125 = 100 + 25 \tag{13}$$

The value of the embedded call option increases when interest rates drop. If rates decline sufficiently, the borrower will want to exercise the call option and refinance the debt at a lower interest rate. For example, suppose all interest rates drop and the interest rate on new par debt (callable at par) is 7 percent. Then the old debt can be replaced with a new debt with the same call price, but a coupon $3 lower for each future period. The savings are shown in table 11.13. The present value of the savings is $3/0.07 = $42.86. The costs of refinancing must be subtracted to arrive at the net benefit of refinancing. In general, the net refinancing

Table 11.13 Coupon savings in general

	Points in time			
	0	1	2	$\cdots$
Old coupon		C_{OLD}	C_{OLD}	C_{OLD}
New coupon		C_{NEW}	C_{NEW}	C_{NEW}
Savings		$C_{OLD} - C_{NEW}$	$C_{OLD} - C_{NEW}$	$C_{OLD} - C_{NEW}$

Table 11.14 Coupon savings example

	Points in time			
	0	1	2	$\cdots$
Old coupon		10	10	10
New coupon		7	7	7
Savings		3	3	3

benefit equals the interest savings discounted at the interest rate on new callable debt minus the refinancing costs.

$$\text{Refinancing benefit} = [C_{OLD} - C_{NEW}]\begin{bmatrix} \text{Present value} \\ \text{of an annuity} \\ \text{for remaining life} \end{bmatrix}$$
$$- \begin{bmatrix} \text{Refinancing} \\ \text{costs} \end{bmatrix} \qquad (14)$$

In our example, if the costs of refinancing are 1.25% of par, then

$$\text{Refinancing benefit} = [10 - 7]\left[\frac{1}{0.07}\right] - [(100)(0.0125)] \qquad (15)$$

$$= 42.86 - 1.25 = \$41.61$$

In the case where the remaining life of the bond is a finite number, the present value of an annuity is found from a present value table or on a calculator.

Refinancing costs include the call premium, underwriter fees, loan initiation fees, points, appraisal fees, survey fees, taxes, and search time. For mortgages, refinancing costs can be 3% to 6%, with 5% being quite common. For marketable bonds, refinancing costs generally include a call premium plus underwriter fees ranging from 1 to 5%.

A borrower gains from refinancing a callable debt instrument after a drop in interest rates. Whatever the borrower gains from refinancing is a loss to the lender. When a loan is called-in, the lender receives the par value plus a call premium, which then must be reinvested at the new, lower interest rate. If lenders are intelligent and aware of the possibility of the debt instrument being called, the present value of potential losses is included in the original loan. A callable debt has a higher coupon (and possibly a call premium) to reflect this risk of refinancing.

Following a decline in interest rates, a borrower with an embedded call option faces the problem of finding the right time to exercise the call option. If the borrower exercises the option after a small decline in interest rates, the gain from refinancing is small. It is better to wait until the decline in interest rates is considerable and the refinancing gain is larger. But, if the borrower waits too long, interest rates may go back up and the gain from refinancing may be lost.

A small proportion of debt instruments contain a put option, which allows the lender to redeem the par value of the loan. Generally, these put options can be exercised only if a specificied event occurs. The triggering events are typically mergers that reduce the protection of the bond-holders against default. If the triggering event occurs, the bondholders have the option to redeem the bonds. The options are often called poison puts, because they make mergers more difficult, or "poison" them.

Summary

The market for put and call options has expanded greatly since 1975. Since these options are one-sided rights, they allow investors to protect themselves against one-sided risks. For example, the purchase of a put option allows the buyer to protect against the risk of a particular security dropping in price. The purchase of a call option allows the buyer to protect against the possibility that a security's price may rise.

For every option buyer, there is an option writer who takes the exactly opposite position. The option buyer is playing a zero-sum game against the option writer. Whatever one wins, the other loses. Put–call parity shows the relationship between the prices of a call option, a put option, the underlying security, and the present value of the exercise price.

A large proportion of debt instruments contain an embedded call option. The call option gives the borrower the option to pay off the debt at par (plus a call premium). If interest rates have fallen, the old debt can be replaced with a new debt with lower interest costs. The gain from refinancing is the present value of the interest savings less the costs of refinancing.

Notes

1 If the options are American, put–call parity may break down if the underlying security makes cash payments such as dividends. With cash dividends, there is a possibility that an American put option might have a higher value if exercised rather than held until expiration.
2 This overlooks the impact of the interest rate upon the value of the underlying security – clearly an important factor in the case of bonds.

Questions and Problems

1 A call option with exercise price of $90 sells for $8. The call option has three months until expiration. The underlying asset sells for $90. A put with the same exercise price sells for $6.

   (a) Draw a profit profile for buying the call option.
   (b) Draw a profit profile for writing the call.
   (c) Draw a profit profile for writing the call and buying the underlying security. Compare your answer with that to part (b).
   (d) Draw a profit profile for buying the put.
   (e) Draw a profit profile for writing the put.
   (f) Draw a profit profile for shortselling the underlying asset.
   (g) Draw a profit profile for shortselling the underlying asset and buying the call. Compare this with your answer to part (f). How does this position compare to issuing a callable bond?
   (h) Draw a profit profile for buying the underlying asset and buying a put option. Compare this with your answer to part (a).
   (i) Draw a profit profile assuming you bought the underlying security at $80 and wrote a call (with exercise price of $90) for $8.
   (j) Draw a profit profile assuming you bought the underlying security at $95 and wrote a call (with exercise price of $90) for $8.
   (k) Draw a profit profile assuming you buy a call for $8 and buy a put for $6.
   (l) Draw a profit profile assuming you write a call for $8 and write a put for $6.
   (m) Draw a profit profile assuming you buy a call for $8 and write a put for $6. Redo assuming that the call has an exercise price of $90 and the put an exercise price of $80.
   (n) Draw a profit profile assuming you write a call for $8 and buy a put for $6. Redo assuming that the call has an exercise price of $90 and the put an exercise price of $80.

2 On the expiration date of a call option, the price of an underlying security is $115, the exercise price is $100, and the call sells for $5. What arbitrage opportunity is available?

3   A call option has an exercise price of $100, the underlying security sells for $150, and the call sells for $200. Is this consistent with equilibrium? Are there any arbitrage opportunities?

4   A one-year put with exercise price of $100 sells for $13, the underlying security sells for $90, and the interest rate is 10 percent. What is the price of a call with the same exercise price? Assume no premature exercise of the options.

5   Explain why a call option has a larger percentage change than the underlying security.

6   Explain the impact of each of the following upon the value of a call option:

   (a)   Price of the underlying.
   (b)   Exercise price.
   (c)   Time to expiration.
   (d)   Volatility of the underlying.

7   Suppose a firm has a perpetual callable debt with a coupon of 10%, callable at par. Interest rates fall so that new callable debt can be sold at 8%. Selling new debt incurs underwriting fees of 1%. Compute the net benefit of refinancing.

8   Redo the previous problem assuming that the bond is a ten-year bond, not a perpetual bond. The replacement bond also has ten years to maturity.

12
Mortgages

A mortgage is a loan with real estate pledged as collateral. If the borrower defaults on the loan, the lender has first claim upon the real estate. The pledged real estate can be residential property or commercial property.

Interest rates on mortgages can be fixed over the life of the mortgage (fixed-rate) or the interest rate may be tied to some interest rate index and vary over time (called variable-rate, floating-rate, or adjustable-rate). With fixed-rate mortgages, the lender bears the risk of changing interest rates. With floating-rate mortgages, the borrower bears the risk of changing interest rates. The interest cost is lower, on average, for floating-rate loans. The fixed-rate borrower pays a higher interest cost to lock-in the interest cost.

Virtually all mortgages allow the borrower to repay the principal before final maturity. Repayment occurs primarily for two reasons: (1) sale of a property, (2) refinancing of the mortgage after a decline in interest rates.

In the past, mortgage loans were originally made and held until maturity by thrifts and commercial banks. Today, a large proportion of mortgages are sold by the originators to mortgage investors. We call these marketable mortgages. Marketable mortgage loans are originated (or originally granted) by thrifts, commercial bankers, or mortgage brokers. Marketable mortgages are insured against default by the borrower. They are then pooled together and claims on the pools are sold to investors. These claims are highly marketable. Since the underlying mortgages serve as security for the pools, claims on the pools are often called securitized debt.

With marketable mortgages, the mortgage market has become a national market where borrowers raise funds in the large, impersonal market for funds. A national market is undoubtedly more efficient since borrowers and lenders can be matched more easily. The result is a reduction in the interest cost to borrowers and an increase in interest rates earned by lenders.

In the past, the mortgage market was much more of a localized market. Individuals made deposits in local banks and thrifts, which made mortgage loans locally. The lender typically held the mortgage until maturity. With these localized markets, disparities in interest rates occurred. Mortgage borrowers in some areas paid higher rates than in other areas. With a national mortgage market, borrowing rates are much more uniform.

Active national markets in mortgages require homogeneous mortgages, that is, mortgages that are interchangeable. The biggest obstacle to homogeneous marketable mortgages is default risk. If a borrower defaults, the lender has the messy problem of seeking legal redress. This default problem has been overcome by the guaranteeing of mortgages by government agencies and by private insurance companies. Once a mortgage has been guaranteed, the guaranteeing agency bears the default risk and the ultimate mortgage buyer is not concerned with default. The resulting guaranteed mortgage trades as if it is default-free.

Mortgage Mathematics

Suppose a borrower takes out a mortgage loan for a principal amount, P, and repays it in equal installments of M. The interest rate would be fixed at y. To simplify the discussion, we assume n annual installment payments. The present value of the installment payments must equal the mortgage principal, P, that is:

$$P = \frac{M}{1+y} + \frac{M}{(1+y)^2} + \cdots + \frac{M}{(1+y)^n} \tag{1}$$

This may be expressed as:

$$P = \left[\frac{M}{y}\right]\left[1 - \frac{1}{(1+y)^n}\right] \tag{2}$$

$$P = M[present\ value\ of\ annuity] = M[PVA_n] \tag{3}$$

PVA_n denotes the present value of an annuity of \$1 per period for n periods at the interest rate y. Given the maturity, n, the interest rate, y, and the amount of the principal, P, the preceding equation can be solved for the installment payment, M:

$$M = \frac{P}{PVA_n} \tag{4}$$

Consider a numerical example with a principal of $100, an interest rate of 10 percent, and a 20-year repayment period. Then the annual installment payment is:

$$M = \$\frac{100}{8.5136} = \$11.75 \qquad (5)$$

Since there are 20 annual mortgage payments of $11.75, the total amount paid over the entire life of the mortgage is $235. $100 of this total is repayment of the original loan. The remaining $135 is interest. Even though the total amount of interest is quite large, these payments represent a fair price for an interest rate of 10 percent. The borrower is paying for receiving the $100 principal of the loan immediately.

Each mortgage payment, M, includes a payment for interest and repayment of part of the principal, sometimes called amortization of principal. As the principal is reduced, the total interest on the principal is reduced, and more of the mortgage payment is repayment of principal.

The interest and principal repayment may be computed recursively. The interest payment is the previous period's principal times the interest rate. The repayment of principal is the mortgage payment minus the interest. The computations are illustrated in table 12.1.

In general, for an n-period loan with mortgage payment of M and interest rate y, the principal repayment and interest for period j are:

$$Principal\ repayment = M\left[\frac{1}{(1+y)^{n-j+1}}\right] \qquad (6)$$

$$Interest\ payment = M\left[1 - \frac{1}{(1+y)^{n-j+1}}\right] \qquad (7)$$

The loan balance remaining after j payments is equal to:

$$Remaining\ principal = M\sum_{i=1}^{n-j}\frac{1}{(1+y)^i} = M[PVA_{n-j}] \qquad (8)$$

where PVA_{n-j} is the present value of an $n-j$ period annuity. This formula says that the remaining principal is merely the present value of the remaining $n-j$ mortgage payments of M dollars per period discounted at the interest rate y. The percent of the original principal remaining after j periods is the remaining principal divided by the original principal. That is,

$$\%\ of\ original\ principal\ remaining = \frac{M[PVA_{n-j}]}{P} = \frac{M[PVA_{n-j}]}{M[PVA_n]} = \frac{PVA_{n-j}}{PVA_n} \qquad (9)$$

Table 12.1 Computation of interest and principal repayment

Point in time	Principal	Interest = principal at previous point in time times the interest rate	Repayment of principal = mortgage payment minus interest
0	$100.00		
1	$98.25 = 100 − 1.75	$10.00 = 0.1(100)	$1.75 = 11.75 −10.00
2	$96.34 = 98.26 − 1.92	$9.83 = 0.1(98.25)	$1.92 = 11.75 − 9.83
3		$9.63 = 0.1(95.34)	

Note: Principal = $100.
Interest rate = 10%.
Maturity = 20 years.
Mortgage payment = $11.75.

This formula implies that the percentage of an n-period mortgage repaid after j periods is

$$\% \ of \ principal \ repaid \ after \ j \ periods = \frac{[PVA_n - PVA_{n-j}]}{PVA_n} \quad (10)$$

To illustrate these formulas, consider our example of a mortgage with principal of $100, maturity of 20 years, and interest rate of 10 percent. The annual mortgage payment is $11.75. Suppose we want to know the amount of the principal repayment and interest in year 10 (i.e. $j = 10$ and $n - j = 20 - 10 = 10$). Then:

$$Principal \ repayment = \$11.75 \left[\frac{1}{(1.10)^{20-10+1}} \right] = \$4.12 \quad (11)$$

$$Interest \ payment = \$11.75 \left[1 - \frac{1}{(1.10)^{20-10+1}} \right] = \$7.63 \quad (12)$$

Notice that the principal repayment plus the interest payment sum to the total mortgage payment of $11.75. The loan balance remaining after j payments is equal to:

$$Remaining \ principal = \$11.75 \sum_{i=1}^{10} \frac{1}{(1.10)^i} = \$11.75[PVA_{10}]$$

$$= \$11.75[6.1446] = \$72.20 \quad (13)$$

$$\% \text{ of original principal remaining} = \frac{PVA_{n-j}}{PVA_n} = \frac{PVA_{10}}{PVA_{20}}$$

$$= \frac{6.1446}{8.5136} = 72.2\% \qquad (14)$$

$$\% \text{ of original repaid after } j \text{ periods} = \frac{PVA_{20} - PVA_{10}}{PVA_{20}}$$

$$= \frac{8.5136 - 6.1446}{8.5136} = 27.8\% \quad (15)$$

Variable-Rate Mortgages

With fluctuating interest rates, lenders have incentives to pass on interest rate risk in the form of variable-rate (floating-rate, adjustable-rate) loans. The interest rate charged to borrowers can be tied to the rate on a widely quoted money market rate, perhaps the 1-year Treasury bill rate plus 2 percent. The lender's cost of raising funds varies with this rate, possibly equalling the 1-year bill rate plus 0.5 percent. By setting the loan rate at the 1-year bill rate plus 2 percent, the lender can lock-in a profit of 1.5 percent minus operating costs and default risk.

On the other side of the coin, the borrower bears the risks and possible returns of changing interest rates. In the long term, the benefits from borrowing short-term may be considerable because long-term interest rates are typically higher than short-term rates. A bank borrowing short and lending long-term earns this term premium on average. By making variable-rate loans, banks pass on these potential profits to borrowers. With variable-rate loans, the bank avoids possible catastrophic losses when short-term interest rates exceed long-term rates; in addition, the bank loses possible large profits if short-term interest rates drop.

Assumable Mortgages

When a real estate property is sold, some mortgages allow the new owner to take over (or assume) the existing mortgage. From the buyer's viewpoint, an assumable mortgage has the advantage of avoiding loan initiation fees on a new mortgage. From the seller's view, the assumable mortgage avoids possible prepayment penalties. These advantages of an assumable mortgage should be reflected in a higher selling price for the property in a perfect market.

If an assumable mortgage has a lower interest rate than the interest rate on a new mortgage, the selling price of the property should reflect this advantage. For example, suppose a house with an assumable 25-year mortgage with $500 principal and 6 percent interest rate is sold when interest rates on new mortgages are 10 percent. The interest payments on the mortgage are $39.11 (i.e. $500/12.7834, where 12.7834 is the present value of a one-dollar annuity at 6 percent for 25 periods). A 10 percent mortgage with principal of $500 has annual payments of $55.08 (i.e. 500/9.077, where 9.077 is the present value of an annuity at 10 percent for 25 periods). The difference in interest has a present value of $144.97 (i.e. [55.08 − 39.11][9.077], where 9.077 is the present value of a 25-period annuity at 10 percent) that should be reflected in a higher selling price.

Nonassumable mortgages have a due-on-sale clause making the principal amount of the mortgage due if the property is sold. In addition, the seller must pay any prepayment penalties.

The Prepayment Option

Mortgages normally contain an option allowing the borrower to repay the remaining principal. Prepayment options are important for homeowners who need to sell a home when moving. Without a prepayment option, the homeowner would be forced to renegotiate the loan with the lender under unfavorable conditions.

Prepayments also occur following a decline in interest rates because an old mortgage at a high interest rate can be replaced by a lower-rate mortgage. In order to decide whether to refinance a mortgage, the borrower needs to compare the present value of the savings to the costs of refinancing.

The benefit of refinancing

We will first present a general framework for determining the benefit of refinancing and then work through a detailed example. Suppose at time 0 a mortgage is taken out with a principal of P_0, maturity of n periods, an interest rate of y_{OLD}, and a periodic payment of M_{OLD}. After j periods have elapsed, the interest rate has dropped to y_{NEW}. The old mortgage has a remaining principal of P_j and is replaced by a new mortgage with $n - j$ periods until maturity. The new mortgage has periodic payments of M_{NEW}. The interest rate on the new loan is y_{NEW}. There are refinancing costs of REF. The refinancing benefit is computed as follows. The old mortgage payment is:

$$Refinancing \; benefit = [M_{OLD} - M_{NEW}]PVA_{n-j,y_{NEW}} - REF$$

$$= \begin{bmatrix} Periodic \\ savings \end{bmatrix}\begin{bmatrix} Present \; value \\ of \; annuity \end{bmatrix} - \begin{bmatrix} Refinancing \\ costs \end{bmatrix} \quad (16)$$

$$M_{OLD} = \frac{P_0}{PVA_{n,y_{OLD}}} \quad (17)$$

The new mortgage payment is:

$$M_{NEW} = \frac{P_j}{PVA_{n-j,y_{NEW}}} \quad (18)$$

To illustrate, suppose that ten years ago a homeowner took out a 20-year mortgage that now has 10 years remaining. The old interest rate was 10 percent. Refinancing costs are 6 percent of the remaining principal. For simplicity assume a principal of $100. From earlier calculations, the mortgage payment is $11.75 and the remaining principal is $72.20. Interest rates have now dropped to 7 percent and the new mortgage payment is:

$$M_{NEW} = \frac{P_j}{PVA_{n-j,y_{NEW}}} = \frac{\$72.20}{PVA_{10,0.07}} = \frac{\$72.20}{7.0236} = \$10.28 \quad (19)$$

The savings from refinancing are computed as follows:

$$Refinancing \; benefit = [M_{OLD} - M_{NEW}]PVA_{n-j,y_{NEW}} - REF$$

$$= [\$11.75 - \$10.28][7.0236] - [0.06][\$72.20] \quad (20)$$

$$= \$5.99$$

In this case, refinancing results in savings after deducting refinancing costs.

Although a current refinancing may be advantageous, waiting to refinance in the future may be better. If future interest rates are lower, the benefit of refinancing can be larger. If future interest rates are higher, the opportunity to gain from refinancing is lost.

Prepayments

Although a typical long-term mortgage might have a 30-year maturity, a large proportion of the mortgages are prepaid by 10–12 years when homeowners move or when mortgages are refinanced after interest rates drop.

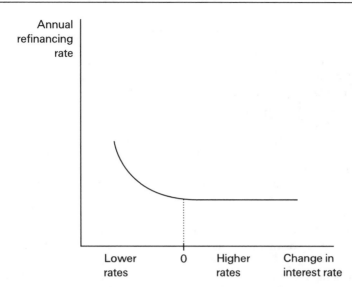

Figure 12.1   Annual refinancing rate and the change in the interest rate

The resulting pattern of prepayments is shown in figure 12.1. The vertical axis shows the annual prepayment rate. The horizontal axis shows the change in interest rates from the original mortgage rate. In figure 12.1, some prepayments occur because some homeowners move and repay their mortgages. These moving prepayments are largely independent of changes in interest rates. As the pace of economic activity increases in an economic expansion, interest rates increase at the same time that demand for labor increases. More job opportunities cause greater labor mobility, more home sales and more mortgage prepayments. Thus, interest rate increases may be associated with some increase in moving prepayments.

When interest rates increase above the original mortgage yield, refinancing does not pay; prepayments are largely moving prepayments. When interest rates fall sufficiently, homeowners refinance to take advantage of lower interest rates on new mortgages. The decline in interest rates has to be large enough to cover refinancing costs to trigger a refinancing. A small decline in interest rates does not cause refinancings. For larger drops in interest rates, more homeowners find refinancing attractive. Thus, for declining interest rates, prepayments have a moving component and a refinancing component.

Prepayment assumptions

When figuring the value of a mortgage, the possibility of prepayment should be included. Typically, analysts assume a particular pattern of prepayments and then figure the value of the mortgage given these prepayments. Several types of prepayment assumptions are used.

The Public Securities Association (PSA) approach assumes low pre-payments in the beginning since new home buyers are unlikely to move immediately after buying a home. As time goes by, homeowners are more likely to move. Interest rates are more likely to change. The annualized prepayment rate increases until month 30. Thereafter, the prepayment rate is 6 percent per year.

The constant prepayment rate (CPR) assumes a constant percent of the remaining principal is prepaid annually over the life of the mortgage. The advantage of this approach is its simplicity.

When mortgages are valued, some assumption is made about the prepayment pattern. The value of the mortgage or the derivative securities can be dramatically affected by the payment assumption. An assumption of prepayment of 100 percent of PSA gives markedly different cash flows from 300 percent of PSA. With prepayments of 300 percent of PSA, the prepayment rate is 3 times the prepayment rate with 100 percent of PSA and the mortgages prepaid much faster.

Marketable Mortgages

Figure 12.2 illustrates several alternatives for mortgage financing. The traditional approach for financing is for a borrower to receive a mortgage loan directly from a commercial bank or a thrift institution, which finances the loan with deposits. Since these deposits can be withdrawn on short notice, the bank or thrift is financing a long-term mortgage with short-term funds and bearing the risk of rising interest rates.

In the second type of mortgage loan, the borrower approaches a mortgage originator (that is, a commercial bank, thrift, or mortgage company), who submits the loan application to a guarantor. As discussed below, there are private mortgage guarantors and government agencies (that is, the Federal Housing Administration or FHA and the Veterans Administration or VA) that guarantee payments if the borrower defaults. If the guarantor accepts a mortgage, the mortgage is included in a mortgage pool. Mortgage pools can be organized by private firms. However, the majority are organized by government

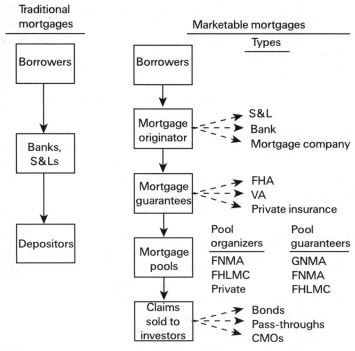

Figure 12.2 Methods of mortgage financing

agencies (discussed below) created to promote the flow of funds from the bond market into the mortgage market. These agencies provide a guarantee of payment of interest and principal on their mortgage pools. Thus, there are two layers of protection against default by the borrower: the insurers (FHA, VA, or private insurer) and the pool organizers (GNMA, FNMA, or FHLMC). GNMA pools have FHA and VA insurance. FHLMC and FNMA pools have private insurance. This double layer of insurance is necessary for two reasons. First, the insurers (FHA, VA) put limits on the amount of their liabilities. Second, long legal delays can occur in trying to collect funds. The pool organizers guarantee timely payment of interest and principal and thus bear the risks of delays. Because of these dual guarantees, the buyer does not have to be concerned with default risk.

Pools of guaranteed mortgages are put together by government agencies or by private institutions. Claims on the pool of mortgages are then sold to investors. Since these claims have no default risk and have standardized features, they are highly marketable. Highly marketable securities are attractive to investors, implying relatively low interest rates. This process of putting mortgages into pools and selling claims or the pools has been called securitization of mortgages. Such securitization benefits homeowners since at least part of the reduction in interest rates is passed on to the mortgage borrower.

Some mortgage pools may be formed through a sale of mortgages to the pool organizer. FHLMC and FNMA pools are formed in this way. In other mortgage pools, the pool guarantor does not actually purchase the mortgages. GNMA pools are formed in this way. GNMA does not actually purchase mortgages.

The pool organizer has three alternatives for selling claims to finance the mortgage pool. First, bonds can be sold to finance the mortgages; this procedure is used by FNMA on some of its mortgages. Second, pass-through securities (discussed below) can be sold; this the most common procedure. Third, derivative securities (discussed below) can be issued.

The introduction of marketable mortgages with default guarantees has had several important consequences. (1) Because savings and loan institutions hold fewer mortgages directly (and bear the default risk), the failure rate of savings and loans has been reduced. (2) Interest rates available to borrowers have become far more uniform. Before marketable mortgages, local conditions significantly affected the interest rates in many areas. (3) The introduction of marketable mortgages has allowed more money to flow into the mortgage market, making interest rates on mortgages lower than they would have been otherwise.

Default and Mortgage Guarantees

Some proportion of mortgage borrowers default. In the event of default by the borrower, the lender then has first claim upon the property and can take legal action to seize and sell it to cover the mortgage principal. This process is costly and time-consuming, and lenders prefer to screen loan applicants to reduce the probability of default.

Default probability is closely related to two factors. First, the default probability increases as the loan to property value ratio increases. When the loan is less than 80 percent of the property value, defaults are rare. Defaults are far more common when the loan is more than 90 percent of the property value. Second, default probability increases as the ratio of mortgage payments to income increases. When mortgage payments are more than 30 percent of income, the default probability is high.

Two government agencies guarantee mortgages: the Federal Housing Administration (FHA) and the Veterans Administration (VA). The operations of both are quite similar except that the FHA insures mortgages to qualified borrowers, whereas the VA guarantees mortgages for veterans only. Each agency sets standards for approving loan applications and the loans have standard terms with respect to maturity, assumability, prepayment, and so on.

There are a number of private insurance companies for mortgages. The private companies developed for several reasons. First, FHA and VA loans have caps on the maximum amount of the loan. Private insurers do not have these caps and serve a segment of the market. Second, FHA and VA loan applications take a long time to process, perhaps as much as two months. Private insurers can process loan applications much faster. Third, government guarantors have very rigid requirements on loans, whereas private insurers can be more flexible. An appraiser examines homes applying for coverage. FHA and VA guarantees require rigid specifications. Homes failing to meet these specifications may still be perfectly safe and sound. Private insurers have the flexibility to account for these differences. For example, the FHA may require certain types of gutters. A home with different gutters would not qualify for FHA insurance, although private insurers would have no problem insuring the home.

Private mortgage insurance has the advantage of flexibility over the FHA and VA. However, private insurance has a disadvantage; the private insurance company itself can go bankrupt and default on its insurance obligations. If a severe recession or depression occurs, a very large number of mortgage defaults would undoubtedly occur. If the total obligations of the insurance company to pay defaulted mortgages exceeds the reserves available, the insurer may be forced to default on the insurance. Whereas the risks of default by individual borrowers can be diversified away in a large portfolio of mortgages, the risk of a major downturn in the economy cannot be diversified away. In effect, private mortgage insurance represents only partial protection against mortgage default.

Three government agencies are involved in the creation of marketable mortgage claims: the Government National Mortgage Association (GNMA or Ginnie Mae), the Federal National Mortgage Association (FNMA or Fannie Mae), and the Federal Home Loan Mortgage Corporation (FHLMC or Freddie Mac). FNMA and FHLMC actually purchase mortgages to put into pools; GNMA does not purchase the mortgages but guarantees mortgages in a pool created by a mortgage originator. All three agencies guarantee the payment of interest and principal. FNMA also purchases mortgages which they hold as investments, using bonds as financing.

GNMA is a government agency, that is, a part of the United States government. The other two, FNMA and FHLMC, are government-sponsored agencies, that is, private entities which have the backing of the federal government. Because of the view that the government will come to the rescue of a sponsored agency, the security markets probably perceive little difference between a government agency and a government-sponsored agency.

Derivative Mortgage Products

If mortgages are put into a pool, there are a number of ways of handling prepayments. First, a claim on a mortgage pool may entitle the holder to a pro-rated share of all payments. These claims are called **pass-through securities** because the mortgage payments are merely passed through the pool to the final investor. The term participation certificate (PC) is also used. In this case, each claimant shares in the prepayments. Sharing in prepayments means that each claim gets a percentage of the principal repaid. When the principal is reduced, future interest payments are reduced. Pass-through securities are generally standardized contracts. This makes them highly liquid, with an active resale market. Investors who purchase or sell pass-throughs are able to change their holdings rapidly in the market without affecting prices.

A second possibility is to partition prepayments. Some investors want to avoid prepayments and others do not. To accommodate these investment needs, pool organizers have developed many ways of partitioning the prepayments. The resulting securities are called derivative mortgage products, collateralized mortgage obligations (or CMOs), or real estate mortgage investment conduits (or REMICs). The major varieties are discussed below. They include sequential pay securities, Z bonds, planned amortization classes, and principal-only or interest-only derivatives.

Partitioning of prepayment cash flows is a two-edged sword. The prepayment risk to some investors is reduced and they receive a lower risk position and lower expected returns. But, the prepayment risk to other investors is increased; they have a higher risk position and higher expected returns. For high-risk investors, the gains and losses from interest rate movements can be considerable. Sometimes interest rates will move in favor of the high-risk investors and sometimes against them. The realized returns may be very favorable or very bad.

The partitioning of mortgage cash flows produces a net benefit to mortgage borrowers. Each class is purchased by investors who want to hold a mortgage with a particular expected prepayment pattern. The buyers of individual classes can be expected to accept somewhat lower yields for separate classes than buyers of a claim on the entire pool. In effect, dividing a mortgage pool into parts increases the value of the mortgages and reduces their yields. The yield reduction is at least partially passed on to borrowers. Part of the yield reduction is realized as (arbitrage) profit by the pool organizer.

The primary disadvantage of partitioning is reduced marketability because of the large variety of different securities. The terms of derivatives, especially the number of classes, are not standardized. The number of classes has varied from 3 to 10. A 3-class derivative is quite different from a 10-class derivative. This situation may easily change if some set of terms with large market appeal becomes standard. In spite of the lack of marketability, issues of derivatives have increased dramatically. The reduction in the uncertainty surrounding prepayment is apparently very important to many buyers of derivatives.

Sequential pay or "plain vanilla" derivatives

A sequential pay derivative divides the prepayments into classes (or tranches). The most common pattern is for all principal payments to be used to pay down the nearest remaining class.[1]

Imagine principal payments broken into 4 classes. The first 25 percent of payments are used to pay off the principal of class 1. As part of the principal is repaid in class 1, future interest payments to class 1 are reduced as well. When all of the principal of class 1 is paid, this class ceases to exist. The next 25 percent of principal payments goes to class 2. When all of these principal payments are made, class 2 ceases to exist, and so on.

Z bonds

A Z bond is the lowest-priority class. It accrues interest until all other classes are repaid their principal. Then the Z bond receives interest and principal.

Z bonds are extremely high-risk for two reasons. First, they have long effective maturities. As interest rates change, the present value of the cash flows fluctuates sharply because each cash flow is discounted for many periods. Second, uncertainty about the timing of prepayments is very large for this class with a residual claim on the cash flows. Z bonds should have high yields because of the high risk. But the realized returns will have great variability.

Figure 12.3 shows the cash flows for a 4-class sequential pay derivative. Class A receives interest until all of its principal is repaid. Class B receives interest until all of class A's principal is repaid; then class B begins to receive principal and interest. Class C receives interest until

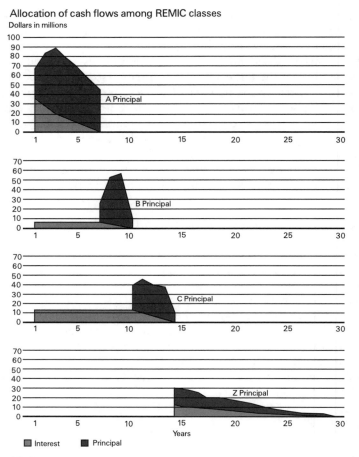

Figure 12.3 A sequential pay derivative (from Federal National Mortgage Association, *REMICS and Mortgage-Backed Securities*, Washington, DC, 1995)

class B's principal is completely repaid; then C receives principal and interest. The last class is a Z bond. Notice that the Z bond gets no cash flows until all of the principal for the first three classes is completely paid off.

Planned amortization class (PAC)

A planned amortization class or PAC has a fixed principal payment schedule that must be met before other classes receive principal

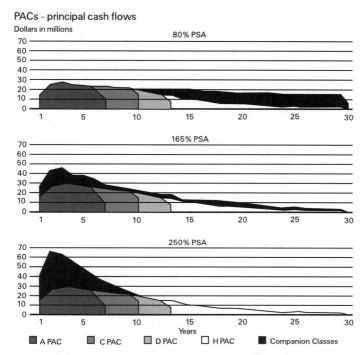

PACs - principal cash flows

Figure 12.4 Planned amortization class (PAC) (from Federal National Mortgage Association, *REMICS and Mortgage-Backed Securities*, Washington, DC, 1995)

payments. The PAC payments are made from scheduled amortization and prepayments. The pool organizer estimates the probable prepayments. Then part of the pool is sold as PACs. The PAC class is small enough so that the PAC payments are made under most interest rate scenarios.

Figure 12.4 shows the cash flows from a mortgage pool with four classes of PACs and companion classes, which receive the residual cash flows after PACs are paid. The cash flows are shown for several scenarios of PSA. Expected prepayments are 100% of PSA. The top segment shows 80% of PSA, close to the expected prepayments. The four PAC classes get paid as scheduled, but the companion classes get paid at the end. In the lowest segment, the prepayments are fast, 250% of PSA. Then the companion classes get repaid rapidly.

The buyers of the companion classes face considerable uncertainty about the timing of their cash inflows. If interest rates rise, the companion classes are paid in the distant future, and the present value is low because of the higher interest rate used to discount the cash flows. If interest rates drop, the companion classes are paid rapidly, and the low interest rate contributes to a relatively high present value. Obviously, the value of the companion classes fluctuates dramatically as interest rates change.

Principal-only (PO) and interest-only (IO) derivatives

Some mortgage pools are divided into separate segments receiving principal only (PO) and interest only (IO). As unscheduled prepayments occur, the holders of POs receive the added cash flows. Since the remaining principal is reduced, holders of IOs receive reduced interest payments.

Buyers of IOs and POs assume some pattern of prepayments in valuing their securities. If the actual prepayments differ, values are significantly affected.

Falling interest rates If prepayments are faster than anticipated because of falling interest rates, principal payments are received sooner and discounted at a lower interest rate; the value of POs rises. Earlier principal payments reduce interest payments to IOs. These interest payments are discounted at a lower interest rate, partially offsetting the decline in payments. For small declines in interest rates, IOs might actually increase in value. For larger declines in interest rates, prepayments are substantial and IOs decline sharply in value. If large drops in interest rates occur in the early life of the mortgage, IO holders may actually receive less money than they invested – for a negative rate of return.

Rising interest rates With rising interest rates prepayments are slower than anticipated. For POs, principal payments are deferred and discounted at higher interest rates; the value of POs drops. For IOs, interest received is higher than anticipated, although discounted at a higher interest rate. IOs can increase in value unless interest rates increase sharply.

Summary

Mortgages are used to finance real estate properties, both homes and commercial properties. Fixed-rate mortgages have a constant interest rate over the life of the mortgage. Floating-rate mortgages have an interest rate that moves up and down as market interest rates change. Borrowers have the option to prepay a mortgage loan before maturity.

Prepayment most often occurs because of moving or a drop in interest rates.

The growth of marketable mortgages with default guarantees has created a large investment market for mortgage-backed securities or derivatives. A variety of mortgage derivative securities have been developed that partition the prepayment risk.

Notes

1 The principal payments can be handled in two ways. First, all payments of principal, including both scheduled amortization and prepayments, are made to the nearest remaining class. This procedure is the most common one. Second, all remaining classes can share in the scheduled amortization of principal, but prepayments go to the nearest remaining class.

Questions and Problems

1 For a standard fixed-rate mortgage, compute the annual mortgage payment for a 15-year annual mortgage loan with principal of $100 and interest rate of 10 percent.

2 In problem 1, break each mortgage payment into interest on remaining principal and amortization for the first three years. Also, compute the remaining balance on the mortgage at each point in time. What is the total amount of interest paid over the mortgage's life? Does this seem high or low, fair or unfair?

3 Assume that you take out a 15-year mortgage at a 10 percent interest rate and $100 principal. Compute the amortization in year 13. Compute the percentage of the mortgage principal repaid by year 13. How many years does it take for half of the original principal to be repaid?

4 Suppose Susan has a 15-year mortgage with $100 principal. In year 8, the amortization of the principal is $5.93. Use the present value tables to compute the interest rate on the mortgage.

5 Assume that you take out a 15-year mortgage at a 10 percent interest rate and $100 principal. After one year, the interest rate on new loans is 7 percent. If you refinance, there are refinancing costs of 6 percent. Compute the immediate gain from refinancing. Also, compute the refinancing benefit if the refinancing occurs five years after the mortgage is taken out.

6 Suppose Jasmine inherits a house from her grandfather. When the house was originally purchased by grandpa 20 years ago, the mortgage was for 30 years. The original mortgage principal was $100. The remaining principal is now $50.23. The current interest rate is 6 percent and refinancing costs are 3 percent. Does it pay to refinance? (Hint: First find the interest rate on the existing loan.)

7 Explain what it means to originate a mortgage loan. Who are the originators?

8 A bank has a choice of making a 2-year loan at 10 percent or a variable-rate loan at the 1-year Treasury bill rate plus 2 percent. Currently, the Treasury bill rate is 7 percent. Under what circumstances is the 2-year loan better than the variable-rate loan and vice versa?

9 An investor buys a claim on a pool of 15-year mortgages at 10 percent and $100 principal. Compute the interest and principal repayments for the first three years assuming no prepayments. Next, assume that 6 percent of the original principal is prepaid every year. Compute the interest and the scheduled principal payments and the prepayments for the first three years.

10 A thrift institution decides to sell all its mortgages and use the proceeds to purchase pass-through securities. What is the gain to the thrift institution? Whatever the thrift gains, someone else loses. Who takes the other side of this transaction and what are the consequences for this party? Is there any net gain to the system from shifting risks in this way?

11 Explain the differences between a mortgage guarantee from FHA or VA and insurance from a private insurance company.

12 Look in your local newspaper for interest rates on a long-term fixed-rate and a variable-rate mortgage. Report the loan initiation costs. How is the interest rate adjusted on the variable-rate mortgage?

13
Futures Contracts

For many years, futures contracts on physical commodities have been traded. In recent years, active markets have developed for financial futures contracts. This chapter describes futures contracts for physical commodities and the use of futures contracts in risk reduction and hedging. Chapter 14 examines financial futures contracts and their uses.

A futures contract involves a contractual agreement to purchase or sell something at a future point in time, called the **delivery month**.[1] The buyer is called the **long** and the seller is called the **short**. Futures contracts are **zero-sum games**; that is, the short and the long are playing against each other. The long's gains equal the short's losses and vice versa.

The actual purchase of the commodity is not scheduled to take place until the delivery month, as shown in figure 13.1. For example, suppose a contract is signed for the short to deliver one ounce of silver in one year for a price of $8.00. Figure 13.2 shows the futures obligations.

In fact, most futures contracts are closed out by an offsetting position before delivery occurs. A long offsets by going short; a short offsets by going long. Imagine an investor who has taken a short position in silver

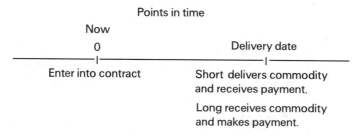

Figure 13.1 Futures contracts

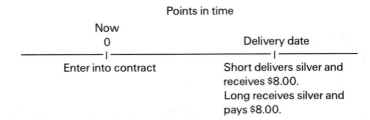

Figure 13.2   Short position in silver futures

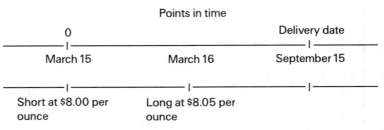

Figure 13.3   Offsetting a short futures position

futures at $8.00 per ounce on March 15 as shown in figure 13.3. The scheduled delivery date is September 15. Any time before that delivery date, the short can offset the short position by going long. For example, suppose that on March 16 the short decides to close the position by offsetting, that is, going long at $8.05 per ounce. Going long one contract offsets the original short position for a loss of $0.05 per ounce. There is a loss because the investor has sold (shorted) at $8.00 and bought (gone long) at $8.05. Had the position been closed at a price below $8.00, the short would have gained.

Offsetting does not involve any incremental brokerage fees because the fee to establish the initial short position includes the commission to take the offsetting long position – a so-called **round trip commission**. If actual delivery is made on the contract on September 15, silver has to be purchased and delivered to the location specified in the futures contract. Sizable transactions costs are incurred. Even with financial futures contracts in which the short has to deliver securities, the transactions costs involved in purchasing the securities in the spot market generally exceed the cost of an offsetting futures position.

A particular contract is traded in a designated "pit" at the exchange. A pit is a series of steps above the trading floor. The traders stand on the steps and engage in open outcry and hand signal trading. Because of the rapid ups and downs in futures prices, the pressures of being a trader are quite intense.

Open Interest

The total number of outstanding contracts is called the **open interest**. For every outstanding contract, one person is short and one is long. For the open interest to change, the number of shorts and longs must change. Consider the example in figure 13.4. On March 15, the open interest is 30 contracts. In total, investors are long 30 contracts and short 30 contracts. For every contract long, there must be a contract short.

On March 16, Jones decides to offset one long contract by going short, reducing Jones' net position to 19 contracts long. When Jones goes short one contract, someone else must be going long. The identity of this long determines the change in the open interest.

The first possibility occurs if the long is one of the existing shorts. Then, a short is also offsetting at the same time as Jones. Suppose Peters decides to offset one contract. Then the new open interest is shown in figure 13.5. In the second possibility, when Jones offsets one contract by shorting one contract, the long is another investor, Smiles. Then, the open interest remains at 30 contracts. See figure 13.6.

To summarize, if a particular transaction involves a new long *and* a new short, the open interest increases by one contract. If a transaction involves offsetting by an existing long *and* offsetting by an existing short, the open interest declines by one contract. If a transaction entails

Longs		Shorts	
Jones	20	Smith	15
Roberts	10	Peters	15
Total	30	Total	30

Figure 13.4 Open interest – March 15

Longs		Shorts	
Jones	19	Smith	15
Roberts	10	Peters	14
Total	29	Total	29

Figure 13.5 Open interest – March 16

Longs		Shorts	
Jones	19	Smith	15
Roberts	10	Peters	15
Smiles	1		
Total	30	Total	30

Figure 13.6   Open interest – March 16

offsetting by an existing short or long, and if the other side of the transaction is a new investor, the open interest remains unchanged. Each futures exchange has a **clearinghouse** to keep track of the short and long positions. The clearinghouse cancels the offsetting positions.

The amount of trading is different from the open interest. For example, if 50 longs decided to offset by going short and the other sides of the transactions were taken by 50 new long investors, we would have 50 trades and an unchanged open interest.

Margin and Marking-to-Market

Every long and short position is required to post a performance bond called **margin** with the clearinghouse. The margin allows the clearing-house to guarantee the financial integrity of contracts. If one side defaults, the clearinghouse should have sufficient margin funds to ensure that the other side of the contract does not suffer financially.

Because an investor in futures markets must put down margin equal to only a small proportion of the market value of the underlying commodity, the investor's position is highly levered and quite risky. A small percentage change in the price of the futures contract brings about a much larger percentage change in the value of the margin. If the investor puts down m percent of the futures price, the margin will change $1/(m$ percent) for every 1 percent change in the futures price. For example, if an investor puts down 10 percent of the futures price, the margin will change 1/0.10, or 10, times as fast as the futures price.

Each day the exchange computes a **settlement price**. The settlement price is not the closing price, the price from the very last trade of the day. Instead, the settlement price is an average of the prices near the end of trading.[2]

If the settlement price increases (decreases) from one day to the next, the long has a gain (loss) and the short has a loss (gain). Consider an example for silver futures as shown in figure 13.7. The settlement price

Figure 13.7   Silver futures

on March 15 is $8.00 per ounce. At the end of trading on the next day, March 16, the settlement price is $8.20. This means that the long gains $0.20 per ounce and the short loses $0.20 per ounce. The clearinghouse transfers funds between the accounts of the short and the long in a process called **marking-to-market**. In the futures markets, every contract is marked-to-market every day. Every day, the longs and the shorts must "settle up."

The funds used to settle the accounts of the shorts and the longs come from the collateral deposited by investors with the clearinghouse. When prices increase, the collateral of the longs is increased and the shorts' collateral is reduced by the same amount. If an individual investor's collateral becomes too small as a result of market price changes, the investor is required to put up more margin or the position is closed. Thus, marking-to-market helps to guarantee performance on the contract.

Futures exchanges set **price limits** on individual futures contracts except during delivery months. Price limits restrict the change in price on a particular day to some maximum amount up or down. For example, if a futures contract settles on Monday at $8 and if a price limit of $1 is applicable, on Tuesday the contract is not allowed to trade at less than $7 or more than $9. The motivation for price limits is to restrict the price volatility of futures contracts. If a contract is up or down the limit, trading may stop until the following day, allowing the traders some time to cool down. The price limits also allow the clearinghouse time to collect more collateral from traders who have taken losses. Thus, price limits help to maintain the financial integrity of traders' positions. Instead of having price limits, the clearinghouse could require greater amounts of collateral.

In addition, limits are set on the total number of contracts in which a position can be taken. Position limits are motivated by the desire to keep markets competitive. There is fear that price manipulation might occur if one trader, or a syndicate of traders, controls too many contracts. These position limits, combined with price limits and margin requirements, guarantee the financial integrity of contract positions. Thus, one side of a contract can expect to suffer no financial harm if the other side defaults.

Forward versus Futures Contracts

In some markets, forward contracts are traded. Forward contracts have a number of similarities and differences with futures contracts, as summarized in table 13.1.

Forward markets exist in the foreign exchange markets. Typically, banks regularly dealing with each other write forward contracts on foreign currencies. The forward market is a small, private market. Since the banks dealing in these forward markets know each other quite well and have many interactions, default on a particular contractual agreement is unlikely. Consequently, these forward contracts do not involve collateral, although compensating balances may be expected. No cash flows occur between the initiation of the forward contract and the delivery date. The parties merely agree to exchange currencies at some future date. Delivery is usually made on forward contracts. Terms on particular contracts are tailor-made to meet the specific needs of the parties, making individual contracts unattractive to other parties and creating a thin resale market for forward contracts.

Futures contracts are standardized and actively traded on impersonal exchanges. Since the short and long do not know each other, the risk of default is real. To reduce the likelihood of default, futures contracts require a performance bond and marking-to-market. As further protections, daily price limits and position limits are also used. With futures contracts, cash flows occur before the delivery date as the gains or losses from marking-to-market are settled daily.

In the theoretical forward contracts discussed in this book, default is impossible. In practice, the chance for default on a forward contract can

Table 13.1 Forward versus futures contracts

	Forward	Futures
Collateral	None	Yes
Marking-to-Market	None	Daily
Compensating balances	Usually	None
Resale	Limited	Active trading on organized exchanges
Contract terms	Custom made	Standardized
Delivery	Usually delivered	Usually offset
Market size	Small, private. Participants know each other	Large, public, impersonal

be considerable. To illustrate, suppose a speculator enters into a forward contract to sell wheat at $2 per bushel for delivery next October 1. On the delivery date of October 1, the spot price of wheat is $4. Making delivery requires the speculator to buy wheat in the spot market and then sell it in the futures market to satisfy the short position, for a loss of $2 per bushel. Default on the forward contract is tempting.

The markets for forward foreign exchange attempt to solve the problem of default by having a small and private market in which the parties are unlikely to default because of their close ties. In contrast, futures markets attempt to solve the problem of possible default and contractual nonperformance by requiring margin and by marking-to-market. In the example of the previous paragraph, if the speculator shorts futures (instead of a forward contract) at $2 and prices rise to $4, the short pays the long the amount of the price increase on a daily basis because of marking-to-market. If the speculator's margin on the futures contract is too low, more margin is posted or the speculator's position is closed out. Thus, the financial integrity of the futures contract is protected.

If all interest rates are certain, futures and forward prices are identical, even though futures contracts have marking-to-market. Since interest rates are uncertain in practice, a difference between futures and forward prices may exist. However, there is a powerful theoretical argument of the equivalence of futures and forward contracts even with uncertainty. Empirically, any difference between futures and forwards appears to be a second-order effect – perhaps a fraction of a percent. The following discussion of futures markets overlooks the possible differences between futures and forward contracts created by collateral requirements and marking-to-market.

Determinants of Futures Prices

On the delivery date, a futures contract and a spot market contract are identical. Therefore, the futures price equals the spot price of the deliverable commodity. If not, arbitrage opportunities are available from buying in the lower-priced market and simultaneously selling in the higher-priced market. If the futures price is higher than the spot price, an arbitrager can make a profit by shorting futures, buying the commodity, and delivering it into the futures contract for an immediate risk-free profit. If the futures price is below the spot price, an arbitrager can go long futures and shortsell the commodity; when delivery occurs on the futures contract, the delivered commodity can be used to close the short position.

Before the delivery date, there are two cases to consider. First, for a nonstorable commodity, the futures price is determined by the market's expectation of the future spot price on the delivery date. As an example, consider a futures market for tomatoes with a delivery date 1 year into the future. Since tomatoes are storable only for short periods, the futures price for delivery 1 year hence is set by the market's expectations of demand and supply for tomatoes on the delivery date. These expectations depend upon population trends, weather conditions, availability of substitutes, etc.

Second, the commodity may be storable. In practice, existing futures contracts are for storable commodities. Let the current futures price be F and the current spot price be P. Then, for storable commodities such as grains and metals, arbitrage will force the relationship:

$$F = P + interest + storage \ until \ delivery \qquad (1)$$

In other words, purchasing a futures contract is the equivalent of borrowing the purchase price of a commodity, buying the commodity, and storing it until the delivery date (see table 13.2). At the delivery date, the loan principal, interest charges, and storage costs must be paid. The total of these three costs equals the futures price.

Arbitrage forces equation (1) to hold. To prove equation (1), the cases where the futures price is above (below) its equilibrium value are shown shortly to provide arbitrage opportunities. This arbitrage forces the prices back to their equilibrium values in equation (1).

Equation (1) shows that the futures price is the spot price plus interest and storage until the delivery date. Expectations of market prices on the delivery date do not appear directly in equation (1). However, expectations are implicitly incorporated in the equation because arbitrage forces expectations of the prices on the delivery date to affect both the futures price and the current spot price.

Table 13.2   Creating a forward position from a spot position

Actions	Points in time	
	0	Delivery date
		Cash flows
Borrow	$+P$	Repay $-[P + $ interest $+$ storage$]$
Buy commodity	$-P$	
Net cash flows	0	$-[P + $ interest $+$ storage$]$

Table 13.3 Arbitrage if futures price is above equilibrium level

Actions	Points in time	
	0	Delivery date
		Cash flows
Short futures		$+F$
Borrow	$+P$	
Buy commodity	$-P$	
Repay loan + interest		$-P(1+R)$
Deliver commodity in futures market		
Net cash flows	0	$F-P(1+R)$

Futures price above equilibrium level

Table 13.3 shows the arbitrage if the futures price rises above its equilibrium price. The arbitrager can short futures, borrow money, purchase the commodity in the spot market, and store until the delivery date. On the delivery date, the arbitrager delivers the commodity, gets paid by the long, and repays the loan plus interest. There is a sure profit. To simplify the discussion, the storage cost is assumed to be zero. R is defined as the total interest from time zero until delivery expressed as a percentage.[3]

If $F-P(1+R)$ is positive, there is a sure arbitrage profit. The actions of arbitragers shorting futures and buying in the spot market drive the futures price F down and the spot market price P up until $F-P(1+R)$ equals zero. Consider the following numerical example of arbitrage. If the spot price of gold is $400 and the 1-year spot interest rate is 10 percent, the futures price for delivery in 1 year should be $440 [i.e. 400(1.10)]. If the futures price is actually $500, arbitrage profits are available from shorting futures, borrowing $400, buying gold, and storing it until the delivery date. The actions and cash flows are shown in table 13.4.

Futures price below equilibrium level

Table 13.5 shows the arbitrage. The arbitrager goes long futures, shortsells the commodity, and invests the proceeds from the shortsale. On the delivery date, the arbitrager purchases the commodity through

Table 13.4 Arbitrage example if futures price is above equilibrium level

Actions	Points in time	
	0	Delivery date
		Cash flows
Short futures		+500
Borrow	+400	
Buy commodity	−400	
Repay loan + interest		−400(1.10)
Deliver commodity in futures market		
Net cash flows	0	500 − 400(1.10) = 60

Table 13.5 Arbitrage if futures price is below equilibrium level

Actions	Points in time	
	0	Delivery date
		Cash flows
Long futures		−F
Short commodity	+P	
Invest proceeds	−P	+P(1 + R)
Take delivery on futures and close short position		
Net cash flows	0	−[F − P(1 + R)]

the futures contract, uses this to close the short position, and receives the amount lent plus interest for a sure profit.

If the futures price F is less than the spot price plus interest, $P(1 + R)$, the net cash flow from this arbitrage is positive with complete certainty. The actions of arbitragers repeatedly profiting from this arbitrage force the futures price up and the spot price down until the arbitrage profits are eliminated, that is, until the futures price equals the spot price plus interest.

Consider the arbitrage opportunities for the following numerical example. The spot price of gold is $400 and the 1-year interest rate is 10 percent, again implying a futures price of $440. If the futures price is actually $400, the arbitrage opportunity is as shown in table 13.6.

Table 13.6 Example of Arbitrage if futures price is below equilibrium level

Actions	Points in time	
	0	Delivery date
		Cash flows
Long futures		−400
Short commodity	+400	
Invest proceeds	−400	+400(1.10)
Take delivery on futures and close short position		
Net cash flows	0	−[400−400(1.10)] = 40

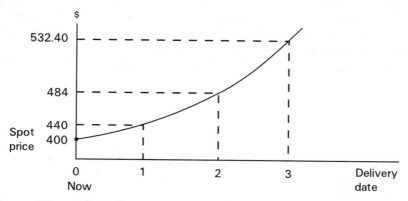

Figure 13.8 Futures prices for more distant delivery dates

The length of time until delivery

In equation (1), futures contracts for more distant delivery dates have higher price quotations because of higher interest and storage costs for carrying the commodity for a longer time period. To illustrate, consider the case where storage costs are zero. Then, the futures price for delivery in d periods is the spot price times 1 plus the spot interest rate to the power d [i.e. $(1+R_d)^d$]. Figure 13.8 shows the futures prices for several delivery dates for a flat term structure of 10 percent and spot price of $400.

For precious metals such as gold, silver, and platinum, the storage costs are relatively small compared to the market price. For these precious metals, the differences in futures prices are largely determined by the term structure of interest rates. There is a close relationship between futures prices and the actual term structure of interest rates.

Thus, the futures price for gold for delivery d periods from now (assuming zero storage costs) is:

$$F_{GOLD} = P(1 + R_d)^d \qquad (2)$$

Convenience yield

For most futures contracts, the futures price increases as the delivery date becomes more distant because the total interest and storage costs increase as the delivery date becomes more distant. For some commodities, possession of the commodity may have a convenience value to a firm. This convenience yield reduces the futures price below the spot price plus interest and storage. Figure 13.9 illustrates the impact of convenience yield. In a perfect market there would be an arbitrage from going long in the futures, shorting the commodity in the spot market, lending the proceeds, and closing all positions at the futures delivery date. For commodities with convenience yield, shortselling the commodity in the spot market is impossible in practice. For such commodities,

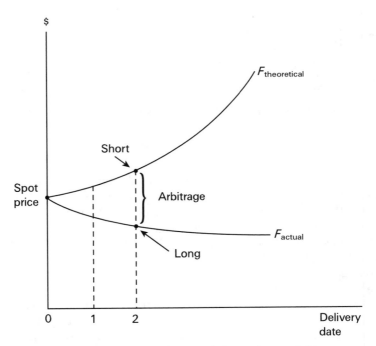

Figure 13.9 The impact of convenience yield

Table 13.7 Futures price of light sweet crude oil observed on September 28, 1990

Delivery month	Futures price ($ per barrel)
November 1990	39.51
December 1990	38.31
January 1991	36.72
February 1991	35.40
March 1991	34.15
April 1991	33.00
May 1991	31.95
June 1991	31.00
July 1991	30.20
August 1991	29.55
September 1991	29.05
October 1991	28.62
November 1991	28.27
December 1991	27.98
January 1992	27.71
February 1992	27.45
March 1992	27.20
April 1992	26.96

the actual futures price lies below the theoretical futures price in a perfect market.

The case of oil futures prices during the war with Iraq in the fall of 1990 is a striking example of convenience yield. Table 13.7 presents the futures price per barrel for light sweet crude oil observed on September 28, 1990, for various delivery dates. At the time, the spot price of oil was approximately $41 per barrel.

If equation (1) is correct, the futures price for distant delivery dates should exceed the spot price by the amount of interest and storage until the delivery date. With the spot price of oil at $41 in September 1990, the sum of the spot price plus interest and storage until April 1992 is considerably higher than $41. Yet, the futures price for April 1992 delivery was only $26.96. Consequently, the convenience yield exceeded $14.04 ($41 − 26.96).

The earlier discussion indicated an arbitrage opportunity if the futures price was less than the spot price plus interest and storage costs (see tables 13.5 and 13.6). The arbitrage was to (short)sell the commodity, invest the proceeds, go long futures, and use the oil purchased from the futures contract to cover the shortsale.

One version of the arbitrage is to shortsell the commodity. To shortsell, a lender of the commodity has to be found. Given fears about oil shortages resulting from the war, no lenders of oil were available. The potential lenders of oil were unwilling to lend because the convenience yield of oil was very high. A second version of the arbitrage is for holders of oil to sell their own oil, lend the proceeds, and buy back oil in the futures market. Again, the war uncertainties made holders of oil unwilling to give up the convenience yield of their inventories. In short, the war and the resulting high convenience yield made arbitrage impossible.

Speculative Futures Positions

Going short or long in futures without any offsetting position is often described as taking a **speculative position**. As an example, suppose you anticipate a sharp rise in the price of silver and go long in silver futures for 1,000 ounces at $5.00 per ounce. Happily, you are correct. The futures price goes to $6.00 and you make a profit of $1.00 per ounce, or $1,000.[4]

To set up your original futures position, margin is required in the form of marketable securities or cash. The broker will inform you of the exact amount of margin. For simplicity, assume that the initial margin is $500 (10 percent of the original value of the contract). If, in fact, the actual gain on your short position is $1,000, the percentage gain is 200 percent of the initial margin. The percentage gains and losses on futures can be very large. All your margin can be lost in a few days. For this reason, speculative positions (i.e. either short or long with no offsetting position) in futures contracts are very risky.

The percentage changes in collateral (or equity) are related to the percentage changes in the underlying futures price in the following way (overlooking interest and dividends):

$$\frac{\% \ change}{equity} = \frac{\% \ change \ futures \ price}{\% \ put \ down} = \frac{(new - old)/old}{\% \ put \ down} \tag{3}$$

For example, if the margin percent is 5%, then:

$$\frac{\% \ change}{equity} = \frac{\% \ change \ futures \ price}{0.05}$$

$$= 20[\% \ change \ futures \ price] \tag{4}$$

since $1/0.05 = 20$. Thus, your collateral changes 20 times as fast percentagewise as the futures price.

Hedging with Futures Contracts

In a futures **hedge**, an investor offsets a position in the spot market with a nearly opposite position in the futures market with the objective of reducing the overall risk of the position. The hedged position also has a lower expected return than an unhedged position. Hedges allow those unwilling or unable to bear the risk to transfer the risk to another party willing and able to take on the risks and possible rewards. This risk transfer function of futures markets is socially desirable.

In a **long hedge**, the investor takes a long position in futures. In a **short hedge**, the investor takes a short position in futures. A very important type of short hedge occurs when an investor with a long position in the spot market simultaneously shorts futures contracts. This variety of a short hedge is illustrated by the following example.

Suppose a farmer plants a wheat crop in the spring, expecting to harvest and sell the wheat in the fall. Effectively, the farmer has a long position in wheat. Because the price of wheat at the harvest time is uncertain, the farmer bears considerable risk about the eventual profits earned on the wheat.[5] To protect against this risk, the farmer shorts wheat futures (a short hedge) and locks-in the selling price of the wheat. If the futures price is $6.00 per bushel and production costs are $4 per bushel, the farmer's short position in wheat futures allows the wheat to be sold at $6.00 per bushel, locking-in a profit of $2.00 per bushel.

The short futures position is a two-edged sword. While the farmer can avoid losses if the wheat price at harvest is low, the farmer also gives up large profits if the wheat price is quite high at the harvest date. The farmer is willing to give up the chance of large profits in order to avoid possible catastrophic losses on the downside. The futures contract allows the farmer to transfer the risks to someone else better able to bear these risks.

As an example of a long hedge, consider a bread manufacturer in need of wheat to make the bread. To lock-in the purchase price of wheat on the harvest date and guarantee a profit from making bread, the bread manufacturer goes long wheat futures (a long hedge). The bread manufacturer forgoes windfall gains if the wheat price is low on the harvest date. In exchange, potentially large losses are avoided if wheat prices are high on the harvest date. The futures contract permits the bread manufacturer to pass on the price risks of wheat. Bread manufacturing becomes a more stable industry as a result.

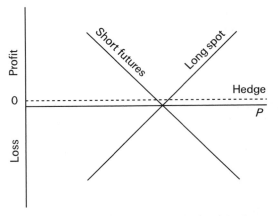

Figure 13.10 Profit profile for short hedge

Fine-tuning the hedge

In short hedging, the hedger may be able to find a futures contract for a virtually identical item as the hedger's spot position. Then, the gains (losses) in the spot market are offset by the losses (gains) in the futures market. This offset is shown in figure 13.10, which shows profit profiles. The investor goes long in the spot market at $10. As the spot price increases (decreases), the investor gains (loses) dollar for dollar. The profit profile for a short futures position in the identical item is also shown. Gains (losses) in the spot position are offset dollar for dollar by the short futures position. The profit profile for the net position is a horizontal line, indicating no change in the value of the net position as the spot price changes. This flat profit profile represents a perfect hedge.[6]

Very often, highly similar futures contracts do not exist. The hedger must utilize a short position in a similar, but different, item. This is called a cross hedge. Suppose a farmer is long in the spot market in grade A wheat but futures trade for grade B wheat. Grades A and B are related, but different. Suppose the farmer engages in a one-for-one hedge. For every bushel of grade A wheat in the farmer's long spot position, the farmer shorts one bushel of grade B wheat futures. Figure 13.11 shows the profit profiles for long spot grade A wheat, short futures grade B, and the net position. Grade B wheat prices are assumed to move half as fast as grade A wheat. The slope of the profit profile for long spot grade A is 1.0; the slope of the profit profile for short grade B wheat is -0.50. The net position has a slope of $+0.50$. Thus, the gains and losses on the spot position in grade A wheat are cut in half by the short hedge.

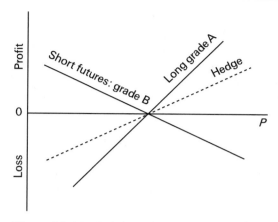

Figure 13.11   Profit profile for a cross hedge

Price grade B

Figure 13.12   Relationship between grade A and grade B

The relationship between grade A wheat and grade B wheat is shown in figure 13.12. For every dollar change in grade B, grade A changes $2. Using this information, the farmer can construct a perfect hedge by shorting two bushels of grade B wheat for every bushel long of grade A wheat. For every dollar decrease in grade A wheat, grade B falls by $0.50. But the total drop in the two short positions in grade B is $1.00 for a perfect offset.

In practice, the relationship between a spot position and a futures contract in a cross hedge is not a perfect straight line but the dots shown in figure 13.12. Using regression analysis, the hedger can estimate the slope of the best-fitting relationship, often called β. For every unit of the spot commodity, the hedger shorts β units of the futures. β is called the optimal hedge ratio. The optimal hedge is not a perfect hedge, since the link between the spot and futures is not perfect. The optimal hedge is the best hedge in the sense that the expected change in the hedged position is zero.

Summary

Futures contract are obligations to buy and sell commodities at future delivery dates. These contracts allow businesses and individuals to transfer price risks to those who choose to bear the risks. The short is obligated to sell the commodity at a fixed price. The long is required to buy the commodity at the contractually agreed price.

The futures price of storable commodities equals the spot price plus interest and storage until the delivery date. Arbitrage guarantees this result in the absence of convenience yield.

In a hedge, a position in the spot market is offset with a futures position to reduce the overall risk. A short hedge involves a short futures position. A long hedge includes a long futures position.

Notes

1   For futures contracts, the delivery date is actually a month. The seller has the option to pick the exact day during the month to make delivery of the contract and be paid.
2   Use of a settlement price instead of a closing price is motivated by the practice of marking-to-market, discussed below. The settlement price is used to figure the amount of cash transfer between shorts and longs after trading closes. If the closing price were used, some traders might be able to manipulate prices at the close to their advantage.
3   For example, if $100 is borrowed at time zero and $101 is repaid in 1 month, R will be 1 percent. R is not an annualized rate.
4   Because of daily price limits, this gain will not occur over one day but will be spread out over several days. Each day there will be marking-to-market, and some gains (or possibly losses) will be realized daily.
5   Besides price uncertainty, the farmer also bears quantity risk. At planting time, the farmer does not know the exact number of bushels that will be harvested.
6   This profit profile assumes the futures price changes only because the spot price changes. Formally, since $F = P(1 + R_d)^d$, the profit profile assumes that the change in R_d and the change in d are zero.

Questions and Problems

1   The open interest includes:
    Longs
        Bob   15 contracts
        Lois   5 contracts
    Shorts
        Bill   10 contracts
        Helen   10 contracts
    Determine the new open interest under the following assumptions:
    (a)   Bill goes long 1 contract and Gene shorts 1 contract.
    (b)   Bill goes long 1 contract and Bob shorts 1 contract.
2   Explain the differences between forward and futures contracts.
3   What are price and position limits on futures contracts? What are the purposes of price and position limits?
4   Suppose you go long in gold futures at $300 per ounce. Your broker requires you to put up 5% of this price as collateral. The net day gold futures settle at $320. Compute the gain as a percent of your equity in the position. What is the general relationship between the percent change in the investor's equity and the percent change in the futures price?
5   Assume the following information about the futures price for gold:

	Delivery dates (number of years into future)		
	1	2	3
Current price of futures contract per ounce of gold	$300	$350	$400

If the current spot price of gold is $260, determine spot interest rates for periods 1, 2, and 3, and forward interest rates for periods 2 and 3, assuming no marking-to-market and no storage or transactions costs.

6   Assume no marking-to-market or storage costs. The spot price of gold is $300 and the futures price for delivery in 1 year is $360. The annual interest rate is 10 percent. Is the preceding information mutually consistent? If not, how can investors exploit the situation for their own profit?
7   Suppose that oil in the spot market is selling for $30 per barrel. Oil futures for delivery in two years are quoted at $20 per barrel. The two-year spot interest rate is 8%. Explain the perfect market arbitrage to profit from this situation. In practice, what would prevent this arbitrage from occurring?
8   Investors can reduce their risk by using a futures market hedge to offset a spot market position. What happens to this risk? What are the consequences for the hedger?

9   A farmer plants enough wheat to harvest 1000 bushels. The cost of planting the wheat is $2.50 per bushel. On the harvest date, the wheat price will be one of three prices with equal probability: $2.00, $4.00, or $6.00. Compute the farmer's profit for each of these possibilities. The futures price for wheat is $3.80. Compute the farmer's profit for this price. When is hedging with futures the best choice for the farmer?

10 You buy gold in the spot market at $280 per ounce. You decide to hedge the gold position with a cross hedge in platinum futures. Suppose platinum futures are quoted at $400 per ounce. For every dollar that gold advances (or declines), platinum futures are likely to change by $1.25. Draw a profit profile for a one-to-one hedge – one ounce of short platinum futures for each ounce long spot gold. Then, derive the hedge ratio for a perfect hedge and draw the profit profile.

11 Look up the *Wall Street Journal* prices for gold futures. From the spot and futures prices for gold, determine the term structure of interest rates under the assumption of zero storage costs. Compare your answers with the yields on Treasury securities and explain the differences.

14

Bond Futures

Bond futures contracts allow market participants to agree to buy or sell bonds at delivery dates in the future. Investors who are long in bond futures are able to lock-in future lending interest rates. Investors taking short positions in bond futures are able to lock-in future borrowing interest rates. This chapter concentrates on Treasury bond futures contracts because these are widely traded. The analysis can be easily adapted to handle other bonds futures contracts.

Treasury Bond Futures

The Chicago Board of Trade (CBT) has a US Treasury bond futures contract calling for the delivery of $100,000 par value of Treasury bonds with at least 15 years to maturity or first call date, whichever is sooner. For a number of years, this so-called T-bond futures contract has been one of the most actively traded futures contracts. This contract is extremely attractive as a hedging tool to bond dealers, underwriters, banks, and other financial institutions.

Treasury bond futures are quoted per $100 of par value in 32nds of a dollar. The quote is a percentage of the par value of $100,000 per contract. As an example, if the quotation is 81–10, the dollar amount is $81,000 plus 10/32 of $1000, which is $312.50. Thus, a quote for Treasury bond futures of 81–10 translates into $81,312.50.

Futures price on the delivery date

On the delivery date, the futures price must equal the spot price of the deliverable commodity. If a particular bond is deliverable into the

T-bond futures contract, arbitrage forces the futures price to equal the spot market price. If the futures price is too high, the arbitrager shorts futures, buys the deliverable bond, and delivers the bond into the futures contract. If the futures price is too low, the arbitrager goes long futures and shorts the bond in the spot market; the bond acquired from the long futures position is used to cover the short position.

In practice, a sizable number of bonds are eligible for delivery into the T-bond futures contract. The large number of bonds makes it hard for anyone to manipulate prices. It also adds a number of complications covered later in this chapter. In the text, one deliverable bond is assumed for simplicity.

Futures price before the delivery date

The CBT Treasury bond futures contract is different from metals futures contracts because the underlying bond pays coupons. The coupon affects the futures price. Let us consider several cases. Initially, take the simple case of one deliverable bond and no marking-to-market (implying identical futures and forward prices).

Delivery in one year and deliverable bond matures in two years For this case, the futures cash flows are as shown in table 14.1.

The futures price, F_{BOND}, should be the time 1 value of the coupon and par values discounted at the forward interest rate $f_{0,2}$. That is,

$$F_{BOND} = \frac{c + Par}{1 + f_{0,2}} \tag{1}$$

where F_{BOND} = the futures price and $f_{0,2}$ is the forward interest rate for period 2. A little algebra indicates that

$$F_{BOND} = P_{0,2}(1 + R_{0,1}) - c \tag{2}$$

Table 14.1 Delivery in 1 year and 2-period bond

	Points in time		
	0	1 (delivery date)	2 (bond maturity)
Action	Contract signed	Futures price paid	Coupon + par value received
Cash flows	0	$-F_{BOND}$	$+c + Par$

where $P_{0,2}$ is the spot price of a 2-period bond and $R_{0,2}$ is the 2-period spot interest rate. The futures price is mathematically equivalent to the time 1 value of the current bond price, $P_{0,2}$, minus the coupon paid at time 1. The time 1 coupon is subtracted since the buyer of futures is not entitled to this coupon. The buyer of the futures contract is entitled only to the time 2 coupon and the par value.

As an example, assume the following term structure: $R_{0,1} = 4$ percent, $R_{0,2} = 8$ percent, implying that $f_{0,2} = 12.15$ percent. Suppose a deliverable bond has an \$8 coupon and \$100 par value. The current or spot price of the bond is \$100.28. Then,

$$F_{BOND} = \frac{108}{1.1215} = 100.28(1.04) - 8$$

$$= \$96.29 \tag{3}$$

Delivery in one year and deliverable bond matures in n years   The futures cash flows in this case are as shown in table 14.2. The buyer of the futures contract receives the coupons from time 2 until time n and the par value at time n. The futures price is the time 1 value of these cash flows.

$$F_{BOND} = \frac{c}{1+f_{0,2}} + \frac{c}{(1+f_{0,2})(1+f_{0,3})} + \cdots + \frac{c+Par}{(1+f_{0,2})(1+f_{0,3})\cdots(1+f_{0,n})} \tag{4}$$

The person who is long futures is entitled to receive the bond cash flows from time 2 through time n. To arrive at the time 1 value, each of these cash flows must be discounted by the appropriate forward interest rates. A little algebra indicates that the futures price may be expressed in terms of the current spot price of the bond as follows:

$$F_{BOND} = P_{0,n}(1 + R_{0,1}) - c \tag{5}$$

Table 14.2   Delivery in 1 year and n-period bond

	Points in time				
	0	1 (delivery date)	2	$\cdots$	n (bond maturity)
Action	Contract signed	Futures price paid	Coupon received	Coupon received	Coupon + par value received
Cash flows	0	$-F_{BOND}$	$+c$	$+c$	$+c+Par$

The futures price is mathematically equivalent to $P_{0,n}(1+R_{0,1})-c$. The intuition is that the buyer of futures pays the time 1 value of the bond less the value of the time 1 coupon, which is not received. As a numerical example, suppose the following term structure: $R_{0,1}=4$ percent, $f_{0,2}=f_{0,3}=8$ percent. Assume an $8 coupon and par value of $100. Then,

$$F_{BOND}=\frac{8}{1.08}+\frac{108}{(1.08)(1.08)}=103.85(1.04)-8=100 \qquad (6)$$

Delivery in d years and deliverable bond matures in n years The futures cash flows in this case are as shown in table 14.3. The buyer of the futures contract receives the coupons from time $d+1$ until time n and par value at time n. The futures price is the time d value of these cash flows. The forward price can be derived by looking at the time d value of each individual cash flow. The coupon c received at time $d+1$ must be discounted one period to time d at the forward rate $f_{0,d+1}$ for a time d value of $c/(1+f_{0,d+1})$. The coupon received at time $d+2$ has a value at time d of $c/(1+f_{0,d+1})(1+f_{0,d+2})$. In general:

$$F_{BOND}=\frac{c}{1+f_{0,d+1}}+\frac{c}{(1+f_{0,d+1})(1+f_{0,d+2})}+\cdots$$
$$\cdots+\frac{c+PAR}{(1+f_{0,d+1})(1+f_{0,d+2})\cdots(1+f_{0,n})} \qquad (7)$$

This equation is mathematically equivalent to the following:

$$F_{BOND}=(P_{0,n}-cA_{0,d})(1+R_{0,d})^d \qquad (8)$$

Table 14.3 Delivery in d years and n-period bond

				Points in time			
	0	1	$\cdots$	d (delivery date)	$d+1$	$\cdots$	n (bond maturity)
Action	Contract signed			Futures price paid	Coupon received	Coupon received	Coupon + par value received
Cash flows	0	0	0	$-F_{BOND}$	$+c$	$+c$	$+c+Par$

where $P_{0,n}$ is the spot price of an n-period bond, $A_{0,d}$ is the present value of an annuity of \$1 per period for d periods, and $R_{0,d}$ is the spot interest rate for d periods. The forward price is equal to the current spot price $P_{0,n}$ of a bond with coupon c and maturity n minus the annuity of \$$c$ of coupons from time 1 to time d (i.e. $cA_{0,d}$) times $[1 + R_{0,d}]^d$ to adjust for the fact that the cash flows are received at time d.

To illustrate, suppose the futures delivery date is in two years. The deliverable bond has a maturity of 4 years and a coupon rate of 8 percent. Assuming $R_{0,1}$ is 4 percent, $R_{0,2}$ is 6 percent, $R_{0,3}$ is 8 percent, $R_{0,4}$ is 10 percent, the current price of the bond is 94.93.[1] The futures price is:

$$F_{BOND} = \left[P_{0,4} - c \left(\frac{1}{1 + R_{0,1}} + \frac{1}{(1 + R_{0,2})^2} \right) \right] (1 + R_{0,2})^2$$

$$= [94.93 - 8(0.9615 + 0.8900)](1.06)^2 = 90.92 \qquad (9)$$

Hedging with Financial Futures

In a futures hedge, a spot position is (partially) offset with hedging in a futures position. The net position has reduced risk. The futures market allows many types of investors to transfer risks to other investors more willing to bear these risks.

There are many types of hedges. The ensuing discussion concentrates on short hedges, in which a long position in the spot market is offset by a short position in futures. Chapter 13 presented profit profile diagrams for short hedges. These may be used by any investor who has a long position in the spot market. Apart from small investors, many financial institutions might hedge, including underwriters, bond dealers, banks, insurance companies, and pension funds.

Short hedge for Treasury bond futures

Suppose an underwriter has purchased a bond issue with a \$100,000 par value for resale to the public. The underwriter purchases the bond expecting to be able to sell it for \$100,000. Because the issue must be registered with the SEC, the underwriter anticipates a two-week period between making a firm commitment to buy the bond and sale to the public. During this period, interest rates might rise considerably and the value of the underwriter's bond decline. To protect against this risk, suppose the underwriter shorts one contract of T-bond futures at 96–00.

Table 14.4   Gains and losses from a short hedge

		Points in time			
	0	1	$d=2$ (delivery date)	$d+1$ $\cdots$	n (bond maturity)
Action	Long spot & short futures	Sell spot & long futures			
Cash flows	$-P_{0,n}$ & $+F_0$	$+P_{1,n-1}$ & $-F_1$			

At the end of the two-week period, interest rates have risen and the underwriter is forced to sell the bonds at $95,000 for a $5000 loss. During the same period, the futures contract declines in value to 92–00, resulting in a gain of $4000 on the short futures position. The net loss on the hedge position is $1000. The underwriter has moderated the downside risk by having a partially offsetting position in futures.

Table 14.4 shows the gains and losses from a short hedge. $-P_{0,n}$ is the value of the spot position purchased at time 0, $P_{1,n-1}$ is the value of the spot position sold at time 1, $+F_0$ is the value of the futures position shorted at time 0, $-F_1$ is the value of the long futures position at time 1.

The net gain or loss on the hedge is

$$Net\ Gain\ (Loss) = -P_{0,n} + P_{1,n-1} + F_0 - F_1 \qquad (10)$$

In the numerical example,

$$Net\ Gain\ (Loss) = -100{,}000 + 95{,}000 + 96{,}000 - 92{,}000$$

$$= -1000 \qquad (11)$$

Hedging is a two-edged sword. Losses are reduced by hedging, but so are gains. If interest rates drop, the underwriter makes a profit on the bonds, but suffers a loss on the short futures position. The net gain is smaller, or negligible. Hedgers are willing to forgo both losses and gains because the hedger is risk-averse. For a hedger, the penalties from losses are greater than the advantages of gains. Large losses from a sharp increase in interest rates might bankrupt an underwriter. To avoid this adverse possibility, the hedger is willing to forgo large gains.

Hedges can be fine-tuned by changing the number of futures contracts in the hedge. In the underwriter hedge, the bond price changes $1.25 for every $1.00 change in the futures price. The hedge can be improved by shorting 1.25 futures contracts for every bond ($100,000 par) purchased.

The difference between the futures price and the spot price (i.e. $F - P$) has been called the basis (B). Note that the net gain (loss) on a hedge equals the change in the basis. That is,

$$Net\ Gain\ (Loss) = +F_0 - P_{0,n} - [+F_1 - F_0] = +B_0 - B_1$$

$$= basis\ change \qquad (12)$$

where B_0 is the basis at time 0 and B_1 is the basis at time 1. Hedges are effective if the change in the basis is relatively small. The hedge is perfect if the change in the basis is zero. Then the change in the futures and spot prices exactly offset.

Cheapest Deliverable Bond

The investor who is short CBT Treasury bond futures contracts is allowed to deliver any US Treasury bond with $100,000 par value. A delivered bond must also have at least 15 years to the smaller of maturity or first call date.

The purpose of having many bonds deliverable is to reduce the likelihood of a corner by increasing the total supply of deliverable securities. A **corner** occurs if one investor is able to purchase most of the deliverable supply of a commodity in the spot market and at the same time have large long positions in the futures markets. At the delivery date, the shorts are required to cover their positions either by purchasing the commodity in the spot market or by offsetting their futures market positions. To offset, the shorts would have to go long in futures. In either case, the shorts are at the mercy of the cornering investor, who is able to charge them a very high price to extricate themselves. Corners are illegal, and both the regulatory authorities (Commodity Futures Trading Commission) and the exchanges have the obligation and the power to break up corners. There are several things that an exchange can do to break a corner by the longs. First, the exchange can raise margin requirements. Second, the exchange can declare that there be trading for liquidation only. Then the longs cannot add to their positions and can only close out their positions with the shorts. Third, the exchange can determine a price and close out all positions at this price.

The Hunt brothers attempted to corner the silver futures market. The first step in this corner was acquiring large amounts of silver in the spot market at low prices. The second step was taking very large long positions in the futures market at rising prices. During a relatively short period, the spot and futures prices more than quintupled, resulting in enormous paper profits. At this point, the exchanges stepped in and increased margin requirements on futures positions. A sharp decline in both spot and futures prices followed, as the alleged cornering group was forced to liquidate some of their positions to meet margin requirements. The corner was foiled.

Invoice price

The long pays the short the invoice price for delivering a particular bond. The **invoice price** is equal to the settlement futures price times an **adjustment factor**. In trying to figure the best bond to deliver, the short has to do the following calculation for every bond:[2]

$$Proceeds = (F)(adj) - P$$

$$= \begin{bmatrix} futures \\ price \end{bmatrix} \begin{bmatrix} adjustment \\ factor \end{bmatrix} - \begin{bmatrix} spot \\ price \end{bmatrix}$$

(13)

where F is the settlement futures price, adj is the adjustment factor, and P is the market price of the bond. The best or **cheapest bond to deliver** from the short's viewpoint is the bond for which the proceeds in the preceding expression are the largest. In general, the proceeds are negative for all bonds. If the proceeds are positive, there are arbitrage profits from shorting futures and delivering the bond with positive proceeds. In equilibrium, all arbitrage opportunities should be eliminated, resulting in the net proceeds being zero or negative. The short tries to find the bond for which the proceeds are closest to zero; this minimizes the cost to deliver.

On the delivery date, the cheapest bond to deliver is the bond for which the proceeds are zero in frictionless markets. Setting proceeds equal to zero in the preceding expression and solving for the futures price implies that:

$$F = \frac{P_k}{adj_k}$$

$$\begin{bmatrix} futures \\ price\ on \\ delivery\ date \end{bmatrix} = \frac{[Spot\ price\ for\ cheapest\ deliverable]}{[adjustment\ factor\ for\ cheapest\ deliverable]}$$

(14)

In practice, longer-maturity bonds and/or low coupon bonds have been relatively cheap to deliver in the Treasury bond futures contract. The price of these cheap-to-deliver bonds has set the price of the futures contract. Typically, there are several bonds that are relatively cheap to deliver. This makes corners very difficult.

The adjustment factor

To establish a relative value in delivery, the Chicago Board of Trade uses an adjustment factor (adj) for each security. The adjustment factor is computed from the following formula:

$$adj = \frac{c/PAR}{(1.08)} = \frac{c/PAR}{(1.08)^2} + \cdots + \frac{c/PAR + 1.0}{(1.08)^n} \qquad (15)$$

$$adj = \left[\frac{c}{PAR} \right] \left[\begin{array}{c} Present\ value\ of \\ an\ annuity\ at\ 8\% \\ for\ n\ periods \end{array} \right] + \frac{1}{(1.08)^n} \qquad (16)$$

To compute the adjustment factor, the coupon rate (i.e. coupon divided by par) and an assumed par value of 1.0 are discounted at an 8 percent discount rate.[3] The value of the adjustment factor, adj, depends upon the coupon rate. If the annual coupon rate is 8 percent of par, adj equals 1.0. If the annual coupon rate is greater (less) than 8 percent, adj is greater (less) than 1.0. Table 14.5 illustrates the computation of the adjustment factor for 20-year bonds with coupon rates of 6 percent, 8 percent, and 10 percent and par values of $100. Note that the present value of a 20-period annuity at 8 percent is 9.8181 and $1/(1.08)^{20}$ equals 0.2145.

The short has the choice of bond to deliver. The adjustment factor attempts to adjust the invoice price for the relative worth of the bonds. Recall that the invoice price is the futures price times the adjustment factor. Consider the three preceding bonds. The 6 percent coupon bond has the lowest price. The amount that the short gets paid for delivering this bond (i.e. the invoice price) should reflect this lower value. If the highest coupon bond (10 percent) is delivered, the short should receive more money because this high coupon bond has a higher value. The invoice prices for the three bonds are computed in table 14.6, assuming that the settlement futures price is $100.

The preceding discussion can be clarified by the following example. From table 14.6, the invoice prices equal the bonds' market prices. This shows the objective of the adjustment procedure – to adjust the invoice price for the relative value of the bond delivered. In this particular

Table 14.5 The adjustment factor

Coupon (% rate)	Price ($)	Computation of adjustment factor
6	80.41	(0.06)(9.818) + 0.215 = 0.80408
8	100.00	(0.08)(9.818) + 0.215 = 1.00
10	119.68	(0.10)(9.818) + 0.215 = 1.1968

example, the invoice price equals the market price for every bond. In general, this is not true. Typically, bonds have invoice prices below their market prices. The shorts search for the best bond to deliver, the so-called cheapest to deliver. The cheapest bond to deliver has an invoice price very close to the market price of the bond. Frequently, the difference between the invoice price and the market is close to zero for many bonds. Then the deliverable supply of bonds is large and corners are hard to achieve.

Assume the bonds in table 14.7 can be delivered by an investor who is short in Treasury bond futures. In perfect markets, the cheapest bond to deliver has the smallest ratio of bond price to adjustment factor. The computations in table 14.8 use annual coupons discounted at 8 percent annually to compute the adjustment factors. The lowest ratio of price/adjustment factor is for bond 4. The equilibrium futures price equals this ratio of 90.474566. The "Net proceeds" table (table 14.9) shows the invoice price, market price and the proceeds from delivering each bond. The invoice price for each bond equals the equilibrium futures price (90.474566) times the adjustment factor for each bond. For example, for bond 1 the invoice price is (90.474566)(0.82881).

For the cheapest bond to deliver, bond 4, the invoice price exactly equals the market price of the bond. Therefore, the proceeds from delivering that bond are zero. Every other bond has a lower invoice price

Table 14.6 Invoice price versus market price

Coupon (% rate)	Invoice price = (futures price) × (adjustment factor)	Market price ($)
6	(100)(0.80408) = 80.41	80.41
8	(100)(1.0) = 100.00	100.00
10	(100)(1.1968) = 119.68	119.68

Table 14.7 Example of five deliverable bonds

Bond	Maturity (years)	Coupon (annual, $)	Market price ($)
1	15	6	90.50
2	18	7	92.25
3	21	8	96.375
4	24	9	100.00
5	30	8.50	101.00

Table 14.8 Computing adjustment factor

Bond	Adjustment factor	Price/adjustment	
1	0.82881	109.19269	
2	0.906283	101.78939	
3	1.00000	96.375	
4	1.105283	90.474566	←cheapest equilibrium price
5	1.05593	95.6503	

Table 14.9 Net proceeds

Bond	Invoice price ($)	Market price ($)	Proceeds from delivery ($)
1	74.986025	90.50	−15.51
2	81.995561	92.25	−10.25
3	90.474566	96.375	−5.90
4	100.00	100.00	0.0
5	95.5348	101.00	−5.47

than market price. For these bonds, the proceeds from delivering the bond are negative, implying that these bonds are inferior to deliver.

Other Aspects of the Delivery Process

The delivery process for CBT Treasury bond futures has some other interesting complications. As with most futures contracts, there is a delivery month.[4] The short position has the option to deliver at any point during the month.

In the beginning of the month, the settlement price for that day is used for deliveries initiated on that day. On the seventh business day before the end of a delivery month, the settlement futures price is determined and this price is used for computing the invoice price for deliveries made in the rest of this delivery month. The fixing of the futures price gives the short an option to choose the day for delivery. This delivery option may turn out to be quite valuable. If the futures price is fixed at 90 seven days before the end of the month and spot prices subsequently decline, the short may be able to buy a deliverable bond for much less than its invoice price and deliver it for a profit. If bond prices subsequently rise during the last seven business days, the short would have to buy a bond at a high price and suffer a loss at delivery.

During most of the delivery month, the settlement futures price is set every day at 3 p.m. central time. The short has the option to deliver until 8 p.m. If the short chooses not to deliver, the same position is simply maintained until the next day, when the same choice is made. The option to initiate delivery between 3 p.m. and 8 p.m. has value to the short, since the trading of bonds continues after the futures markets close.[5] This option is called the **wildcard option**. If bond prices go down after 3 p.m. and the adjustment factor on the cheapest deliverable bond is greater than 1.0, the short's option has positive value, and delivery may be desirable. It has been suggested that this wildcard option tends to push the 3 p.m. futures price below the price that would prevail without the wildcard option.

Summary

Treasury bonds futures contracts are widely traded. The futures price for delivery on a particular delivery date equals the coupon payments plus par value discounted back to the delivery date at the appropriate forward interest rates. Treasury bonds futures are widely used to hedge spot positions by investment banking firms, bond dealers, banks, and mortgage brokers. Treasury bond futures allow the short to deliver one of several bonds. The short will choose the cheapest bond to deliver. This cheapest to deliver bond sets the futures price.

Notes

1   The price is $8(0.9615 + 0.8900 + 0.7938 + 0.6830) + 100(0.6830)$.
2   This overlooks accrued interest. The long must pay the short the invoice price plus accrued interest. The short delivers a bond which entitles him to the accrued interest. Technically, the accrued interest should be added to the invoice price and added to the bond price. But, these two terms cancel.
3   In practice, n represents the number of quarters, rounded down to the nearest quarter from the futures delivery date, until the shorter of the bond's maturity or first call date. In addition, in practice the adjustment factor is computed using semiannual coupons discounted at 4 percent semiannually. We overlook these technicalities.
4   Treasury bill futures have a single delivery date.
5   The actual delivery process covers three business days. On day 1, the short position gives notice that delivery is being initiated. Actual delivery of the commodity and payment of the invoice price occurs on day 3.

Questions and Problems

1 A bond futures contract with one deliverable bond has a maturity date in 2 years, par value of $100, and annual coupon of $8. If the futures delivery date is in 1 year, determine the futures price if

   (a) $R_{0,1} = R_{0,2} = 8$ percent.
   (b) $R_{0,1} = 5$ percent, $R_{0,2} = 10$ percent.

2 Consider a bond futures contract with one deliverable bond having a maturity date in 3 years, par value of $100, and annual coupon of $8. If the futures delivery date is in 1 year, determine the futures price if

   (a) $R_{0,1} = R_{0,2} = R_{0,3} = 8$ percent.
   (b) $R_{0,1} = 5$ percent, $R_{0,2} = 7$ percent, $R_{0,3} = 9$ percent.

3 A bond futures contract has one deliverable bond with a maturity date in 3 years, par value of $100, and annual coupon of $8. If the futures delivery date is in 2 years, determine the futures price if

   (a) $R_{0,1} = R_{0,2} = R_{0,3} = R_{0,4} = 8$ percent.
   (b) $R_{0,1} = 5$ percent, $R_{0,2} = 7$ percent, $R_{0,3} = 9$ percent.

4 Suppose a bond futures contract has one deliverable bond with a maturity date in 30 years, par value of $100, price of $95, and annual coupon of $8. If the futures delivery date is in 1 year, determine the futures price if $R_{0,1} = 4$ percent.

5 Assume that the price quotation of the CBT Treasury bond futures contract changes from 96–14 to 97–09. What are the gains and losses to the short and long as a result of marking-to-market for 1 contract with $100,000 par value?

6 An individual owns a 21-year maturity bond with an annual coupon of 10 percent, a face value of $100,000, and a price of $95,000. To protect against rising interest rates, this individual shorts one CBT Treasury bond futures contract with a delivery date 2 years hence and a futures price of 92–16. In the course of the next year, interest rates change. The bond price drops to $88,000 and the futures price drops to 86–16.

   (a) Overlooking bond coupon and marking-to-market, compute the gains or losses on the bond position, the futures position, and the net position.
   (b) Suppose we knew the relationship between the futures and spot prices. For every dollar change in the futures, the spot price changed $1.10. Determine the optimal hedge ratio.

7 A bond dealer owns a 21-year maturity bond with an annual coupon of 5 percent, a face value of $100,000, and a price of $95,000. To hedge

against rising interest rates, the dealer shorts one CBT Treasury bond futures contract with a delivery date 2 years hence and a futures price of 92–16. In the course of the next year, interest rates drop. The futures price goes to 97–16. At what interest rate on the bond would the hedge just break even?

8   Suppose that there are three deliverable bonds for a bond futures contract with delivery date in one year. Each bond has 2 periods until maturity. A bond with a 6 percent coupon has a price of $94.72. A bond with a 7 percent coupon has a price of $96.48. A bond with an 8 percent coupon has a price of $98.24. Suppose that the quote on the futures contract is 99. Which is the cheapest bond to deliver? If these three bonds were the only bonds deliverable, what would be the equilibrium futures price?

15

Other Derivatives

This chapter briefly describes some of the more common types of derivative financial instruments not covered earlier. These include floating-rate notes, interest rate swaps, convertible bonds, and preferred stock.

While many new types of securities have been introduced, only a portion have lasted. Lasting security types provide some significant and fundamental value to a sizable group of issuers or investors. The advantages of new instruments include one or more of the following. First, innovations may reduce transactions costs. Second, innovations may allow investors to create a new type of security which divides the cash flows from one investment into a set of derivative securities. The resulting derivatives may appeal to a new group of investors. The total value of the derivatives may be greater than the value of the underlying components. An example is the decomposition of Treasury bonds into Treasury strips. Third, new instruments (e.g. options) may allow the transfer or limiting of risks. Fourth, some products (e.g. futures contracts) allow investors to diversify more efficiently. Fifth, some new financial instruments are responses to changes in tax laws and regulations.

Floating-Rate Notes

A floating-rate note is a bond with a variable interest rate. The coupon on the floating-rate note is tied to a particular short-term interest rate. Periodically, perhaps every six months, the coupon on the bond is reset to equal the short-term rate plus x percent.

As an example, suppose the bond's coupon is tied to the 6-month Treasury bill rate plus 3 percent. When the bond is issued, the Treasury bill rate is 6 percent and the bond pays a coupon of 9 percent.

Six months later, the Treasury bill rate is 4.5 percent; the bond's coupon is reset to 7.5 percent.

A floating-rate note is a long-term bond with a short-term interest rate. A floating-rate note is a substitute for repeated short-term loans. To the issuing firm, the advantage of a floating-rate note is avoidance of the transactions costs of repeatedly rolling-over the short-term loan. To the bond buyer, the floating-rate note has low price risk. Since the coupon is reset periodically (for example, every six months) to bring the bond price close to par, the bond price is unlikely to depart markedly from par during the time between the reset dates.

The default premium for a long-term floating-rate loan differs from the default premium for a sequence of short-term loans. With repeated short-term loans, the default risk premium in the new loans is renegotiated at each rollover. If the firm becomes riskier, the default risk component of the interest rate rises. With a floating-rate instrument, the default risk premium is set initially and not changed. Thus, a floating-rate bond combines the default premium of a long-term bond with the sensitivity of a short-term bond to changes in the default-free interest rate. At the issue date, rational lenders incorporate all available information concerning possible future changes in the issuer's default risk. These anticipations become part of the permanent default risk premium.

The periodic resetting of the bond's coupon brings the bond price to par if the default risk of the firm remains unchanged. If the market perceives new information about default risk, the bond price does not adjust to par. For example, consider again the floating-rate bond where the coupon equals the 6-month Treasury bill rate plus a 3 percent default premium. If the default risk of the firm increases so that a new short-term note would have a 5 percent default premium, resetting of the floating rate's coupon does not bring the market price to par but instead somewhat below par to reflect the higher default premium. As you might expect, this discount increases as the bond's maturity gets longer.

Another way to engineer bond cash flows is through the use of reset notes, which are a special variety of variable-rate notes. With reset notes, the coupon is reset periodically (perhaps every two years) by an investment banker to bring the market price to par. Thus, if the default risk increases, the reset coupon reflects the higher default risk. After resetting, the bond sells at par. With a standard floating-rate note, the default premium is fixed; after resetting to reflect changes in the default-free interest rate, the bond price can deviate from par.

Interest Rate Swaps

An interest rate swap is an agreement to exchange the cash flows from debt obligations with different maturities. In a typical interest rate swap, one firm borrows long-term. The second firm borrows at a floating(variable) rate. Then the two firms agree to swap the interest payments. This is a fixed/floating rate or "plain vanilla" swap. The interest payments are swapped but the principal payments are not. Thus, if one party defaults, the default involves the interest payments only. This reduces the risks to all parties.

In general, a commercial bank or an investment bank serves as an interest rate swap dealer as shown in figure 15.1. The term **counterparty** is used to describe the participants. Typically, the fixed-rate borrower swaps with a dealer as counterparty. In turn, the dealer swaps with the floating-rate borrower as counterparty. The dealer makes a commission for carrying out both ends of the swap.

Floating-rate loans are tied to a widely used interest rate index, for example, the London Interbank Offer Rate (LIBOR). LIBOR is the rate at which Eurocurrency deposits are exchanged between banks. The floating rate might be expressed as LIBOR plus 0.50 percent.

A simple (or plain vanilla) interest rate swap is shown in figure 15.1. Assume that firms L and S can borrow on the terms shown in table 15.1.

Firm L has a 2 percent advantage borrowing fixed-rate and a 1 percent advantage borrowing floating-rate. Suppose firm L borrows long-term at the fixed rate of 9 percent and swaps with the swaps dealer. The swaps dealer pays firm L 9.15 percent and firm L pays the swaps dealer LIBOR plus 0.10 percent. The total interest payments paid and

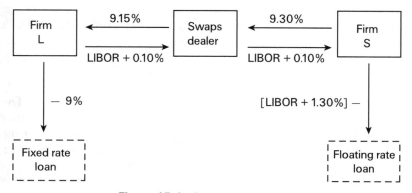

Figure 15.1 Interest rate swap

Table 15.1   Fixed and floating rates for firms L and S

	Firm L	Firm S
Fixed rate	9%	11%
Floating rate	LIBOR + 0.30%	LIBOR + 1.30%

Table 15.2   Interest paid and received by firm L in the swap

Pays interest on long-term fixed-rate bond	−9%
Receives fixed rate from swaps dealer	9.15%
Pays floating rate to swaps dealer	−[LIBOR + 0.10%]
Net	−[LIBOR − 0.05%]

Table 15.3   Interest paid and received by firm S in the swap

Pays interest on short-term floating-rate loan	−[LIBOR + 1.30%]
Pays fixed rate to the swaps dealer	−9.30%
Receives floating rate from the swaps dealer	+LIBOR + 0.10%
Net	−10.50%

received by firm L are shown in table 15.2. As a result of the swap, firm L has a net position of a floating-rate loan at LIBOR minus 0.05 percent. Firm L saves 0.35 percent compared to borrowing directly at the floating rate of LIBOR + 0.30 percent.

In figure 15.1, firm S borrows floating rate at LIBOR plus 1.30 percent. Firm S swaps with the swaps dealer agreeing to pay 9.30 percent fixed rate and receive from the dealer LIBOR + 0.10 percent. The cash flows are shown in table 15.3. The swap results in a net fixed-rate loan for firm S at the interest rate of 10.50 percent, a saving of 0.50 percent compared to a direct fixed-rate interest rate of 11 percent.

The swaps dealer

The swaps dealer benefits by a commission of 0.15 percent. The commission compensates the dealer for the costs of matching the parties in the swap. In addition, the commission compensates the dealer for the risk of default by the counterparties. If there is a default, the dealer replaces the defaulting party by a new counterparty.[1]

The dealer's risk of default depends upon which counterparty defaults and the course of interest rates since the swap was originated. Suppose firm L defaults. Firm L is supposed to pay the dealer LIBOR + 0.10 percent (floating rate) and the dealer pays firm L 9.15 percent (fixed rate). If interest rates have not changed since the swap was originated, firm L is simply replaced by another firm; the dealer is unaffected except for transactions costs. If interest rates have gone down since the swap was issued, the dealer gains since the dealer can pay less than 9.15 percent to the new counterparty.[2] If interest rates have risen, the dealer loses. For example, the new counterparty may be paid 9.50 percent by the dealer. The dealer loses 0.35 percent, the difference between 9.50 percent and 9.15 percent.

Suppose firm S defaults. The dealer is supposed to pay firm S LIBOR + 0.10 percent (floating rate) and receive 9.30 percent (fixed-rate). If interest rates rise, firm S is replaced with a new counterparty paying more than 9.30 percent to the dealer; the dealer gains. If interest rates decline, a new counterparty paying less than 9.30 percent is found and the dealer loses.

Many swaps dealers are commercial banks. Bank regulators are concerned about the potential impact upon the entire bank's financial condition if widespread defaults occur in the swaps portfolio of a commercial bank. The swaps dealer loses if interest rates rise and companies such as L (which pay the dealer floating rate) default or if interest rates fall and companies such as S (which pay the dealer fixed rate) default. The dealer can reduce the risk by diversifying the swaps portfolio across many unrelated counterparties.

Reasons for interest rate swaps

The market for interest rate swaps is huge. Over one trillion dollars of par value of bonds have been swapped in the US alone. Several explanations are offered for the growing popularity of swaps.

Swaps are claimed to have a comparative advantage. Referring to the example in figure 15.1 and table 15.1, firm L has an absolute advantage in both long-term fixed-rate debt and in floating-rate debt. By borrowing fixed-rate where firm L enjoys a comparative advantage, and by swapping, both firms enjoy lower borrowing costs.

Market imperfections are a possible cause of comparative advantage. Market imperfections allow firm L to borrow at a favorable fixed rate. Although firm L really wants to borrow short-term, it can reduce its costs by borrowing fixed-rate and swapping. While the market imperfections – comparative advantage argument can explain some individual swaps, imperfections widespread enough to generate over one trillion dollars of swaps seem doubtful.

Low transactions costs of swaps may induce firms to swap rather than refinance their existing debt. Suppose a firm has an existing debt issue.

Because of changed circumstances, the firm wants to retire this issue and replace it with a different issue. This procedure involves considerable transactions costs. A cheaper alternative is to swap the existing debt for a desired debt position. If the commission paid to the swap dealer is sufficiently small, swapping is cheaper.

Complicated swaps contracts allow some firms to significantly alter their capital structures. For example, many callable bonds have a period of call deferment. If interest rates fall during this call deferment period, the firm is unable to call the bond and realize refunding benefits. The firm can make a tender offer for the bonds. Tender offers have two drawbacks – the refunding benefits must be shared with the bond-holders and transactions costs are incurred. A lower-cost alternative may be to engage in a forward swap. With a forward swap, the swapping of cash flows does not begin until some future date.

Convertible Bonds

A sizable number of corporate bonds are convertible into common stock at the option of the bondholder. The bond indenture explains the conversion terms. In addition, the bonds are usually callable at par plus a call premium. A convertible bond is in-the-money if the stock value of the bond exceeds the call price. It is out-of-the-money if the stock value is less than the call price. The call feature is included to allow the firm to force conversion into common stock. Forced conversion works in the following way. Suppose a convertible bond has a call price of $110 for a $100 par value. If the value of the bond as stock is $150, calling in the bond at $110 gives the convertible bondholders the choice of $110 in cash or common stock which can be immediately sold for $150. Rational bondholders prefer to convert.

Conversion can be forced only if the bond is in-the-money. Call of an out-of-the-money convertible induces the bondholders to turn in their bonds at the call price. Sometimes voluntary conversion occurs if the convertible is in-the-money and the dividend yield on the stock exceeds the current yield on the convertible.

Figure 15.2 shows the relationship between the stock value, the straight bond value, and the price of the convertible. The stock value is initially below the par value and the stock value is assumed to grow over time. The straight bond value gradually approaches the par value as the bond gets closer to maturity. The call price declines over time to the par value. As the stock value rises above the call price, the premium of the convertible over the bond value declines and the market price of the convertible approaches the stock value.

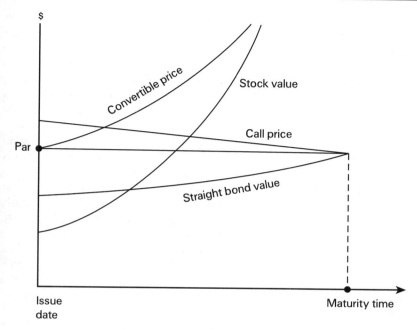

Figure 15.2 Convertible bonds

The market price of the convertible must exceed the higher of the straight bond value or the stock value. Otherwise, arbitrage occurs. For example, suppose the stock value is $115 and the present value of the coupons and par is $100. The convertible must sell for at least $115. If it sold for $110, an arbitrager could buy the convertible for $110, convert it, and sell the common stock for $115 – a risk-free profit of $5.

Why issue convertibles?

In an efficient market, securities are fairly priced. At the margin, there is no advantage or disadvantage to issuing a convertible. Consequently, one argument for convertibles is that they have no disadvantage. Why not issue them?

Other arguments concerning convertibles focus on asymmetric information. The managers of the firm may have superior information compared to outside investors and find some advantage from convertibles. One possibility is that negative private information is available to the management. By issuing convertibles, the firm is able to sell common stock at an inflated price.

Another possible asymmetric information argument is that positive private information is available to the management.[3] Suppose the managers are aware of a great new product for which the firm has a competitive advantage. The new product will increase sales and earnings in the future; the firm will have a high growth rate. Since the security markets are unaware of these favorable prospects, the current stock price does not reflect the true value of the stock. Selling stock at the current price is unwise.

Since the typical convertible is issued when the stock value is substantially less than par, issuing a convertible allows the firm to effectively sell stock at a higher price. For example, suppose the value of the convertible as stock is only 60 percent of par when the bond is issued at par. With the growth opportunities incorporated, the value is actually double, 120 percent of par. Issuing the convertible allows the firm to effectively sell stock at a price above the current market value.

When convertible bonds are issued, the stock price tends to decline somewhat. This evidence is consistent with the view that issuing convertibles is a negative signal to the market. This evidence supports the position that convertibles are issued when the management has negative information.

A substantial literature examines the best time to call a convertible. In perfectly efficient markets, the convertible can be called as soon as the stock value reaches the call price. In practice, most convertibles are called long after this point. Several explanations have been offered. First, there may be no real disadvantage in leaving the convertible outstanding. In addition, the firm has the advantage of the tax deductibility of the interest on the convertible. Second, the call of a convertible bond may force down the stock value below the call price. Then, bondholders will not convert but instead redeem their bonds for the call price. To avoid this possibility, firms may wait until the stock value is well above the call price. When an issue of convertibles is called, the call is often backed by an underwriter who guarantees conversion to common stock.

Bonds with detachable warrants

Some bond issues include a straight bond with a detachable long-term call option, or warrant. When a warrant is exercised, the exercise price must be paid. For some warrants, exercise requires payment of the exercise price in cash. Many warrants allow the bond from which they were detached to be presented in lieu of a cash exercise price. If the warrant can be exercised by presenting the bond, the package of a bond with a detachable warrant is virtually the same as a convertible bond.

LYONs

A LYON (which stands for a Liquid Yield Option Note) is a corporate zero-coupon, convertible, callable, and puttable bond. Since a LYON is a zero-coupon bond, the interest accrues. Consequently, the call price and the put price must increase over time as the interest accrues. Each issue of LYONs has a schedule of call prices and a schedule of put prices. Since the LYON is a zero-coupon bond, the minimum share price for which holders would convert to stock changes over time. LYONs appeal to a subset of investors who would like to have an option to convert to common stock if the common does well, who want to own a zero-coupon bond without reinvestment risk, and who favor a put option as protection against a deterioration of the issuer's credit standing.

Preferred Stock

Preferred stock is a hybrid – somewhere between a bond and a stock. Preferred stock pays dividends instead of interest. The amount of the dividend is specified. If the dividend is not paid, the firm is not in default. The dividend is "in arrears," that is, owed with cumulative interest.[4] The firm cannot pay common stock dividends until all preferred dividends and arrearages are paid. If the dividend is not paid, the preferred stockholders may get voting rights for the board of directors.

In the event of a bankruptcy, preferred stockholders have a prior claim on the firm's assets ahead of common stockholders. The order of priorities is bondholders first, then preferred stockholders. Common stockholders have a residual claim on the firm's assets.

Preferred dividends are not tax-deductible for corporate income tax purposes. In contrast, interest on bonds is deductible for corporate income tax purposes. Because of this difference in tax deductibility, preferred stock occurs largely in regulated industries, such as electrical utilities. Apparently, regulated firms are able to pass on the higher after-tax cost of preferred stock to their customers.

Convertible preferred stock is preferred stock that is convertible into common stock. Convertible preferred is very similar to convertible debt, except that preferred stock pays dividends and bonds pay interest.

Summary

This chapter discusses several specialized financial instruments which have low transactions costs or allow the trading of risks. Floating-rate securities have coupon rates tied to a particular short-term interest rate. The borrower bears the risk of changes in the short-term default-free interest rate.

Interest rate swaps allow borrowers to trade debt obligations of different maturities. They may allow some firms to take advantage of relatively low borrowing rates. In some cases, swapping of debt obligations is cheaper than refinancing.

Convertible bonds are, in essence, a combination of a straight bond and a call option. Growing firms may be able to effectively sell common stock above the current market price by issuing convertibles.

Notes

1   The dealer can also sue the defaulting party and may recover part of any loss incurred.
2   Default by firm L is unlikely after a drop in interest rates.
3   The arguments of positive and negative private information are contradictory. They could logically apply for different firms issuing convertibles, but not for the same firm.
4   The typical preferred is cumulative. Some preferred is noncumulative.

Questions and Problems

1   Describe a floating-rate note. There are two components of an interest rate – changes in the general level of interest rates and changes in the default risk of a particular issuer. How does each of these affect the interest rate on floating-rate debt? How does a reset note differ from a floating-rate note?
2   Explain the reasons why firms might swap their debt obligations.
3   Describe the impact of changing interest rates upon the default risk of a swaps dealer.
4   What are the possible motivations behind issuing convertible bonds?
5   Describe the differences between preferred stock and bonds.

16

Exchange Rates and International Investments

The purpose of this chapter is to provide an understanding of the relationships between exchange rates and international investing. The factors determining currency exchange rates are discussed, as well as the impacts of exchange rates upon international trade and investment.

International Investment

International investment increases portfolio diversification if the investment returns in different countries are less than perfectly correlated. Internationally diversified portfolios have lower risk than purely domestic portfolios, if the economies in individual countries are affected by some factors unique to those countries. Returns on international investments are affected by changes in exchange rates. The ensuing discussion examines the impact of exchange rates in detail.

Besides the risk of changing exchange rates, investing in foreign securities has several special costs and risks. First, acquiring information about investments in other countries is more difficult and expensive than obtaining information about domestic investments because of distance and language differences. Travel to foreign countries to acquire information can be quite expensive. Understanding foreign information requires fluency in a foreign language or ready access to a translator. Second, financial disclosure standards differ by country. In some foreign countries, firms are neither required nor expected to reveal nearly as much information to the public as in the United States. Third, accounting definitions are country-specific. As an example, earnings may mean quite different things in individual countries.

Fourth, international investors face political risks as governments and their policies change. In some countries the risk of radical political change is quite considerable. A recent example is South Africa, a country beset with major racial conflicts. The resolution of these conflicts will significantly alter the business environment. Clearly, international inves- tors with funds committed to South African firms bear some of this risk.

Fifth, countries that have balance of payments problems may impose exchange controls in the future. These controls typically limit the transfer of funds out of the country. The chance of exchange controls introduces the possibility that funds invested in a particular country may be difficult or impossible to get out of that country.

Exchange Rates

Each country has its own currency, which is used domestically for pur- chases of goods and services. When someone wants to purchase a good or service from another country or transfer funds to another country, the domestic currency is exchanged for the currency of the foreign country. The rate at which one currency is traded for another currency is called the exchange rate.

There are two ways of quoting exchange rates shown in table 16.1. First, the exchange rate can be expressed as the number of units of foreign currency per unit of domestic currency. For example, 125 yen equals $1 or 0.67 pounds equals $1. Second, the exchange rate can be expressed as the number of units of domestic currency per unit of foreign currency. For example, $1/125 equals 1 yen or $1.50 equals 1 pound. Either way of quoting exchange rates is conceptually OK. As a matter of custom, some exchange rates are quoted one way and some the other way. The US dollar/Japanese yen exchange rate is usually quoted as yen per dollar. The US dollar/British pound exchange rate is usually quoted as dollars per pound.

Table 16.1   Quoting exchange rates

	Number of units of foreign currency per unit of domestic currency	Number of units of domestic currency per unit of foreign currency
Japanese currency	125 yen = $1	$1/125 = 1 yen
British currency	1/1.50 pounds = $1	$1.50 = 1 pound

The rest of this chapter quotes the exchange rate in terms of the number of units of foreign currency per dollar (i.e. yen per dollar, pounds per dollar, pesos per dollar). The exchange rate between two countries is denoted by X.

Impact of Changing Exchange Rates on Imports and Exports

A currency depreciates in value if fewer units of that currency are required to buy the same number of units of foreign currency. Suppose the exchange rate is 125 yen equals $1. Then the dollar depreciates to 100 yen per $1. That is, a dollar buys fewer yen.

If the exchange rate changes, the relative costs of imports and exports change. To illustrate, suppose there are originally 125 yen to $1, and then the dollar depreciates to 100 yen to $1. The impact upon United States exports and imports is shown in table 16.2.

The depreciation of the US dollar makes exports from the US to Japan cheaper; residents of Japan pay fewer yen for a US cigar. Imports from the Japan to the US are more expensive; a US resident, buying a radio made in Japan, pays a higher price for the radio after the dollar depreciates. Depreciation of the dollar is appreciation of the yen. Exports from Japan to the US are more expensive and imports into Japan are cheaper.

Exchange Rates and Investment Returns

Changes in exchange rates affect the realized rates of return on foreign asset holdings. Consider a simple case where the one-period spot interest rate in the US is 6 percent and the one-period spot interest rate in Japan is 8 percent. A US investor has $1 and two ways to invest it. See table 16.3.

1 Invest in US dollar-denominated bonds. At the end of one year, the investor has $1.06.

Table 16.2 Impact of depreciation in US dollar on US exports and imports

	Exports from US to Japan One cigar costs $1	Imports from Japan to US One radio costs 12,500 yen
Time 0: 125 yen = $1	1 cigar costs 125 yen	1 radio costs $100
Time 1: 100 yen = $1	1 cigar costs 100 yen	1 radio costs $125

Table 16.3   Investing in US versus Japan

	Time 0	Time 1
Invest in US bonds	$1	$1.06
At time 0, exchange for yen and invest in Japanese bonds	125 yen	(125)(1.08)/100
At time 1, exchange yen for dollars		= $1.35

2   Exchange $1 for 125 yen at the exchange rate of 125 yen per dollar Invest the yen at 8 percent for one year with a resulting value o 135 yen. Convert the yen to dollars. The dollar value of these yer depends upon the exchange rate in one year. If the dollar depreciate: and the exchange rate changes to 100 yen per dollar, the 135 yen car be exchanged for $1.35 for a rate of return of 35 percent. The depre ciation in the dollar has raised the rate of return in US dollar terms.

Suppose that the rate of return on the foreign investment strategy ir Japan is denoted by ROR_{FOR}. Then,

$$1 + ROR_{FOR} = \frac{(125)(1.08)}{100} \qquad (1$$

Rewrite this as

$$1 + ROR_{FOR} = \frac{(125)}{100} + (0.08)\left[\frac{125}{100}\right]$$

$$= 1.25 + (0.08)[1.25] \qquad (2$$

Subtract 1 from both sides to arrive at the rate of return on the foreign investment strategy.

$$ROR_{FOR} = 0.25 + (0.08)[1.25]$$

$$= 0.25 + 0.10 = 0.35 \qquad (3$$

There are two components of the return on this investment. Twenty-five percent is earned because the dollar value of the principal increases a: the dollar depreciates. The Japanese bond earns 8 percent interest anc there is an additional gain of 2 percent because of the depreciation o the dollar.

In general, a US investor gains from the foreign investment strategy i the dollar depreciates. If the dollar appreciates, the investor has a foreigr xchange loss. These results can be shown by the following expression.

$$ROR_{FOR} = \left[\frac{X_{0,s}}{X_{1,s}} - 1\right] + R_{0,J}\left[\frac{X_{0,s}}{X_{1,s}}\right]$$

$$= [\% \text{ change of dollar value of principal}]$$
$$+ [\text{Foreign currency return}][\text{Exchange rate adjustment}] \quad (4)$$

where

$X_{0,s}$ = the spot exchange rate at time 0.
$X_{1,s}$ = the spot exchange rate at time 1.
$R_{0,J}$ = the one-period spot interest rate in Japan
(observed at time 0).
ROR_{FOR} = rate of return on the foreign investment strategy.

f the dollar depreciates, the time 0 exchange rate is greater than the ime 1 exchange rate, $X_{0,s} > X_{1,s}$, and

$$\frac{X_{0,s}}{X_{1,s}} > 1, \quad \frac{X_{0,s}}{X_{1,s}} - 1 > 0 \quad (5)$$

If the dollar depreciates, the first term on the righthand side of quation (4) $(X_{0,s}/X_{1,s} - 1)$ is positive and adds to the US dollar return rom the exchange rate gain on the principal. The second term in quation (4) is the foreign currency return $(R_{0,J})$ times an additional gain $X_{0,s}/X_{1,s})$ if the US dollar depreciates.

If the dollar appreciates, the first term in equation (4) is negative because the dollar value of the principal decreases. The second term is ositive, but its size depends upon the size of the foreign currency return $R_{0,J})$ times the ratio of the exchanges rates $(X_{0,s}/X_{1,s})$, which is less than if the dollar appreciates. The sum of the two terms can be negative. little algebra shows when the return on the foreign investment strategy s negative.

$$ROR_{FOR} < 0 \quad \text{when } X_{1,s} > X_{0,s}(1 + R_{0,J}) \quad (6)$$

n our example, the total return on the foreign investment strategy is egative if the time 1 exchange rate exceeds 135 yen to $1 US, i.e. 125)(1.08).

Inflation, Interest Rates, and Exchange Rates

Chapter 1 discussed the link between inflation rates and interest rates. n the case of complete certainty and no taxes, the inflation rate is added n to the interest rate so that lenders preserve their purchasing power.

The rate of inflation in individual countries affects the exchange rate Suppose we compare two countries. According to **relative purchasing power parity**, the currency of the country with the higher inflation rate depreciates by the difference in inflation rates. Let p_{US} = the US inflation rate, and p_{FOR} = the inflation rate in the foreign country. According to relative purchasing power parity:

$$rate\ of\ depreciation\ of\ US\ dollar = p_{US} - p_{FOR}$$

$$= \begin{bmatrix} US \\ inflation \\ rate \end{bmatrix} - \begin{bmatrix} Foreign \\ inflation \\ rate \end{bmatrix} \quad (7$$

If the US inflation rate exceeds the foreign inflation rate, the US dollar depreciates by the difference in inflation rates. If the foreign inflation rate exceeds the US inflation rate, the US dollar appreciates (i.e. negative depreciation).

The total impact of inflation upon foreign investment depends on its impact upon the foreign interest rate and upon the change in the exchange rate. To simplify things, suppose that the US inflation is zero If the interest rate in the foreign country increases by the inflation rate and the US dollar appreciates by the foreign inflation, the net impact upon the foreign investment strategy is zero.

In practice, relative purchasing power parity does not hold precisely Interest rates typically do not increase by exactly the anticipated inflation rates, and exchange rates do not change by the difference in exchange rates. However, countries with high inflation rates tend to have both high interest rates and high rates of depreciation in their currencies.

Spot and Forward Exchange Rates

Spot exchange rates are time 0 transactions. Forward exchange rates are contracts signed at time 0 for an exchange to take place in the future In a forward contract, both parties agree to set the price today for delivery at a future date.

Forward foreign exchange contracts allow investors and businesses to lock-in values in another currency. Imagine a firm expecting to receive $1,000,000 in 90 days and planning to invest this money in Japan. If the firm waits 90 days before exchanging dollars for yen, the exchange rate might change adversely. For example, the dollar may depreciate from 125 yen to one dollar to a new rate of 120 yen to one dollar. At this new rate, the firm receives fewer yen for each dollar and the investment has reduced profitability. Instead of waiting 90 days, the firm can buy yen in 90 days with a forward contract. A forward exchange contract allows the firm to lock-in immediately an exchange rate for 90 days into the future. The forward contract allows the firm to avoid the risk of an adverse change in the exchange rate. The forward contract is a two-edged sword; the firm cannot benefit if the exchange rate changes favorably.

Forward contracts are actively traded by a number of banks that are dealers in the foreign exchange markets. These contracts can typically run up to 180 days. Thus, businesses can lock-in foreign exchange rates 180 days into the future.

Covered Interest Arbitrage

Interest rates in individual countries are closely linked with forward exchange rates. Assume some spot interest rates in the US ($R_{0,US}$) and in Japan ($R_{0,J}$) and spot ($X_{0,S}$) and forward exchange rates ($X_{0,f}$). A US investor has two investment choices as shown in table 16.4.

1 the investor invests in US bonds for one period and earns the interest rate $R_{0,US}$.
2 the investor exchanges US dollars and receives $X_{0,S}$ yen, which are invested for one period at the spot interest rate of $R_{0,J}$. At time 1, the yen are exchanged for dollars at the forward exchange rate $X_{0,f}$. Note that the spot interest rates and the spot and forward exchange rates are known with complete certainty at time 0. The entire transaction is certain.

Since both strategies start with the same amount and there is no risk in either strategy, the values at time 1 must be equal. That is:

$$(\$1)(1 + R_{0,US}) = \frac{(X_{0,s})(1 + R_{0,J})}{X_{0,f}} \tag{8}$$

Unless this condition holds, arbitragers enter the market, making profits until this condition holds.

Table 16.4 Covered interest arbitrage

	Time 0	Time 1
Invest in US bonds	$1	$1 + R_{0,US}$
At time 0, exchange for yen and invest in Japanese bonds	$X_{0,s}$ yen	$(X_{0,s})(1 + R_{0,J})/X_{0,f}$
At time 1, exchange yen for dollars		

Covered interest arbitrage shows that interest rates in different coun tries are related. The relationship does not provide any information abou the direction of causation. Does the US interest rate determine th Japanese, or vice versa? As a practical matter, the interest rate in a ver large economy has a significant impact upon the interest rate in a very smal economy, but not vice versa. For two countries of the same size, th interest rates are probably determined by factors in both countries.

Solving the preceding equation for the forward exchange rate gives us

$$X_{0,f} = \frac{(X_{0,s})(1 + R_{0,J})}{(1 + R_{0,US})} \tag{9}$$

This equation shows that the relationship between the forward exchang rate and the spot exchange rate depends upon the interest rates in th two countries. That is:

$$X_{0,f} > X_{0,s} \quad when \ R_{0,FOR} > R_{0,US}$$

$$\begin{bmatrix} forward \\ exchange \\ rate \end{bmatrix} > \begin{bmatrix} spot \\ exchange \\ rate \end{bmatrix} \quad when \begin{bmatrix} foreign \\ interest \\ rate \end{bmatrix} > \begin{bmatrix} US \\ interest \\ rate \end{bmatrix} \tag{10}$$

$$X_{0,f} = X_{0,s} \quad when \ R_{0,FOR} = R_{0,US}$$

$$\begin{bmatrix} forward \\ exchange \\ rate \end{bmatrix} = \begin{bmatrix} spot \\ exchange \\ rate \end{bmatrix} \quad when \begin{bmatrix} foreign \\ interest \\ rate \end{bmatrix} = \begin{bmatrix} US \\ interest \\ rate \end{bmatrix} \tag{11}$$

$$X_{0,f} < X_{0,s} \quad when \ R_{0,FOR} < R_{0,US}$$

$$\begin{bmatrix} forward \\ exchange \\ rate \end{bmatrix} < \begin{bmatrix} spot \\ exchange \\ rate \end{bmatrix} \quad when \begin{bmatrix} foreign \\ interest \\ rate \end{bmatrix} < \begin{bmatrix} US \\ interest \\ rate \end{bmatrix} \tag{12}$$

Covered interest rate arbitrage has a drawback as an explanation of th interest rates in different countries. Forward contracts are necessary fo the arbitrage to hold. Since forward contracts exist only for relativel short maturities, covered interest arbitrage does not hold for long matur ities. Thus, the long-term interest rates in two countries can diverge.

Time Series Properties of Exchange Rates

In an efficient market, investors seek out profit opportunities. Position with abnormally high returns on a risk-adjusted basis attract man investors. The profit-seeking actions of these investors drive returns to a fair level, given the risk.

The foreign exchange markets are highly competitive. A sizable number of very sophisticated financial institutions continually monitor the markets for profit opportunities, making abnormal profits hard to achieve. If a significant future change in exchange rates is highly likely, competition for profits makes investors take action immediately. The impact of the future change is instantly reflected in the spot and forward exchange rates. Consequently, in a perfectly efficient market, exchange rates should be unbiased predictors of future exchange rates.

International Bond Markets

In recent years, the market for international bonds has become quite sizable. International bonds are of two varieties: foreign bonds and Eurobonds. Foreign bonds are issued by a foreign borrower in the currency where the bond is issued. For example, General Motors might issue foreign bonds in Switzerland denominated in Swiss currency. A foreign bond is subject to the regulations in the country of issue.

Eurobonds are denominated in a particular currency but sold in several countries. For example, IBM might issue Eurobonds denominated in US dollars but sold in many different countries (a Eurobond denominated in US dollars is often called a Eurodollar bond). In general, Eurodollar bond issues are not subject to regulation. In contrast, a public offering of bonds by IBM in the US would have to be registered with the SEC, so registration costs and restrictions would be involved. Eurobonds are frequently bearer bonds, meaning that there is no formal record of the owners of these bonds. Owners receive interest by presenting coupons to the issuer. Anonymous ownership may have the advantage of avoiding taxes.

Investment in international bonds may have the advantage of allowing investors to diversify their portfolios. However, this advantage must be weighed against the disadvantages of international investments, including exchange rate risk and higher information and transactions costs.

For many investors, mutual funds represent the best choice for international investing. Mutual funds allow diversification and provide a professional investment manager to analyze the foreign markets.

Summary

Exchange rates are affected by international investment and international trade. International investment provides diversification benefits and production and marketing advantages. International trade occurs because of countries' absolute or relative advantages in production. Currency exchange rates are interrelated with inflation, economic growth, and monetary policy in different countries. The US currently allows its exchange rate to fluctuate freely as market conditions change. Forward exchange rates are determined by domestic and foreign interest rates.

Questions and Problems

1 Explain the terms *depreciation* and *appreciation* of the US currency.
2 The exchange rate between US dollars and British pounds is 0.6 pounds per dollar. The exchange rate between US dollars and Japanese yen is 100 yen to the dollar. Determine the exchange rate of yen per pound and pounds per yen.
3 The US/Canadian exchange rate is $0.90 Canadian equals $1 US. The US/UK exchange rate is $2 US equals 1 pound. How many $ Canadian are in 1 pound?
4 The exchange rate between US dollars and British pounds is 0.6 pounds per dollar. You can invest in the US for one year at the spot interest rate of 8 percent. Alternatively, you can exchange dollars for pounds and invest in Britain at 12 percent. After one year, you exchange the pounds for dollars at the prevailing exchange rate.

   (a) At what exchange rate would your total return on the British investment be 15 percent?
   (b) At what exchange rate would the returns on the US and British investments be equal?
   (c) What should the forward exchange rate be?

5 Bobby Boyd is considering investing in US 1-year bonds at 8 percent or Canadian bonds at 12 percent. The current exchange rate is $0.80 Canadian equals $1 US. If the Canadian bonds are chosen, Bobby intends to exchange US dollars for Canadian today in the spot market; then in one year, Bobby would exchange the $ Canadian for $ US at the spot exchange rate. At what spot exchange rate in one year would the two investments earn the same US dollar returns?
6 The spot exchange rate is $0.85 Canadian equals $1 US. The forward exchange rate for delivery in one year is $0.90 Canadian equals $1. The one-year spot interest rate in the US is 6 percent. What is the one-year spot interest rate in Canada?
7 Assume the US interest rate is 6 percent, the US inflation rate is 4 percent, the British inflation rate is 12 percent, and the current exchange rate is

0.60 pounds to one US dollar. If relative purchasing power parity holds, what should happen to the exchange rate?

8 Assume that relative purchasing power parity holds. The current exchange rate is $1 US = 300 Mexican pesos. The inflation rate in the US over the next year will be 5 percent and the inflation rate in Mexico will be 55 percent. If so, what should the exchange rate become in one year, other things held constant? $1 US equals how many Mexican pesos?

9 Suppose Robert Connors is a Canadian investor. The one-year spot interest rate in Canada is 10 percent and the one-year spot interest rate in the US is 8 percent. The spot exchange rate between Canadian dollars and US dollars is $1 US equals $1.25 Canadian. Suppose Mr Connors exchanges Canadian dollars for US, invests at the one-year spot interest rate in the US, and then exchanges the US dollars for Canadian currency. At what future exchange rate will the return on the US investment strategy equal the return from investing in Canada at the one-year spot interest rate? Please state the exchange rate two ways – Canadian dollars per US dollar and US dollars per Canadian dollar.

10 Suppose that interest rates in Japan are 1 percent for all maturities and interest rates in the US are 5 percent for all maturities. A US investor borrows money in Japan for one year, exchanges for US dollars at an exchange rate of 130 yen to one US dollar, and buys 30-year US bonds. After one year the US bonds are sold, the money exchanged for yen at the exchange of 110 yen to one US dollar, and the loan repaid. Compute the rate of return on this strategy. Decompose this return into two parts, the exchange rate effect and the difference in interest rates.

Select Bibliography

American Bar Foundation, *Commentaries on Model Debenture Indentures* (Chicago, IL, 1971).

Bierwag, G. O., *Duration Analysis: Managing Interest Rate Risk* (Cambridge, MA: Ballinger, 1987).

Fisher, I., *Appreciation and Interest* (New York: Macmillan, 1896).

Fisher, I., *The Theory of Interest* (New York: Macmillan, 1930).

Hansen, A. H., *A Guide to Keynes' "General Theory"* (New York: McGraw-Hill, 1953).

Hickman, W. B., *Corporate Bond Quality and Investor Experience* (New York: National Bureau of Economic Research, 1958).

Homer, S., and Liebowitz, M. L., *Inside the Yield Book* (Englewood Cliffs, NJ: Prentice-Hall, 1972).

Hull, J. C., *Options, Futures, and Other Derivatives* (Englewood Cliffs, NJ: Prentice-Hall, 1997).

Jackson, T. H., *The Logic and Limits of Bankruptcy Law* (Cambridge, MA: Harvard University Press, 1986).

Keynes, J. M., *The General Theory of Employment, Interest and Money* (New York: Harcourt, Brace, Jovanovich, 1936).

Livingston, M., *Money and Capital Markets*, 3rd edn (Cambridge, MA: Blackwell, 1996).

Livingston, M., and Gregory, D. W., "The Stripping of US Treasury Securities," New York University Salomon Brothers Center for the Study of Financial Institutions, Monograph Series in Finance and Economics, monograph, 1989.

Macaulay, F. R., *Some Theoretical Problems Suggested by the Movements of Interest Rates, Bond Yields, and Stock Prices in the United States since 1856* (New York: National Bureau of Economic Research, 1938).

Malkiel, B. G., *The Term Structure of Interest Rates* (Princeton, NJ: Princeton University Press, 1966).

Morningstar, *Mutual Fund Sourcebook* (annual).

Nelson, C. R., *The Term Structure of Interest Rates* (New York: Basic Books, 1970).

Solnik, B., *International Investments*, 2nd edn (Reading, MA: Addison-Wesley, 1991).

Stewart, James B., *Den of Thieves* (New York: Touchstone, Simon & Schuster, 1992).

Stigum, M., *The Money Market* (Homewood, IL: Dow Jones Books, 1990).

US Government Printing Office, *Monthly Statement of the Public Debt* (various years).

US Government Printing Office, *Treasury Bulletin* (various years).

Weisenberger & Co., *Investment Companies* (New York, annual).

Index